WORLD OF WORDS

WORLD OF WORDS

The Personalities of Language

GARY JENNINGS

New York   1984   *Atheneum*

Originally published in somewhat different form under the title
Personalities of Language

Library of Congress Cataloging in Publication Data
Jennings, Gary.
    World of words.
    Rev. ed. of: Personalities of language. New York:
Crowell, c1965.
    Bibliography: p.
    Includes index.
    1. Language and languages. I. Jennings, Gary.
Personalities of language. II. Title. III. Title:
Personalities of language.
P112.J45   1984   402   84-45030
ISBN 0-689-11518-0 (cloth bound)
      0-689-70678-2 (paperback)

Published simultaneously in Canada by McClelland and Stewart Ltd.
Composition by Yankee Typesetters, Inc., Concord, New Hampshire
Manufactured by Fairfield Graphics, Fairfield, Pennsylvania
Designed by Harry Ford
First Atheneum Edition

In memory of my father, a printer

————————

Preface

E VE R Y time a man opens his mouth he says considerably more than he utters.

Whatever his message, the way he expresses it reveals glimpses of his own background, upbringing and personal qualities. But more than that. Whatever his nationality, he speaks a language that was old, weathered and wise before he was born—and his every word reveals something of *its* heredity, ambiance and individuality. This book is an attempt to show that languages are not all textbook rules and rote, that they have some fascinating things to say and show even to nonlinguists who can't speak a word of them.

I have chosen to treat of the "personalities" of the world of words. That is, rather than play the curator of a linguistic museum, discoursing on mummies, I have tried to act the informal host, introducing the reader to convivial new acquaintances with whom he can mingle at ease. For even the "dead languages" were once alive and lively; like the tongues of today, they talked chit-chat, gossiped, joked and cussed.

The early chapters trace the beginnings and development of speech and writing in general, then of separate languages, to show how they came to differ from one another and manifest their discrete personalities. This portion of the book might be considered an anatomy of sorts.

But the bones and muscles of language are clothed in a skin that is capable of smiles, sneers, frowns and winks. So the book's later chapters deal with this expressiveness and these characteristics—dialects, jargons, slang, taboo words, names of persons, places and things, specialized uses (and abuses) of language—the linguistic freckles and blemishes, pimples and dimples that constitute "personality." For examples of these, I have relied mainly on the language the book is written in, but I have tried to provide enough illustrations from other tongues to show wherein their own characteristics parallel or differ from those of English.

Naturally, no one volume can come anywhere near encompassing *all* the multifarious personalities of language. But the broad purview of the subtitle of this book does enable me to bring between covers some fringe aspects and phenomena of language which, though often interesting, entertaining and sometimes even significant, seldom get discussed in more narrowly focused linguistic texts.

I have tried to ensure that anyone who can read English can read this book—admittedly a most unscholarly approach that will peeve some pedants. I have included two or three fragments of exotic scripts only where necessary for illustration; everywhere else they have been transliterated into the Roman alphabet. In the few instances where I've had to spell out a pronunciation I have invented my own system on the spot, rather than assume that the reader can decipher the International Phonetic Alphabet. Where I have succumbed to using professional jargon, I think the context will make its meaning clear.

In a book of the scope of this one it is obviously impractical to comb every split hair of linguistic theory. Where I've run up against conflicting schools of thought on some subject, I have usually taken my pick of school, and haven't always paused to tell why or to cite all the arguments for and against it. In a few cases I have even dared to make some assertions of my own, with which *no* school may agree. Here and there, I may have neglected to label an instance of folklore or folk-etymology, preferring to let a beguiling myth stand on its own. After all, part of a language's personality is what its makers and users believe and think about it.

Perhaps I should warn that this is not a book for Mrs. Grundy. Languages, like people, don't always dwell in drawing rooms. But I think that today's intellectual climate is (finally) such that the preponderance of readers can view the long-shunned subjects of cuss-words and taboo words as clinically as do the professional linguists, without smirk or shock. In any case, I'm inclined to believe that my examinations of profanity and obscenity, while they may vex Mrs. Grundy, will expose her to no words she didn't already know.

One last remark. The ideal philologist regards the "misuse" of language as a psychiatrist regards murder: just one more phenomenon of human behavior. But parts of this book are forthrightly subjective—opinionated, if you will. I choose to believe that there *is* such a crime as slovenliness of speech and writing, hence ultimately of thinking. Though a frequent sinner myself, I still rue and deplore it. Further, I believe that language is a tool of communication, and I abhor the calculated use of it to hide the truth or make lies presentable, to erect or buttress false barriers between man and man. These views may occasionally put me outside the pale of objective scientific discipline. But a book on the personalities of language inevitably deals with human personality as well, and that includes the author's.

G. J.

Contents

WORLD OF WORDS

Let clerks indite in Latin, and let Frenchmen in their French also indite their quaint terms, for it is kindly to their mouths; and let us show our fantasies in such wordes as we learned of our mother's tongue.

—THOMAS USK

The View from the Babel Tower

WHEN Christopher Columbus set sail into the sunset on his first voyage in 1492, one of his ships carried an under-officer specially assigned to the expedition because he spoke fluent Hebrew. Columbus expected to fetch up in Cipangu, Cathay or Ind, and there was no interpreter available to him who knew Japanese, Chinese or any of the Indian tongues. But it was a common belief in Europe at the time that Hebrew, the language of the Scriptures, was the original tongue of all mankind, so Columbus was confident that even among the Far Easterners he would be able to communicate with their scholars.

He must have been dismayed, when he finally landed in what appeared to be a backwater boondocks of the Indies, to find that the natives were as ignorant of Hebrew as they were of the Scriptures, of biblical history and of everything else in Old World experience. At any rate, there is no record of classical interpreters having been supplied for the subsequent voyages to these new Indies.

But the belief persisted until the middle of the nineteenth century that some single original language had been God's gift to man at the time of Creation, and that in happier days "the whole earth was of one language, and of one speech." The theologians took it on faith and the philologists, such as they were, tried piously to confirm it by tortuous rationalizing. In the 1680s Cotton Mather wrote his M.A. thesis at Harvard in a detailed defense of this supposed linguistic revelation. In 1808 the philosopher Friedrich von Schlegel persuaded himself that the ancestor of all modern tongues was the Sanskrit of ancient India. In the 1830s lexicographer

[3]

Noah Webster gave it as his opinion that the prototype language must have been "Chaldee," that is, Aramaic, the language of the Holy Land in Christ's day. At various times Hungarian, German, Danish, Basque, Dutch, Swedish—all of these and many others—have been proved, at least to their speakers' satisfaction, to have been the language of Eden.

The sorry diversity of human languages in the latter-day world was neatly explained by the eleventh chapter of Genesis, and that explanation still suffices for the religious fundamentalists. When the overweening descendants of Shem, Ham and Japheth dared to begin building a tower that should rival the heights of heaven, the Lord chastised them with a thunderclap confusion of tongues. Unable even to call for the waterboy, the tower builders had to abandon their project. Each man of them wandered off, burdened with his individual and lonely language, to some far country where he could beget a whole new people of his own and have somebody to talk to.

The Bible called the city of the ill-fated ziggurat Babel (probably from the Hebrew *bilbel,* "confusion"). Hence the fundamentalists could demonstrate through a plausible folk-etymology that the Babel story was confirmed by echoes in many modern languages—the English word "babble," the Italian *balbettio,* the Spanish *balbuceo,* the French *babil,* etc.

But as the nineteenth century moved into its second half, a new generation of linguists, perhaps no less devout than their predecessors but more disposed to scientific discipline, began to question the concept of a divine Ur-language. At the same time, along came Charles Darwin to dispute the whole concept of Creation. Some scholars were so excited by his theory of evolution that they strained as hard to apply it to the origins of language as they had previously strained to validate Babel. Friedrich Max Müller earnestly suggested that the grunts and squeals of man's animal ancestors all over the earth had gradually evolved toward speech in the same way their brains had evolved toward intelligence, and that thus the world's languages would already have been infinitely various even before the genus *Homo* had attained full sapience.

That exegesis was a little too pat, and was never seriously credited. But Darwin's new timetable did at least give the scholars about a million years of human evolution to maneuver in, as against the paltry few thousand the Bible had allowed them. (According to the sober calculations of Archbishop James Ussher in the seventeenth century, Creation had taken place on an October morning in the year 4004 B.C.

And Gustav Seyffarth, in the 1820s, asserted that "the alphabet of the races of the world" had been invented the day the Deluge ended: September 7, 3446 B.C.)

After Darwin, a host of anthropologists, archaeologists and paleontologists began to turn up evidence that a fair measure of human civilization had been achieved as long ago as 6000 B.C., and that man-creatures must have been living in passably peaceable intercourse—implying some degree of effective mutual communication—a good three quarters of a million years before that.

And yet to this day we are no nearer knowing how language began than are the fundamentalist endorsers of an archetype tongue divine. For all the proof we have to the contrary, we might as well join them in believing that human speech was a direct and recent gift from the Almighty. Linguists now are fairly sure they know the provenances of the major tongues of today, but the primary sources of those languages are shrouded by time past. Too, there are some current languages which refuse to fit comfortably into the linguists' scheme of things, and there must have been untold numbers of other such tongues which flourished and then fell silent over the ages.

There are probably as many different theories about the origin of languages as there are professional linguists, but four of these should suffice to show their general tenor. The linguists, though not normally inclined to persiflage, have described these four hypotheses by rather chucklesome names: the Bow-Wow theory, the Pooh-Pooh theory, the Ding-Dong theory and the Yo-He-Ho theory.

The Bow-Wow theory supposes that man learned to talk by parroting the cries of animals. Considering that man was first a hunter, the notion has a certain plausibility. Once a group of men had agreed, say, that a boar was an "oink" and an aurochs was a "moo," they would eventually have aspired to naming other things.

The Pooh-Poohists believe that man's first meaningful noises were involuntarily jolted out of him by sudden events or situations, somewhat in the manner of a duchess finding a worm in her salad. It's a little hard to believe that a caveman ever uttered anything quite as finical as "pooh-pooh" but, considering his thorny environment, it's not unlikely that he began to talk by saying a frequent "ow!"

The Ding-Dong theory is based on onomatopoeia, like the Bow-Wow, only predicating that man's first words were echoes of natural sounds other than those of animals. For instance, he may have cried "whack!" in merry mimicry of his club bouncing off a rival's skull, or muttered a fearful "bumble-boom" in imitation of the thunder.

The Yo-He-Ho theory maintains that the earliest effective speech was the result of man's beginning to cooperate and coordinate with his fellows. That is, a group of men may have learned to lighten their labors by shouting some sort of cadence count, like sailors' chanteys or soldiers' marching songs, when they were hauling home a sabertooth's carcass or levering boulders down onto an invading war party.

It seems indisputable that sign language by gestures must have long preceded and then accompanied the development of any meaningful grunts and mumbles. We still find gestures handy for beckoning, shooing, threatening, and even as an aid to exposition (ask anybody, "What is a spiral staircase?" and watch). Sir Richard Paget dwelt on this to suggest, in 1930, an offbeat theory of his own as to the beginnings of speech. It was his hypothesis that the first talking man's tongue movements merely imitated his hand gestures, and that his simultaneous expiration of a breath resulted in the articulation of a specific noise to reinforce each gesture.

For example, to indicate "up" a man would point a finger skyward. At the same time he would unconsciously raise the tip of his tongue to touch the roof of his mouth. If at this moment he grunted, the resulting sound would be approximately "ull" or "oll"—or, as it would be written in Latin, *al*.

Sir Richard pointed out that this word element is still widespread in words signifying "up." Latin has *altus* for "high," whence the English "altitude." The Semitic *al* means "to ascend," whence the Israeli airline El Al. The Melanesian *al* means "to climb." The Kwakiutl Indian *allela* means "up." Other grunts with the tongue variously tilted against the palate give the variant sounds of *at*, *an*, *ar* and *atl*. Sir Richard thought it significant that many of the world's upthrusting mountains contain these uptongued noises in their names: the Alps, Atlas, Andes, Himalaya, Allegheny, Ararat, etc.

It's easy enough to find holes in Paget's theory. For one thing, not all speech sounds involve the contortion of the tongue, and the rest of our vocal machinery is not adapted for imitating gestures. But, because we can never know the real story of language's beginning, his theory is no more flimsy than the four previously mentioned. There have been stranger ones; Edgar Sturtevant once suggested that man developed language when he first found it profitable to deceive.

The reason for the impossibility of ever tracing back to the

[6]

beginnings of speech is that there is no "primitive" language surviving on earth for the scholars to study. Early explorers thought they had found something of the sort among the American Indians, the Australian aborigines and such backward peoples. But, crude though their languages sounded to the white man's ear, they proved on investigation to be of a development and complexity easily equal to any "civilized" language. And so the oldest and most basic languages available for scholarly inspection are those whose fragments of writing have been exhumed by archaeologists. But plainly, any ancient language that had attained to writing had already progressed eons beyond the primordial kindergarten.

Most linguistic scholars have ceased to fret over the insoluble. They have contented themselves with visualizing modern-day languages as twigs, so to speak, and with inching backward along them to find the common branches from which the twigs sprouted, thence farther backward to the common limbs from which the branches grew. Thus they have been able to group the world's languages into a system of fairly well-defined families. But if there ever was an archetypal, ancestral language which begat them all—a single trunk to this family tree—it is beyond discovery.

Before we look into the personalities which the various languages developed as they grew, let us briefly see how they *became* separate and disparate.

Our English language is a twig of the so-called Teutonic branch of a limb designated Indo-European. The heftiest and most prolific limb of the language tree, Indo-European has sprouted languages which would seem to be as dissimilar as they are far apart—from Irish in the West to the Bengali of Bangladesh in the East. The belief is that all the Indo-European languages stem from a single prehistoric tongue, and that its speakers must have lived originally in the area which now comprises Austria, Czechoslovakia and Hungary.

How these people came to be there, whether they had evolved there autochthonously from time beyond reckoning, can only be conjectured. But it is possible that they were a Stone Age mixture of even earlier types from both northern and Mediterranean lands, in which case their "original" language must have been an amalgam of still others. To call these people "Indo-Europeans," as most linguists do, is an obvious *ex post facto* misnomer based on the eventual geographic dispersal of their language. But if they had a name for themselves no one knows it, so we will continue to use the term for convenience's sake.

The Indo-Europeans, then, were nomadic. Over the ages

various groups of them went a-roving far, far from home, never to return. As they scattered to all the points of the compass, each group's language began to grow apart from the parent stock and from each of the others'. For example, the Indo-Europeans who first trekked westward gradually developed a proto-Celtic variety of their language during the long march. At one time this must have been the language of almost all western Europe, but it survives today only in its later, splinter languages of Scots Gaelic, Irish, Welsh, Breton on the farthest western coast of France, and the almost extinct Manx.

Following the Celtic groups, a subsequent westward migration spread a Teutonic form of Indo-European all across the northern part of the Continent. This gradually resolved itself into a number of intermediate tongues: Gothic, Old Norse, Englisc, Old Saxon, Franconian—and thence eventually into High and Low German, Dutch, Flemish, the Scandinavian tongues and the various early forms of what finally became English.

Another wave of Indo-Europeans headed straight north to become Lithuanians and Letts. Others moved east and southeast, developing the Slavic body of languages which today includes Polish, Czech, Bulgarian, Serbo-Croatian, the several Russian dialects, etc.

Some of the Stone Age wanderers plodded southeastward all the way across Asia Minor. During this time, they developed a tongue which in a later form became Sanskrit, the oldest Indo-European language with which we are familiar. Various groups dropped out of the line of march here and there, to settle in and bequeath new languages to Armenia, Persia, Afghanistan and Baluchistan. But the most persistently footloose pushed on clear to the Indian subcontinent, where they fanned out into a multitude of settlements and dialects which became the numerous Indic tongues of today.

Still other Indo-Europeans moved southward across the Balkans, developing along the way a proto-Hellenic tongue which was eventually to become classical, then modern, Greek. Another group loitered in Albania, to plant the Thraco-Illyrian still in use there.

Other parties crossed the Alps, developing the Italic languages which eventuated in Latin. Much later, via Roman imperialism, Latin displaced the Celtic tongues of southern Europe to give us the whole body of Romance languages: French, Spanish, Italian, Portuguese, Catalan and Romanian.

My mapping of the spread of the Indo-European tongues is admittedly oversimplified and presumptive; neither mass migrations nor changes in language ever proceed so smoothly. We don't know how long these processes did take, except that they must have occupied glacial ages. We don't know in precisely what order the various migrations took place, or how they might have been affected by rebuffs, checks, retreats and roundabout detours. We don't know how many elementary and intermediate changes the languages may have gone through. We can only trace backward from the numerous language twigs that still are green and from a few dead ones we can recognize as having withered from the same familial branches.

For a small illustration of family resemblance, take the English word "three." In almost every Indo-European language the word for "three" begins with a dental consonant (*t, d* or *th*) followed by an *r*. Among the other languages of the Teutonic branch, for example, it is *thrjá* in Icelandic, *tre* in all the continental Scandinavian tongues, *drei* in German, *drie* in Dutch and Flemish. Among the Romance languages, it is *trois* in French, *tres* in Spanish and Portuguese, *tre* in Italian and *trei* in Romanian. Among the Slavic languages, it is *tri* in Russian, *tři* in Czech, and *trzy* in Polish. It is *tri* in the Celtic languages: Irish, Scots Gaelic, Welsh and Breton; and *tris* in the Baltic languages: Lettish and Lithuanian. It is *tre* in Albanian. It was *tri* in Sanskrit, *treis* in classical Greek, *tres* in Latin and *thri* in Anglo-Saxon.

The prehistoric Indo-European tide submerged what must have been innumerable earlier languages in both Europe and Asia—as in Italy, where we know that it washed away the Etruscan and Messapian. Only one European tongue dating from before the migrations managed to endure to modern times: the Basque of the French-Spanish Pyrenees. But the Indo-European tongues themselves did not everywhere survive. The Macedonian of northern Greece was extinct before history began. The Tocharian evolved by the Indo-Europeans who penetrated farthest eastward, into the Gobi of remotest Turkestan, is known only from scraps of written records.

And even though the Indo-European tongues are spoken today by half of the world's people, there are stubborn islands of unrelated languages flourishing right in the middle of Europe. Basque, for instance, is an entity all to itself, unallied to any other language on earth. Turkish is the European representative of a language group which includes Tataric, Kirghizic and numerous other tongues in use across wide belts of central and northern Asia. What really seems odd is that Hungary, part of the long-ago homeland of the aboriginal Indo-European, should now speak the alien Magyar, a member of a totally unrelated language family (the Finno-Ugric branch of the Ural-Altaic limb) which also includes the Finnish and Lappish of the far north.

Most other languages of the world can similarly be lumped into families whose members all have a common origin. For example, while the two major tongues of India, Hindi and Bengali, are chips off the Indo-European block, the nation also has to cope with some two hundred others, most of them of the Dravidian group: Tamil, Telugu, Canarese, etc. (A ten-rupee note has to proclaim itself in nine different languages.)

The Semitic group once supplied the world with its widest-used languages of commerce and diplomacy: Babylonian-Assyrian, Phoenician, Aramaic. Today its chief representatives are the Arabic of the Near East and Mediterranean Africa, the Amharic of Ethiopia, Maltese and Hebrew, the latter a "dead" language for twenty centuries but successfully resuscitated since 1948 as the national tongue of Israel.

A near limb to the Semitic group is the Hamitic, whose greenest and most fruitful twig was the Egyptian of the pharaohs. A direct descendant, Coptic, is the liturgical language of African Christians, while such relations as Berber, Tamashek and Somali are still spoken by various tribes in the region of the Sahara.

The peoples of the rest of Africa speak some five hundred different tongues, classified by linguists in three main groups— the Sudanese-Guinean group of the Gulf of Guinea coast and the central interior of the continent, the Bantu group farther south, and the Hottentot-Bushman languages of the southwest. It seems probable that the fierce nationalism of Africa's new autonomies will result in a gradual interweaving or lopping off of the lesser language twigs in order to surmount the current communications handicaps. But at this writing Africa is still being hampered by its multiplicity of tongues, from the level of continental progress to that of connubial peace, as witness this letter received by an African newspaper's advice-to-the-lovelorn columnist:

"Being of a different tribe from my wife I do not know what to do every afternoon at four when the radio broadcasts in vernacular. She calls for one tongue, I for another. . . ."

The Sinitic languages of Asia, like the Indo-European, seem to have developed during primeval times when an aboriginal race of people gradually overflowed in all directions from an oriental Eden, situated perhaps in the fertile western valleys of the Yangtze River. The family now includes the myriad spoken dialects of China, plus Tibetan, Burmese, Thai and various other languages of Indo-China. The Japanese and

Korean languages may or may not be related to one another—linguists differ on this—but neither of them is related to Chinese or any other of the Sinitic tongues.

The map of the pre-Columbian Americas is a jigsaw puzzle of vaguely defined linguistic families, some forty each in North and South America. This is a conservative estimate, and the families have been determined more or less by guesswork, but any more rigid classification is probably impossible. There were more than a thousand different tongues spoken in the Western hemisphere at the time the white man arrived, but most of these were dead or dying by the time comparative philologists began to study them.

It may be that the first migrants to cross from Asia via the Aleutian stepping stones brought with them a proto-language like the original Indo-European master tongue. Or perhaps they made the crossing long before any of mankind had any well-developed language at all, and the numerous later tongues evolved independently. Or the crossing may have been accomplished in any number of successive waves, each new migration contributing a new tongue. Some linguists claim to have found affinities between the Eskimo family of languages and the Finno-Ugric which includes Hungarian and Finnish. Other scholars, even more imaginative, believe that the Algonquian Indian languages of northern and eastern North America contain elements borrowed from the speech of Viking explorers who visited the New World five centuries before Columbus.

Like the Amerindian, the more than two hundred native languages of Australia and New Guinea had begun to dwindle before they could be seriously studied, and their familial groupings likewise must remain conjectural. The Malayo-Polynesian tongues are rather better known. This limb of language is second only to the Indo-European in its geographical spread. Its related tongues are spoken from Madagascar, off the coast of Africa, all the way to Easter Island in the eastern Pacific, more than halfway around the world. Its branches and twigs include the Tagalog of the Philippines, the Maori of New Zealand, the fast-disappearing Hawaiian, and numerous other languages of Oceania: Fijian, Tahitian, etc.

Not even professional linguists know how many different languages are in use in the world today. The French Academy, a stickler for precision, used to maintain that there were exactly 2,796, exclusive of local dialects. Other estimates have ranged as high as five thousand, because few scholars can agree on just what *is* a "dialect" or when it qualifies as a "language." And, although most of the however-many thousands of tongues have been tucked cozily into families, there are a number of orphans which deny any kinfolk at all. As already mentioned, Basque is one of them. There's an old legend to the effect that the Devil has never been able to tempt a Basque because the language is so uniquely difficult that he's never learned to speak it.

Korean and Japanese may be orphans, too, unless further linguistic research somehow links them together. Others include a number of hermit languages in Kamchatka and far northeast Siberia, the tongue of the Andaman Islands in the Bay of Bengal, and that of the hairy Ainus of northern Japan.

Even the nonlinguist reader has probably recognized most of the names, at least, of the languages mentioned so far in this chapter, and there are professional linguists who speak, read and write a formidable number of them (Charles Berlitz, former proprietor of the Berlitz Schools of Languages, reputedly speaks thirty languages with varying degrees of fluency). But there are other tongues, currently or formerly in use, whose very names are little known.

Just for a sampling, consider Pis, a language of the Caroline Islands; Kookie, an Indian dialect akin to Bengali; Flup, spoken along Africa's Gambia River; Saliva, an Orinoco Indian dialect; Gah, the tongue of the Malayan Alfurus; Bzub, a dialect of the Caucasus; Zara, a Kurdish tongue of northwest Persia; Cullilan-Cunny, an Amerindian language; Kuzzilbash, a Turkish dialect; Jalloof, language of a Senegal tribe; Miao, the dialect of China's Hunan province; Yairy-Yairy and Watty-Watty, two Australian dialects of New South Wales.

It is a little bit droll, a little bit pathetic, that certain peoples all speaking the same language have seen fit to invent a name for themselves which implies that they are the only people on earth, or at least the most important. This hub-of-the-universe ethnocentrism is oftenest to be found among peoples who inhabit an isolated area, or who are wary or contemptuous of their neighbors. The Eskimos, for example, call themselves the Innuit, which means "the people." The name of China comes eponymously from the dynasty of Ch'in, in turn derived from the word *chin* meaning "man," thus the Chinese are "the men." So are the Gilyads of Siberia (*nibach* in their tongue). So are the Illeni Indians (*illeni*, "the men," gave us the name of Illinois). The African name Bantu means "the men." What we call the Hottentots call themselves Khoi-Khoin, the "men among men."

But no nationality and no language has been able to remain completely aloof and uncontaminated. The men of the Innuit are now well versed in GI slang, courtesy of American military outposts in the Arctic. The Hottentot men among men can probably discourse in Hollywood jargon, learned from the location crews of many a jungle movie epic.

Though separate tongues were developed by the various groups of Indo-European migrants (and by the similar off-shoots of all the other linguistic limbs), these languages did not just achieve variety and then petrify at that stage. They continued to change, and are still continuing to change, with every passing year.

Some of a language's development is internal in nature. Its speakers invent new words to fit new things and concepts, as civilization inevitably grows more complex. They hatch colloquialisms and slang expressions, and a certain percentage of these become fixtures of the language. The natural elisions of everyday speech, vernacular differences or outright mistakes in pronunciation, passing fads in spoken language, all can become accepted and permanent usages. For example, the Middle English word *napron* became, through the slurring of "a napron," the modern English "an apron." In sixteenth-century France it became fashionable, for some queer reason, to pronounce *r* as *z* (Paris: *Pazi*). Though the cuteness eventually became tiresome and petered out, at least one leftover remains in *chaise* for the original *chaire*.

Even arbitrary legislation has occasionally changed the course of a people's language. As recently as 1938 Norway decreed an end to the modified Danish that had been its "literary language" since the Middle Ages, and substituted a standardized version of the everyday vernacular called Landsmaal as its official national tongue. Kemal Ataturk, upon becoming dictator-president of Turkey in 1923, at once set about abolishing the Arabic script that had previously been used for writing Turkish and ordered the use of the Roman alphabet. The result is that Turkish children can begin to read and write now after about six months of schooling, instead of the two or three years it used to take.

And there are external pressures that mold every language: wartime conquests and defeats, intergroup commerce, cultural and technological exchanges, immigration, tourism. Rome's conquest of all western Europe replaced the numerous Celtic tongues with adaptations of Latin. But the long occupation of those territories also affected the speech of the conquerors; the rankers of the legions returned home with their own language considerably mutated, so that eventually the common folk of Rome spoke a plebeian Latin quite different from the patrician language our schools still teach. For instance, *equus* was the highbrow word for "horse," but it survives only in such equally bookish words as "equine" and "equestrian." The legionnaire and the Roman-in-the-street said *caballus*, which is much more widely represented in the Romance languages of today—the French *cheval*, the Italian *cavallo*, the Spanish *caballo*—and in the English "cavalry," "cavalcade," etc.

Switzerland shows one remarkable effect of commerce on language. Traditionally the world's bank, referee and middleman, Switzerland has never aspired to developing a distinctive language of its own, unless one counts the provincial tongue called Romansch spoken by less than 2 per cent of the population. The Swiss have found it more expedient, prudent and profitable to make do with the French, German and Italian of their three abutting neighbors.

The linguistic largesse of immigration is too well known, especially in the United States, to require elaboration here. The linguistic souvenirs brought home by tourists are perhaps best exemplified in the cocktail-party conversation of any debutante just returned from her "finishing" in Europe. As for cultural exchanges of language, the Western world's musical terminology is predominantly Italian (*piano, fortissimo,* etc.), while art critics rely on both French and Italian expressions (*trompe l'oeil, chiaroscuro,* etc.). Because France gave aviation its earliest impetus, the flyer's technology is still full of French terms (*fuselage, aileron,* etc.).

There is no language in the world whose structure or vocabulary does not exhibit the results of one or several internal ferments and external jostlings. And of them all, English is the one which best illustrates the many ways in which language can change, develop and grow.

Whatever tongue the neolithic Britons may have chanted in their dawn-worship ceremonies at Stonehenge, no one knows. We do know that their language gave way to the Celtic brought from the Continent by the so-called Indo-Europeans. And *that* was largely supplanted by the Teutonic dialects of the later invading Angles, Saxons and Jutes. Their Englisc, which became Anglo-Saxon, gave English its basic structure, its grammar and its stock of common words for common things, acts, concepts and emotions. But Anglo-Saxon words, though the oftenest used, are a minority in modern English, because the vocabulary has so often been enriched by other conquerors, skirmishers and settlers—and it is their words we use most in science, art, religion, technology, politics, literature and other supracommon fields.

Latin came with the Roman legions, the later Christian missionaries and the still later cultural cosmopolitanism of the Renaissance. Norse words were contributed by the Vik-

ing invaders. The Norman conquerors brought a sort of bastard French, while Parisian French attended the later succes-
sion of the Angevin kings.

By the fourteenth century, the blend of court French (with
its admixture of Latin) and the London dialect of Anglo-
Saxon (with its traces of Norse and Celtic) had been established as *the* English language. But its speakers continued
to borrow words from all the Continental tongues and, during Britannia's heyday of ruling the waves, her explorers and
colonizers collected still more words from a multitude of
exotic sources.

Meantime, English was constantly enjoying or enduring
every possible change from within: simplification of its grammar, shifts in pronunciation and spelling, the invention of
neologisms, changes in the meaning of many words, the for-
malization of slang, colloquialisms and idioms. It gradually
sloughed off most of the word-endings—indications of gender,
number, case, tense and mood—which still complicate the
Continental languages. The inflections which do remain in
English are few (-s for plural, 's for possessive, -ed for past
tense, etc.) and are seldom irregular (as "men" instead of
mans, "his" instead of he's, "went" instead of goed, etc.). In
the main, English relies on word order and the addition of
modifying words to make its sentences clear. In this it
is structurally more like Chinese than like any of its Indo-
European cousins.

Its insatiable appetite for other people's words and its uninhibited talent for invention have given English, of all languages, probably the widest scope of expression and the
richest potential for euphony. It has a store of synonyms to
convey just about every conceivable nuance of meaning; it
would be possible to write a lengthy monograph on the subject of Love, for instance, without once repeating the word.
And in the rare event that a writer cannot find just the precise locution for his purpose, he can ransack the language's
vast stockpile of word elements to compound a brand-new
coinage of his own.

The one pressure to which English has never bent is that
of legislation, although self-appointed improvers have had a
go at it from time to time. The Norman kings decreed the
use of their brand of French at court, in the courts of law, in
trade and in literature. In 1450 Reginald Pecock sought to
jettison the Gallicisms and Latinisms that had crept into
English, offering pure Anglian alternatives like "ungothrough-
able" for impenetrable and "nottobethoughtuponable" for im-
ponderable. When the Puritans came into the ascendancy in

England they tried to abolish Roman Catholicism from the language by such sleazy stratagems as substituting "Sir" for Saint in church names—Sir Peter's, Sir Mary's (*sic*), etc.—and promoting "Christ-tide" to delete the despised "mass" from Christmas.

Shortly after the American Revolution, several of the United States founding fathers favored setting up an academy like that of France or Sweden, to standardize and sanctify an "official" American language. And there have been meaningless gestures like the 1923 attempt to have Congress establish that "the national and official language of the Government and people of the United States of America . . . is hereby defined as and declared to be the American language, [i.e.] words and phrases generally accepted as being in good use by the people of the United States of America. . . ." But no do-good decree, proposal or ban has ever stopped the English-speaking people from conducting their lives in whatever vernacular they chose.

I should mention here that any praise of the virtues and advantages of English is an automatic appreciation of the many other tongues which have so heavily contributed to it. And also that the foregoing capsule history of English is intended as microcosm; every other language has manifested similar changes, developments and growth. Thus, every language equally testifies to man's adaptability to shifting circumstances and conditions.

But things do not change everywhere in the same direction or degree. One society becomes urbanized, another remains agrarian; a land-cramped people become migrants or marauders, a comfortable people turn to contemplation and aesthetics. This is not to say that every individual person conforms to a societal way of life—but his native language may. Doubtless the Araucanian Indians of the South American pampas have their sages, rascals, idlers, wits and half-wits, but they all speak the same basic tongue. And that language reflects the pitiful rigors of their existence in that it includes a wide vocabulary of words just to express varying intensities of hunger.

The reasonable man is aware that not all Scots are miserly, not all Frenchmen are excitable, not all Russians are gloomy—and ditto for all the other facile labels fabricated by superstition, false tradition and standing jokes. But, while it is impossible to assign a stereotyped temperament to every individual of a specific race, color or nationality, it *is* often possible to detect differing and distinctive "personalities" among their languages.

To a non-Scot, the word "burr" perfectly describes both the

Gaelic pronunciation and the national flower of Scotland: the language and the thistle are equally rough-edged. The liquid vowels of the Polynesian tongues conjure up visions of loveliness and languor, full moon and blue lagoon.

Contrariwise, the gutturals of the German language sound, to a non-German, as harsh and forbidding as winter in the Black Forest. The swoops and swirls of Persian script seem, to a Westerner, as voluptuous and sensual as the quatrains of Omar Khayyám. But Goethe wrote tender and lyrical word-music in German, and Persian is prosaically utilitarian for keeping the accounts of Iranian oil companies. The personality of a language, like that of a man, is the sum of many things not always apparent to the casual eye or ear.

One factor in the makeup of a language is what the Germans call *Sprachgefühl,* or speech-feeling. In *Words and Their Ways in English Speech* philologists J. B. Greenough and G. L. Kittredge define it as "a regular and persistent mode of thought, and consequently of expression, which more or less dominates the form of the language in the mouths of all its speakers. . . . It affects every word that we utter, though we may think that we are speaking as the whim of the moment dictates; and thus it is the strongest and most pervasive of all conservative forces, and has kept [each] language true to itself." They cite as examples Latin's majestic simplicity of style and the epigrammatic scintillation of French, then add, "Men of genius may take great liberties with their mother tongue without offense; but let them once run counter to its characteristic tendencies, let them violate [its] *Sprachgefühl,* and their mannerism becomes, as it were, a foreign language."

While the national language of a people has its own personality, a *Sprachgefühl* distinct from even closely related tongues, it is at the same time a complex of sublanguages—regional dialects, trade jargons and the like—each of which has its own idiosyncrasies. Take a New York stockbroker and an Alabama sharecropper, a Moscow ballerina and a Pskov muzhik—or, for that matter, any teen-ager and his grandfather. Each pair speaks one national language, but with what worlds-apart difference.

It may be hard to imagine a world in which every town or every social group or even every family spoke a separate language—but it could conceivably have happened. Oral language, like gossip, can undergo remarkable changes even across the space of two backyards, let alone across a country or a century. There is every reason to believe that the world's peace and progress have been retarded by its multifarious tongues. But, horrible to contemplate, these thousands of mutually incomprehensible languages might well have wisped and splintered into thousands of thousands—and mankind into even more fragmented, insular and xenophobic subcultures—except for one thing:

Along came writing.

Where preliterate man imposed form diffidently, temporarily—for such transitory forms lived but temporarily on the tip of his tongue, in the living situation—the printed word was inflexible, permanent, in touch with eternity: it embalmed truth for posterity.

—EDMUND CARPENTER

The Moving Finger Writes

THERE is probably not a single part of the human body, mentionable or otherwise, that has not been used as a means of communication, somewhere, sometime. The vocal apparatus is the busiest, of course, but even in our logomanic society the average person spends only an estimated total of twenty-five minutes a day in articulated speech. The rest of his talking is done with hand gestures, smiles, frowns, shrugs and what have you.

The winked eye, the wrinkled nose, the furrowed brow, the cupped ear, the bowed head—all have readable meanings. Lovers in movie balconies commune by playing "kneesies" and "toesies." The depth to which an American girl exposes her frontal cleavage, or a Yemenite girl her face, or a Japanese girl the nape of her neck, can bespeak the extent of her sociability. Balzac called flirtation "that sweet language which the ladies so well understand, that has neither stops, commas, accents, letters, figures, characters, notes nor images."

There have often been meanings assigned to costume and coiffure, rouge and war paint. A Korean girl's hairdo indicates her marital status; a soldier's entire career can be read at a glance in the "fruit salad" of his chest ribbons. The cosmetics lavished on mummies have sometimes been the only "language" to survive its speakers, and this has occasionally given us hints of the way prehistoric people lived and thought. But in general the words that are spoken, gestured, worn or similarly intimated are the most fleeting of human creations. Man could not completely master his environment until he was

[19]

able to preserve some of his astronomical illions of daily utterances for permanent reference.

It is almost certain that he learned to read, in a sense, before he ever learned to write. In order to hunt his intended prey, and to elude whatever might be hunting him, a Stone Age breadwinner had to be able to read spoor. He had to recognize the differences between edible and poisonous plants, potable and polluted waters. And during his foraging expeditions he may have made his earliest attempts at nonvocal communication: perhaps by blazing trees for future trail signs. Anyway, it has aptly been said that man's first signature was his footprint.

His oldest surviving attempts to put his notions on record are cave paintings that were not intended for communication with other men, but with the nature spirits. In drawing a stag transfixed by spears, the artist was practicing imitative magic, invoking the principle of "like begets like" to attract other deer within hunting range. Notwithstanding the primitive superstition involved, this was rather brilliant pragmatism. The caveman had other things to do besides pray for good hunting; he let the drawing do it for him while he attended to more pressing matters. The Tibetan Buddhists still rely on wind-driven prayer wheels in the same manner.

But when game became really scarce, the Stone Age tribe would resort to an all-out session of community prayer to the spirits, and the stag drawing on the cave wall would be the focal piece of the ceremony. It was a reminder to the assemblage of what they were to concentrate on and pray for, and thus was a symbol intentionally conveying a message, or at least a mental nudge. Eons later, the caveman's descendants still acknowledge or obey similar mnemonics: the beads of a rosary, the flag at half-staff, the red and green of a traffic light.

Other early artists set down drawings to commemorate notable events: a record bag of game, a battle victory, a solar eclipse, etc. Such pictorial archives were the only histories compiled by many primitive peoples. Some of them are still as easy to read as a comic strip. But more often, like the illustrations in a book, they depicted only the highlights of an event and had to be explained and filled in by the tribe's hereditary historians. They would have been incomprehensible to later generations if the translations had not been handed down through succeeding storytellers.

Consider the case of the Easter Islanders. Their genealogies and the legends of their long-ago migration from some continental homeland (and perhaps an explanation of the island's famous great stone heads) were preserved in pictograms on what they called "the talking wood," door-sized wooden tablets entrusted to the nobles and priests for safekeeping. But in the nineteenth century marauding slavers carried off the cream of the population, including the few who could read the tablets. Later, Christian missionaries fanatically rooting out "paganism" burned most of the tablets. In effect, Easter Island's history and culture were obliterated; the surviving pictograms are too few to admit of decipherment.

The early picture-writings, in their function of perpetuating a people's history or glorifying individuals, rather tended toward exaggeration and embellishment. The scribe felt free to indulge his imagination at the expense of legibility, and so an inscription's message was likely to get lost in a welter of artistic touches. But as various groups of men abandoned the nomad life of hunting, and settled down to become herders or farmers, they became more businesslike and so did their pictograms.

Among these more settled societies, picture-writing gradually shed its florid fancywork and refined down into a system of quickly written, easily read stylizations. Back when a bull was a wild and fearsome beast to be hunted, a scribe would depict it as seven times the height of a man, wearing awesome horns and an enviable pizzle, and probably snorting brimstone. Now that it had been domesticated into a barnyard commodity, its picture shrank to the meagerest identifiable symbol: a V surmounted by an arc, altogether just three lines to represent head and horns. The vivid, vivacious murals of combat and conquest which had previously adorned tent walls and battle shields were gradually distilled into geometric designs suitable for decorating the rims of pots and hems of gowns.

The farmer and rancher had one necessity which the hunter had not, that of counting and keeping account. The first adding machine was probably a handful of pebbles, one for each cow a rancher owned. The first farmer's almanac was probably a notched stick, perhaps with shallow nicks representing days, deeper ones standing for moon cycles, etc. These primitive tabulations are noteworthy in that they used concrete symbols for intangible, abstract concepts difficult of picturization, and so eventually contributed to the development of writing.

For example, in ancient Peru the Incas' method of counting was to tie knots in a string. Somewhere in prehistory it occurred to them that if a knot could represent a number, another kind of knot could stand for the object being counted.

In time the Incas developed the *quipu,* a complicated bundle of strings capable of conveying quite a variety of information. The *quipu* consisted of a stout rope from which depended tassels of strings of different colors and lengths (some of these bundles weighed ten pounds). The number and kinds of knots, their distance apart, the colors of the strings—all had different connotations. Obviously such a system could quite accurately record dates and figures, but there are some scholars who assert that the *quipus* were equally capable of communicating love letters and literary narratives.

Writing has been done in other modes and media, too—such as the *wampum* bead-belt of the North American Indians, and the *aroko* of the African Nebus: weeds, sticks and pebbles knotted together by a leather thong. Some relics of such systems may still be in use in odd corners of the world; there are some four hundred forms of writing, ancient and modern, known to grammatologists. But the writing systems of civilized society today are all descendants of the prehistoric pictograms. Indeed, some of the pictograms are still very much with us, very little changed. The Roman letter A is simply the bull's-head drawing turned upside down, a pictogram bequeathed to us from the ancient Phoenicians (to whom it was *alf,* "the ox").

While a few of the prehistoric pictures thus maintained some semblance of recognizability, most of them dwindled long ago into standardized pothooks. In other words, they were gradually simplified from pictograms into ideograms, or convenient shorthand scribbles meaning the same thing. In very early picture-writing, the sun was depicted as a fireball emanating prodigious rays, or sometimes wearing wings to indicate its lofty habitat. But eventually scribes found that a simple circle could get across the same idea. And now another factor, that of meaning-by-association, began to give writing even more flexibility of expression. The simple circle for "sun" came to do double duty as an ideogram for "day." Other characters similarly multiplied their usefulness: the symbol for "foot" served for the verb "to go," and so on.

The Chinese were particularly adept at creating words by association, and some of their devisings have an impudent humor to them. A certain Chinese character, standing alone, means "woman." Putting two of these "women" side by side makes the ideogram for "quarrel." Three "women" grouped together is the ideogram for "slander." In Nigeria, the Ibo tribes also had an eloquent ideogram for "quarrel": two lines bent in opposite directions and separated by a straight line—

that is, a man and wife sleeping back to back with a pillow between them.

While ideograms came to be an effective and expressive means of communication, they shared with pictograms one quality that was both a benefit and a bother; namely, they had no connection with the spoken language. On the one hand, this was all to the good, because people speaking different dialects or even totally different tongues could often share and understand the same written language. This attribute is even today the linguistic glue that holds the sprawling Chinese language together. There are four different versions of the basic spoken Chinese, and each of these is splintered into a profusion of dialects and subdialects. A native of Beijing cannot hope to converse with a Cantonese, but the two *can* communicate by handing notes back and forth. Although a particular ideogram may be read aloud by one of them as *nyin* and by the other as *chin*, it means "man" to them both.

There could hardly be three more disparate peoples than the Egyptians, Chinese and North American Indians, yet the ancient symbol for "infant" was the same in many of their writings—the drawing of a small figure sucking its thumb. Even the alphabetic languages of the West today still have use for supralingual ideograms. Scientists of whatever nationality can read each other's chemical formulas and algebraic equations. Musicians can follow each other's scores. Astronomers from every country use the same ideograms to represent the heavenly bodies and their doings.

But the drawback to an ideographic writing was (and is) that although it might serve for everybody's language, it was really nobody's. In order to learn to write, a student had to learn a whole new language different from the one he spoke. Paleographers have managed to decipher numerous pictographic and ideographic writings left by peoples whose spoken languages vanished with them. But though we know what the inscriptions mean, we will never know what they sounded like. Given the drawing of a stick figure stepping into a peaked box, an English interpreter would read, "The man goes into the house," and his German colleague would make it *Der Mann gehen in das Haus*, while, for all we know, the original scribe might have read it aloud as *Etaoin shrdlu*.

Even in the crude form of drawn pictures and representational symbols, writing was a considerable boon to mankind. But, had it remained disjunct from speech, man's oral languages would have continued to flake away into disparate dialects and jargons, an endlessly proliferating Babel. This is exactly what happened in China, where the written language exercised no fixative control over the spoken language. The greatest invention of all time, writing could not begin to fulfill its mighty potential until man perceived that it need not be an art apart—that it could instead be wedded to speech as a permanent transcription of the *spoken* word.

The Egyptians approached this ideal, but stopped short of attaining it. Their hieroglyphic characters included both pictograms and the simpler ideograms abstracted from pictures, but they also came to include symbols used phonetically. For example, the spoken word for sapphire in their language was *khesteb*. To refer to the stone in writing, a scribe would set down the hieroglyphics for the words *khesf* and *teb*. Now, *khesf* properly meant "stop" and *teb* meant "pig," but the scrivener was compounding their sound, not their sense, just as we might draw the picture of a bee and the numeral 4 to make "before." Gradually the scribes went even further and began to use hieroglyphs to stand for just their initial sounds; that is, the ideogram for "pig" (*teb*) would represent the consonantal sound *t*.

Although the Egyptians finally had forty-five symbols representing noises instead of things or ideas, they never took the supreme step of throwing out all the clutter of pictograms and ideograms and converting entirely to a phonetic alphabet. The sound-symbols were used when convenient, or at the whim of the scribes, but the Egyptians were apparently too enamored of the visual beauty of their hieroglyphs to abandon them for a more practical and prosaic system.

The Phoenicians, however, were a practical and prosaic people. It is still not clear where these Near Easteners got their writing system—or whether they ingeniously evolved it on their own. But the Phoenician letters do have unmistakable points of similarity to Egyptian characters, and the Phoenicians were both far-wandering travelers and voracious collectors of anything valuable. A fair guess—unprovable but not yet disproved—is that their traders visited Egypt, admired the local writing system, and cannily appropriated only the part of it they could use: the symbols for separate sounds.

A shrewd, no-sensense, merchant people, the Phoenicians had no more use for a "pretty" writing than a tax collector has for poetry. They found twenty-two symbols ample to transcribe a workable sufficiency of their spoken sounds, and those of the other nationalities they traded with, as well— and so the first phonetic alphabet was born. It was a very brisk and businesslike form of writing, with no pretensions to aesthetic eye appeal. And it fell somewhat short of ideal utility, in that all the twenty-two letters were consonants, and the filling in of vowel sounds was left to the reader to determine from the context of the message. Modern-day Semitic languages still require this extra effort on the part of the reader; the Hebrew characters customarily rendered as "Jehovah," properly transliterate as simply JHVH.

The Phoenicians found their system well enough suited to their mercantile purposes, and never tried to improve it further. It seems ironic that the earliest practical alphabet should have been compiled by a people with no literary aspirations whatsoever, who in fact bequeathed to humanity no writings except accounts, tax rolls and IOUs. But it is slightly gratifying—to anyone who counts commerce a poor inferior to literature—to discover that these granite, grasping people weren't *always* so efficient, even with the aid of the world's first alphabet. One of their wage lists, over four thousand years old, shows the amount of barley paid out by a landowner to his tenant herders for raising his sheep. This clay tablet is notable for two things: it is probably the earliest sample of bookkeeping—and it is added up wrong.*

The alphabet had one further development in prospect, and that was provided by the Greeks. They gladly adopted the Phoenician writing system, but discovered that some of the consonantal characters were unnecessary in their language, and so used them instead to represent vowel sounds. This simple stroke of genius eliminated the ambiguities inherent in the strictly consonantal writing—or most of them anyway—and the alphabet was essentially at the stage of development at which it still stands.

The original Phoenician system traveled in numerous other directions, to influence the alphabets developed in Persia, Armenia, Ethiopia, India, Tibet, Siam and other places—even such faraway lands as Korea and Indonesia. Meanwhile, the Greeks' version spread through Europe and begat further adaptations. In the northern countries, from Britain through Scandinavia to Siberia, it became the thorny-looking alphabet known as *runes*. Carried eastward by the Christian missionary St. Cyril, the Greek alphabet became (with additions)

* It translates:
   "*85 sheep paid for at 1½ measures*
   104 sheep at 1 measure
      An expense of 233 measures."
A quick check of the figures will show that the total should have been 231½ measures of barley.

the Cyrillic used by most of the Slavic peoples. Westward, the Romans adopted and adapted the Greek alphabet, then eventually extended its benefits to the rest of the Western world.

The ideographic writing of the Chinese did not inspire so many borrowings and imitations as did that of the Egyptians, and never has prompted the creation of a phonetic alphabet. The Japanese did appropriate the Chinese characters and, with their talent for improving on other people's inventions, converted them into a syllabary writing. Japanese being a polysyllabic language, with all its elements consisting either of vowel sounds or consonant-plus-vowel sounds (Christmas would be transliterated *Kirisimasu*), separate characters stand for separate syllables, not letters. But Japanese is complicated by the use of Chinese ideograms having the same appearance and meaning as in that language, the only difference being in pronunciation. There are some 1,800 of these used in everyday writing (newspapers, billboards, etc.), but an educated Japanese may make use of 50,000 or more.

Korea also adopted the Chinese ideograms intact, for its "literary language," now pretty much the preserve of academicians and classicists. But the popular language is written with a beautifully simple and functional alphabet, probably introduced by Buddhist missionaries from Southeast Asia. At a time when the Western world's literacy was limited to nobles, priests and soothsayers, in Korea even the rice-paddy workers could read and write, and Korean scholars were compiling the first known encyclopedia.

Everywhere in the world, men built their written languages as they would build a house. First make it sturdy, roomy, functional and comfortable—then make it handsome. The written word has yet to attain its full utility and fluency, but since its very inception its writers have been striving to improve its legibility and enhance its appearance. The Greeks, as usual, had a word for this: *kalligraphia*, the art of beautiful writing—and another word, *hopsis*, meaning an aesthetic delight in same.

The calligrapher has been honored in every land and every time. Chances are that the Stone Age artist was looked up to with awe by his fellow cavemen. Certainly the scribes of ancient Egypt (who, by dint of their medium, had to be artists as well) ranked high in the professional class. The medieval monk who could most artistically illuminate a text to the greater glory of God was the greater glory to his order. The Chinese find as much to admire and contemplate in a single written scroll as an art student does in the whole Louvre; until very recent times the Chinese had shrines where they reverently deposited every scrap of written-on paper after it had served its purpose.

One of the facets of the personality of a language is the look of its written word, but the writing itself can often have a personality of its own, entirely apart from whatever it says or whatever language it says it in. The medium in which a writing was first done has often determined the look of it in perpetuity, and men have written with and on just about everything, from fingertips in the sand to the icing on birthday cakes and smoke trails against the sky.

The angular wedge shapes of Babylonian cuneiform, like a scattering of carpet tacks, were the natural result of punching a pointed stylus into clay. Greek letters were also stiff and cold when they were first scratched on wax tablets; they did not achieve their graceful freehand curves until the scribes turned to the reed pen and papyrus. Gouging letters into a wooden surface developed square scripts, like the linear, chunky characters of the early Chinese; their later writers learned to use brush and ink, and the result was the infinite subtlety of calligraphic Chinese.

When man first learned to write, he seized upon this new talent and, like Stephen Leacock's impulsive hero, galloped gleefully off in all directions. Some people, the Semites for instance, preferred their writing to run in a horizontal direction from right to left. Others, like the Cretans, tried spiral writing, with the characters twining in ever narrowing coils. Some didn't mind which way the writing went; the Egyptians wrote arbitrarily from left to right or right to left, and indicated the direction for the reader by having all the hieroglyphic birds and animals facing the way the writing ran. The Greeks originally wrote *boustrophedon*, "as the ox plows," one line reading from left to right, the next from right to left, and so on alternately. Chinese, Japanese and Korean are read vertically downward in columns proceeding from right to left (and, like the Semitic writings, from the "back" of the book). Other people haven't yet made up their minds about the best direction for writing; the Tuaregs of the Sahara still write at whim, left to right or vice versa, top to bottom or vice versa.

The Roman preference for writing horizontally, left to right, set the direction for the whole Western world. The Romans also, through their predilection for erecting and inscribing monuments at every opportunity, gave us the form of letter most used today; one derivative of it is the type in which this book is set. The Roman monument designers developed a letter "face" in which pleasing proportions, beautifully stated curves, and the balance of thick and thin lines were all combined with its aptitude for being carved in stone. The stone-cutter's finishing stroke of the chisel gave the letters their serifs—those felicitous hairlines at the end of each stroke, which set the crowning touch to the Roman alphabet's artistry and elegance.

Various changes in the look of the alphabet came about through the exigencies of writing it by hand. Monks laboring with quill and parchment gradually eased the upright Roman capitals into the easy-flowing face called uncial ("inch-high," i.e., miniature), the forerunner of lower-case letters. When St. Patrick carried this version of the alphabet to Ireland the scribes there exalted it into the most graceful manuscript hand ever written this side of Suez. Other monks, in Italy, speeded up their copying tasks by developing the slanted, connected cursive script, which influenced both modern handwriting and *this type face, still called italic.*

As the Roman alphabet continued to diffuse throughout Europe, it underwent still further changes in appearance, adapting itself to different peoples' differing standards of beauty. Often, the look of an alphabet seemed to mirror the national character of its users. For example, the peoples of the sunny south gave their writing a rounded, open face that echoed the arches and vaults of their Romanesque architecture. But the habitants of the harsher north thickened the alphabet's thick lines and diminished its thin ones until the letters became the dense and spiky Gothic or Black Letter face. It assumed the ramrod verticality of a Gothic cathedral and the forbidding dignity of the six-barreled, unhyphenated, *zusammengesetzt* German words it is still used to spell.

Johann Gutenberg, credited with inventing printing (in Europe, anyway), was a German, so it was only natural that he should copy his first type faces from the national Black Letter script, and that the rapid spread of printing should disseminate this turbid alphabet throughout the Continent. But the demand for printed material grew so fast that printers very soon were designing and casting new fonts. These early type faces were based on the favored alphabets of the printers' native countries; then came a proliferation of faces copied from every available manuscript style.

No one can count how many type faces have been designed and used in the ensuing five hundred years. Some of them, the grotesque as well as the graceful, have enjoyed an occasional fad during which they've bedizened every piece of paper in sight. An example was the family of "handbill" types ubiquitous in nineteenth-century America. This loud-mouthed face (an Italian import) reduced the actual letters to vestigial scratches and overweighted the terminal serifs into black blobs at top and bottom. But most such outré inventions strutted only briefly in public before retiring to arty letterheads and bohemian coffeehouse menus. Thanks be, the greater portion of printed work today is done in clean and legible types derived from the early classic alphabets.

But even the simplest type faces, like every other form of writing, can manifest individual peculiarities and personalities. Some of their personalities, indeed, have become so well known as to be wearisome. The antique Black Letter, probably because it was the type face Gutenberg employed for the first printed Bible, has kept to this day an aura of sanctity, or at any rate sanctimony. Some version of it (generally the face called Old English) is still used to print every self-important message that aspires to appear *ex cathedra*—from a newspaper's name flag to the undertakers' ads on its obituary page.

While the personality of a style of writing or of a font of type is often easy to perceive in a fairly lengthy inscription, there have been people who've claimed to discern idiosyncrasies, secrets and surprising revelations in isolated words and even in individual letters. Dante saw a human visage in the written word *omo,* in his day the Italian for "man." Rimbaud envisioned vowels as colors: *a* was black, *e* white, *i* red, etc. The early Christians took the Greek *upsilon* (Y) as a text for sermons; they saw in it a road forking into the divergent paths of righteousness and primroses. The Greeks themselves, having forgotten the origins of their alphabet, dreamed up plausible geneses from the shapes of the letters—e.g., that *delta* (Δ) was copied from the female sex organs and *phi* (φ) from the male.

It is a minor wonder that the letter S is still with us; it and its sibilant siblings in other alphabets have long been abhorred by people who perceived in them the shape or sound of the dread serpent or the monogram of the even more dreaded Satan. The Yezedi Arabs won't pronounce the letter. The Hebrew scribes took care not to use it in the opening pages of the Scriptures. The Greek poet Pindar omitted it from his odes. The medieval Romans' use of S as their numeral for 7 may have been intended to take the curse off it by linking it with that traditionally "lucky" number.

No alphabet has yet achieved all that could be desired in the transcription of the spoken word. Even such a voluminous system as the Thai alphabet, with its thirty-two vowels and forty-four consonants, still falls short of optimum utility. The ideal would be the establishment of a single sign for each sound of the human voice and, equally important, the constant use of the same sign for the same sound and *only* that sound.

The Spanish language has one of the most efficient and uncomplicated alphabets—for transcribing its own speech, that is; it cannot easily cope with such foreign sounds as the German *kn,* the English *sh,* the French *u.* English, though praiseworthy in other respects, has one of the most inefficient alphabets of any language. For example, spoken English has twenty or more different basic vowel sounds; written English has only six characters (counting *y*) with which to transcribe them. And consider the various sounds represented by *ough* in such words as bough, through, though, tough, cough and ought. By contrast, the single sound *ee* can be written in at least seven ways: meet, mean, receive, serene, field, marine, people.

Russia, after the 1917 revolution, took steps to skim some of the dross off its system of spelling. The elimination of just one supernumerary character shortened *War and Peace* by seventy pages. Now the only major linguistic renovation of our time is underway, again in the Soviet Union, with a campaign against unnecessary double letters. Such words as *kommunist, appetit,* even *Kyrilliza,* the name of the Russian alphabet, will be shortened to *komunist, apetit, Kyriliza.* Of some twelve hundred words containing double letters, only twelve will stay as is; one of them is *Russia.*

Primitive peoples have always seen magic and mystery in the written (or pictured) word. Even in civilized society, otherwise sensible folk are too often ready to believe any kind of twaddle if it appears in print, and many will endure public humiliation if it means getting their names in print. Such mindless kowtowing to the written word can sometimes perpetuate and even ennoble foolish errors.

According to Etiemble, the Chinese have for centuries misused the character *chouou,* "to speak," with the meaning of *yue,* "to rejoice," simply because "an absent-minded scribe once copied *chouou* for *yue,*" and the Chinese reverence for the written word would not permit of rectifying the error. In England and America, an alphabetical error has been kept alive by people who just adore its quaintness. This is the use of the article "ye," as in such abominations as Ye Wee Tea Shoppe.

There never *was* an article pronounced "ye." Early English scribes borrowed the Anglo-Saxon runic character þ (called "thorn" because it began that word) as a shorthand writing of *th,* which is the way it was always spoken. Later, the first printers, having no þ in their type fonts, substituted y as the closest lookalike, but it was still pronounced "th." Still later, long after that typographic usage had gone out of fashion, antic antiquarians resurrected it for its present affectation, which appears likely to endure as long as tea and simpery shall last.

One final note on the innate personalities of writing per se. As G. K. Chesterton remarked in New York's Times Square, the written word's beauty is often magnified in the eye of a beholder ignorant of its language. Chesterton said of Broadway's blaze of lights, "What a glorious garden of wonders it would be if one could not read." More recently, an American lady tourist arrived in Beirut, Lebanon, just at nightfall, when all over the city the deliciously enigmatic squiggles of Arabic neon signs flashed on, as lovely as frozen fireworks. Enraptured, she turned to her guide and breathlessly exclaimed, "Gorgeous! But what do they mean? That one there, tell me, what does that one say?"

"It says," replied her guide, somewhat sheepishly, "it says Coca-Cola."

The crudest savage may unconsciously manipulate with effortless ease a linguistic system so intricate, manifoldly systematized, and intellectually difficult, that it requires the lifetime study of our greatest scholars to describe its workings.
                                        —BENJAMIN LEE WHORF

A Maison Is Not a Home

U N H A P P Y lovers always should be Frenchmen," wrote Christopher Morley. "So sweet a tongue for any kind of pain."

Most of the Western world seems to agree that French is the language of love—and of diplomacy, culture, gastronomy and aristology in general. We have tags for other tongues, too. German has long been considered the language of science; English, the language of commerce; Chinese, of wisdom; Italian, of the arts; Latin and Greek, the languages of logic; etc. To a linguistic disciplinarian these epithets are merely time-honored whimsies, and easily debunkable. After all, the Chinese manage to make love in their language, and the French to make maxims in theirs. But the various languages didn't get their labels without reason.

Sometimes the identification came about through an early association of language and subject. For example, French has enjoyed its romantic reputation since the twelfth century, when that tongue first sang of chivalry and the cult of "courtly love." This "courtly love" consisted of a rather masochistic, spaniel-eyed worship of some beloved who had to be eternally unattainable. The cult's devotees sublimated their unrequited yearnings into countless *ballades, lais* and *chante-fables* ranging from spoony to spicy. Wandering troubadours broadcast these songs and narratives throughout Europe for centuries afterward, and so established French forever as the "language of love." Just as France instituted the Age of Chivalry, Italy later begat the Renaissance, and gave it an ample Ital-

[32]

ian lexicon—the "language of the arts"—before it spread through the rest of Europe.

But often a language has won its reputation by dint of its own inherent personality. To the popular mind, some aspect of a tongue—its vocabulary, syntax, sound, or just its indefinable *Sprachgefühl*—can make it seem peculiarly suited to some aspect of human endeavor. A passage of Homer's Greek or Horace's Latin can almost persuade a reader that it was composed with a slide-rule. Such spare, clean coolness suggests equally lucid and straightforward thinking; hence the "languages of logic." Chinese seems (to Occidentals anyway) the ideal language for sages and savants because, in verbatim translation, its lack of grammatical inflections makes the tritest aphorism appear laconic, pithy and profound: "Confucius say, 'Better diamond with flaw than pebble without.'"

Since Kepler's day, German innovators have been responsible for a good many of the world's scientific advances, and for the neologisms necessary to describe them. But besides that, the German language—with its formidable compound words and its ponderous Black Letter script—somehow seemed just *right* for verbalizing the arcana of science.

English established itself as the "language of commerce" during the high tide of British imperialism. While Englishmen were staking out colonies, dependencies, treaty ports and trade routes, their language was similarly gobbling up operative words from the tongues of those far-flung outposts—and at the same time insinuating itself as the basis for the pidgin languages of most of the outposts. (The very word "pidgin" means "business.")

But while the vocabulary of a certain language may seem uniquely suited to some specialized category of human doings, it can just as strikingly seem to be inadequate in other categories. Regard the Frenchman, for example. He may live in a house, a castle, a cottage, lodgings, a household (*maison, château, chaumière, logis* or *ménage*) or any other sort of digs. He may even be "at home" (*chez lui*). But nowhere in his vocabulary is there a single, unambiguous substantive meaning simply "a home." Such a phrase as "there's no place like home" defies verbatim translation into French.

Many another language has made do without words which an English-speaker would consider indispensable. The Romans would seem to have had a diplomatic aversion to straight answers; they had no word for "yes" or "no." The Chinese language still doesn't. Another seeming deficiency of Chinese is that it makes no pronominal or verbal distinction among "he," "she" and "it." The only third person singular pronoun is the catch-all *t'a*—"that one."

Neither Hindi nor Urdu, the most-spoken tongues of India and Pakistan respectively, has a verb meaning "to have." Nor has Russian, and this is a fact antedating the collective ownership—or nonownership—of the Communist system. Russian also lacks a word for "business"; it has borrowed the English word (as *biznis*) to mean "black market."

The Portuguese have no names for their weekdays; they number them instead. The Germans give a name to every day except Wednesday, which is simply *Mittwoch*, "mid-week." (In the metropolises of the United States, Friday seems increasingly to be called Getaway Day.) The Eskimos have no word for "snow." Or, rather, they have no one generic word but numerous specific ones, to refer to falling snow, drifted snow, granular snow, etc. The Basque language has no word for "God." (In pagan days, however, it seems the Basques did acknowledge a deity named Jinko—and it may be that the English exclamation "by Jingo!" and the pejorative "jingoism" were somehow derived from that source.)

The Spaniards and the Japanese vie for the palm as the most polite people on earth. But the Spanish language has no single word for "please," and substitutes flowery periphrases like "do me the favor of . . ." and "have the goodness to. . . ." Japanese lacks an expression for "I'm sorry," but makes up for it with even more contrite forms of apology such as "This is poison to your honorable spirit."

Of all people, we English-speakers should be least amazed or amused at the seeming eccentricities of other languages; our own is composed in such large part of borrowings from them. But more to the point, English displays some eccentricities of its own. For instance, its otherwise opulent vocabulary is shy a few pronouns, and the lack is a nuisance. There is no easy pronominal alternative to the clumsy "he or she" construction in sentences like "Every passenger must claim his or her own baggage." Nor does there exist a neuter possessive relative pronoun to replace "whose" in a case like "He held a teapot whose spout was chipped." The word "which's" seems indicated, but there is no such word; and although "whose" is necessarily granted acceptance it has an air of fairy-tale anthropomorphism.

The lack of a word in one language is most often apparent to a speaker of some other tongue which does contain that particular locution. A man's own language is as comfortable and unremarkable to him as the skin he lives in. Unless he dabbles in comparative linguistics, he is not likely to perceive any personality or peculiarity at all in his own tongue; it is always the other fellow's language that he finds interesting or odd, and that mainly insofar as it differs from his own. No matter how many languages a person knows, and no matter how fluently, he tends to use just one of them for his thinking processes (and, incidentally, for dreaming in). That one thus stands as the norm of correctitude and, consciously or not, he is inclined to regard all others as departing from "normal" in some degree.

This is only human nature. But a supercilious attitude toward the other fellow's language can sometimes instigate an unfair opinion of the other fellow himself. It is entirely possible that the French tongue's lack of a word for "home" influenced the rest of the world's unshakable belief that the French are a nation of flighty philanderers. Whatever character one may choose to attribute to the French, and no matter what their dictionary implies, Frenchmen do have homes.

However, while the glaringly "obvious" facets of a language may be superficial and misleading, its less obtrusive characteristics often *can* tell us something about the society of which it is the voice.

Christian missionaries have often had to preach to primitive peoples totally ignorant of concepts taken for granted in the civilized world, and so have had to introduce some tortuosities into their Gospel translations. For example, numerous heathens recoil at the idea of a "kiss," so the Bibles supplied to them render the word in such ways as "to greet by smelling each other's face." A "temple," in a society that never heard of such a thing, may become a "praise-God house." The idea of "worship" is conveyed to one Central American Indian tribe as "to wag one's tail before God."

Each language, from its beginnings, has been molded to fit its society's philosophies, occupations, interests, beliefs, traditions—in sum, to express its total culture. The language becomes an instrument of greater or lesser scope of expression, specialization or generality, flexibility or rigidity. At the same time, the language becomes the main medium by which that culture is perpetuated. As such, it exerts a directing and delimiting influence of its own on the culture's pattern and development. Culture and language progress together down the ages, so commingled that it's moot to say which is the container and which the contained. The cultural influence of language has been described in many and abstruse terms, but perhaps semanticist S. I. Hayakawa has said it most simply: "The way in which we talk about the world shapes our perceptions of that world." And, as shall be shown in the course of this book, the ways in which people talk about the world involve many more factors than the extent of their formal vocabularies.

We don't have to eavesdrop on bushfellows, either, to find examples. The English right under your nose has its infrangible rule that every sentence must contain a subject and a predicate. That is, a verb of being or doing cannot exist without a *something* to be or do it. One result is that we continually invoke the faceless phantom It to wreak such actions as "It is raining." Common to all Indo-European languages, this grammatical insistence that no action can occur independently of an actor is a constant reminder of our Western culture's reverence for the concept of cause and effect. Might not the linguistic structure even have been the *basis* of the causality concept? More than one scholar has suggested that both Aristotelian philosophy and the Newtonian synthesis were the result of their originators' having been nudged by their linguistic conditioning into certain ways of thinking.

In the case of some societies, whose outlooks on life were radically remote from what we would consider "natural," the interconnection of language and culture is even plainer to see. Of course, these societies and their languages are no longer what they were before civilization got at them. But in their pristine state they demonstrated that all mankind need not and did not see the world in the same ways.

The Trobriand Islanders, for example, seem to have had small regard for the relation between cause and effect. Their language had no words like "why" or "because." Any person, event or thing had being and meaning only at the moment it was perceived, used, mentioned or thought about. A thing *was,* that's all, and how it came to be so was inconsiderable. This is not to be construed as brute ignorance; naturally they understood that the sun's rising was the cause of daylight, and that the way to get a fish was to net or hook it. They merely considered any such instances of "how" and "why" so self-evident as not to need discussing—a blithe indifference quite contrary to our passion for analysis, dissection and tinkering to see what makes things tick.

But if the Trobrianders lived in a world of perpetual stasis, the Nootka Indians of Vancouver lived in a world of eternal flux. Their language made no distinction between nouns and verbs, between things and actions. To the Nootkas nothing just *stood* there, it *did* something. Their expression for "a man," for instance, would be an occurrence-word on the order of "it mans." And if the man was doing something besides just manning, they had a stock of affixes to indicate "it walking-mans" or "it sitting-down-mans," or to describe him as "it white-mans" or whatever.

Probably oddest of all, to our view, is a language whose verbs have no past, present or future tenses. The Hopi Indian dialect recognizes only the tenses of fact ("I am eating"), expectation ("I am not yet eating") and nomic regularity ("I do eat"). This is just one of the peculiarities of the Hopi tongue; it has numerous other variances from what we would consider normal and needful. But its verb structure alone says something about the Hopi psychology and their philosophy of life.

Time, to us, is like sand trickling through an hourglass, each day, hour and moment a separate grain: countable, ponderable, manipulable. To the Hopi time was more like water flowing into a lake, each "now" being the lake's accumulation to date of all the moments and millenniums that had flowed in before. The Hopi's existence was geared to this concept of cumulative experience. He venerated his ancestors, treasured tradition and maintained the ancient ways of doing things—because he and his whole immediate world were the sum of them. His life was based on rote; for example, his ceremonial dances were endlessly repeated and danced interminably, because (to his view) every step of them added to the accumulation of prior eons of identical steps, hence to their stored-up "influence" on the weather, the crops or what-not.

With his notion of cumulative time and life, the primitive Hopi would have been ill-equipped—both psychologically and linguistically—to comprehend the white man's concept of sequential time. And our clock-watching preoccupation with records, graphs, contracts, deadlines, stock futures, etc., would have seemed as unrealistic to the Hopi as his raindance to us. On the other hand, it has been suggested that the white man, if he could adopt the Hopi's way of seeing the world as an indivisible space-time continuum, could better grasp such abstract concepts as those of Einsteinian relativity and the fourth dimension.

The cultural differences between less hermitic societies— between the French and the German, say—are naturally not so chasmal as between the Hopi and practically any other people in the world. Nor do the major languages exhibit such striking differences, one from another. But they do have their differences and, even where these are not significant of some cultural peculiarity, they do contribute to the uniqueness of each language's personality.

Anyone with the patience to read through a foreign-language dictionary can discover which of his words that language deems unnecessary, and which ones it includes that his doesn't. But generally not until he starts learning to speak another tongue does he realize that sounds are subject to similar anomalies. Many languages are devoid of vocal sounds which are basic and common to others—not to mention the gestures, grimaces, etc., which some languages find almost as necessary as words.

The Koreans and Japanese have no emphatic *l* sound in their own speech, and consequently find it difficult to pronounce when they essay a tongue like English which does require it. The *r* sound is for them the easiest approximation. ("Rots of ruck!" became a standard parting salute between American GIs in Japan and Korea.) The Chinese have the same problem in reverse. They have no distinguishable *r* sound in their language, and so tend to substitute the *l*—"I am velly ploud to meet an Amelican."

Hindi and Urdu have no long *a* sound (as in "day"). A Greek has trouble learning to pronounce the *b* sound, a German the *w*, an Arab the *p*, a Russian the *h*, an American the unvoiced uvular fricative *ch* (as in Gaelic *loch*). In Spanish the six vowels have fairly fixed and unvarying values, so a Spaniard finds it hard to cope with the inconstant vowels of English. Because the short *i* of "this" is alien to his vocal habits, he pronounces the word "thees." A Frenchman is likewise unaccustomed to the short *i*, and to the voiced fricative *th* as well, so *he* pronounces the word "zees."

Pronunciation is, of course, just one characteristic of oral language; pace, rhythm, stress and intonation are other factors. A German's heartiest greeting to his dearest friend has all the vivacity of an elevator operator calling floors, while a Swede can make a lilting warble out of the fine print in an insurance policy.

The Teutonic languages, such as English, are characterized by clumps of consonants ("twelfths," "latchstring") which tend to chop up an utterance into just-perceptible bursts of one or a few sounds at a time. More liquid languages, such as Spanish, Japanese and Hawaiian, in which the consonantal sounds are separated and softened by vowels, can be articulated without noticeable interruption or modulation. To the nonspeaker, such an utterance often sounds like one long, non-stop word fired off with machine-gun rapidity.

In some cases the vocal intonation of a language is necessary to make it intelligible. The Chinese sing-song way of speaking is no mere mannerism. That language has only a few basic speech sounds; the meaning of each word must depend on its position in a sentence in relation to other words, and equally important, on the pitch at which it is uttered. Mandarin Chinese utilizes four different tones, Cantonese uses nine. Professor Mario Pei has cited one Chinese sentence, a gibber of noises which, without the proper up-and-down-scale intonation, would be as incomprehensible to a Chinese as to a Kickapoo: *Mama chi ma, ma man, mama ma ma.* It means, said Pei, "Mother rides horse, horse slow, mother curses horse."

Even those who can't make sense of a foreign language can form some opinion of it, just from its sound. French got its "language of love" label, as we have seen, from an early identification with the subject. But it could hardly have kept that distinction all this time if it hadn't been melodious enough—even to non-French ears—to befit that tender emotion. It's difficult to imagine German sounding like a "language of love" to anybody but another German. Its gear-grinding gutturals seem more perfectly meshed to mechanical and technical expressions.

Robert, Lord Lytton, once penned a somewhat grumpy verse to declare what foreign languages sounded like to him:

> The Italians have voices like peacocks; the Spanish
> Smell, I fancy, of garlic; the Swedish and Danish
> Have something too Runic, too rough and unshod, in
> Their accent for mouths not descended from Odin;
> German gives me a cold in the head, sets me wheezing
> And coughing; and Russian is nothing but sneezing.

It should be noted that Lytton didn't do much to heighten the stature of his *own* language, what with those sophomoric eye-rhymes. Furthermore, the stanza sizzles with sibilants, thus giving considerable credibility to the epithet that several other nationalities apply to English: "the hissing tongue."

While most individuals of differing nationalities are commendably inclined to tolerate and respect each other's language on a man-to-man level (and often, indeed, to admire the piquancy of a foreigner's accent), nationalities *en bloc* quite often take just the opposite attitude, and contemn or revile the "barbaric" noises made by others. The word "barbaric" itself comes from the term which the ancient Greeks applied to all foreigners, *hoi barbaroi.* It meant "the babblers," the speakers of any uncivilized, brutish tongue; that is, any language other than Greek.

The French epigrammatist Antoine Rivarol once observed, smugly, "Whatever is not clear is not French." To which I will append only one comment: that the original title (and gimmick) of Perrault's "Cinderella" was *La Petite Pantoufle de Vair,* or "The Little *Fur* Slipper." His countrymen confused the sound of *vair* with *verre,* and Cinderella has been wearing a glass slipper ever since.

The French still say of one who mishandles their language, *Il parle français comme la vache espagnol.* This means, "He speaks French as the cow speaks Spanish," and is itself something of a mishandling of the language. The original saying was, "He speaks French as the *Basque* speaks Spanish," because the Basques speak a tongue incomprehensible to anyone else on earth. (The Spaniards compress a similar snide sentiment into a single word: *vasconcear*—literally "to speak Basque," colloquially "to babble.")

To one with no knowledge of a particular language, its sound may be the only discernible aspect of its personality. But a student of that tongue soon sees other characteristic idiosyncrasies in its grammar, syntax and idiom: personality facets peculiar to that language alone—often seeming *most* peculiar. For example, the beginning student of German is frequently stunned by its boxcar words and freight-train sentences, with the verb riding like a caboose at the end.

German capitalizes every noun, as English also did until the early nineteenth century. But English is the only major language which consistently capitalizes two particular pronouns wherever they appear in a sentence—the third person singular He, His, Him, Who, etc., when it refers to the Deity, and the first person singular I. Whether this little conceit implies a megalomaniac sense of me-and-God equality, I don't know; but the fact is that most other Western languages more courteously reserve the pronominal capitalization for You.

English and the other Teutonic tongues are accustomed to putting an adjective in front of its noun. The Romance languages usually reverse that order, though in some cases the relative positions of noun and adjective can make a difference in meaning—as with the Spaniard's sympathetic *pobre hombre* ("poor chap") and more bluntly descriptive *hombre pobre* ("pauper").

Most languages pluralize their nouns by adding a suffix or by changing their endings. But some Arabic words achieve their plural by becoming shorter; a single genie is a *jinni,* a flock of them are *jinn.* Malayan often makes its plural simply by repeating the singular form: *kuda,* "horse," *kuda-kuda,* "horses." And, where most of the world's languages indicate change in number, case, conjugation, etc., at the tail end of a word, the African Bantu makes its changes at the beginning of a word. For example, *mu-ntu* means "man" and *ba-*

ntu means "men." A Korean varies his verb endings according to whether he is speaking to a superior, an inferior or an equal; moreover, the verb endings are influenced by the tenor of the utterance (whether it's casual, weighty, wheedling or whatever) and even by the calendar date ("Happy New Year" takes a different form depending on whether it's spoken on New Year's Eve or New Year's Day).

In King Alfred's time the English language contained a clutter of case, gender and number endings on nouns, pronouns and adjectives. English has since learned to do without most of these, but they are still necessary to many others of the Indo-European language family. To the English-speaker, one of the most wearying aspects of learning a Continental language is the infernal bother of trying to remember whether a chair, say, is masculine, feminine, common or neuter in gender.

Some linguistic scholars claim that the whole business of gender is a remnant of the primitive belief that everything in the world was inhabited by a spirit and that therefore every single object, animate or not, had to be referred to respectfully by the equivalent of "Sir" or "Madam." Others dispute this theory, and maintain that the two or three genders still existent in various languages represent merely a boiling-down or simplification from an earlier time when almost every noun had a separate classification and all its attendant articles, pronouns and adjectives had to wear affixes to agree with it. The student of Latin can be happy, then, while struggling amid its masculine, feminine and neuter genders, that he has *only* three classifications to contend with.

By whatever means gender was engendered, few languages seem to agree on how many of them there should be. The Semitic and Romance tongues recognize masculine and feminine, the Scandinavian languages prefer common and neuter, German follows Latin's lead with masculine, feminine and neuter.

Furthermore, few languages can agree on which nouns should fall into which gender. This disparity offers plenty of room for speculation as to whether the personality of a language does reflect the personality of its speakers. Regard the Frenchman again. His love (*l'amour*) is classified as masculine in gender, while his lovemaking (*la cour*) is feminine. Is the male, then, the guardian of those soft ramparts, and the female the aggressive besieger? Then why is adultery (*l'adultère*) considered strictly a masculine trespass? Why is the Frenchman, when drafted into service as a military sentry, transvested into the feminine gender (*la sentinelle*)

while at home his forlorn wife sulks in her curiously masculine "pouting room" (*le boudoir*)? There are hundreds of
such contrarieties in the Gallic vocabulary. A properly selec-
tive compiler of them could conjecture almost any sort of
personality—weird, wild, wonderful—for the French language and the French people.

And the same goes for every other language that is similarly fragmented into schizoid genders. Why is the German's
wife (*das Weib*) and the Dane's child (*barnet*) sexlessly
neuter? Why does the German see the sun (*die Sonne*) as
feminine and the moon (*der Mond*) as masculine, when they
are considered just the opposite by all other Europeans and
by practically every one of mankind's myths?

Milk, one of the indisputably female contributions to the
universe, has been libeled by the Romance peoples from the
ancient Romans—who deemed it a neuter substance (*lac,
lactis*)—to the French, Portuguese and Italians who, even
more oddly, consider it masculine (*le lait, o leite, il latte*).
Of the Romance peoples, only the Spanish—and no one
knows why—have had the plain good sense to feminize milk
as *la leche*.

English is generally acknowledged the language best supplied with synonyms and neologisms to convey the minutest
gradations of meaning. But English is rather less finicky
about shades of meaning than are some other tongues. To an
Englishman or an American, there is a vast difference,
aesthetically and otherwise, between a leg of lamb and a leg
of dancer-actress Rita Moreno, but the one word "leg" suffices
for both. Not so in Miss Moreno's native Puerto Rico. In
Spanish, a person's leg is a *pierna*, an animal's a *pata*. German makes a like distinction; the verb "to eat" is *essen* for
people, *fressen* for animals. To employ the latter verb to say
that someone is eating (*er frisst*) is to imply that he swills
like a hog.

Conversely, in just about all languages, a single word is
often saddled with double duty through the process of association. The German *Abend* means "the west," and the sun
sets in the west, so the word is also used to mean "evening."
The Hawaiian *aloha* is both a noun ("love") and the world's
loveliest interjection for both "hello" and "goodbye." The Chinese *mai*, depending on its intonation, can mean either "buy"
or "sell"; when both versions are put together (*mai-mai*) it
means "business." The word *mako*, in many Polynesian dialects, means both "tooth" and "shark." The near-extinct Bam-
bara of the Sudan must have been a tuneful tongue; its word
fo meant both "to speak" and "to play a musical instrument."

And some words, through long, devious, often untraceable processes of association, have come to have two or more separate, even contradictory meanings. The English "cleave" is one of these—a husband and wife may cleave together until death cleaves them in twain. "Cleave" at least has some excuse for its Jekyll-Hyde personality. The two meanings derive from two different Anglo-Saxon words: *clifian* ("to adhere") and *cleofan* ("to split").

But the ambiguities of other words sometimes defy exegesis. The German *Reiz* can mean either "charm" or "irritation"; *sperren* can mean "to open" or "to close"; *Handel* can be either a friendly "trade" or an unfriendly "quarrel." The Russian *slovo* can mean either "word" or "secret." The Hebrew *bara* can mean "to create" or "to destroy." The French *se marrer* can be either "to be bored" or, in the words of one French-English dictionary, "to split one's side with laughing." There may be some sly significance in the fact that the Portuguese *requebrat* can mean either "to woo" or "the female posterior."

Some languages concoct unique words and expressions which other tongues are unable to translate exactly, or at least succinctly, and so borrow as is. The French vocabulary has been plundered by many foreigners—notably the English, Americans and Russians (in the old tsarist days)—who consider the dropping of a frequent offhand Gallicism to be *très gentil, blasé* or *risqué*.

Unfortunately, the borrowings quite often get mispronounced. People who render *vichyssoise* as *"vee-shee-swah"* should stick to "cold potato soup." They are the same people who serve "ore-durvs," "crayps," and "canopies." Then there are the concert-goers who talk of having heard Saint-Saëns' *Danse Micawber*. The common mispronunciation of *pied-à-terre* as "peed-a-terre" inspired cartoonist Richard Taylor to illustrate it (in the book *Fractured French*) with a drawing of a gentleman slipping away from a crowded cocktail party to relieve himself on the terrace.

The very sound of foreign words has sometimes inspired imitative coinages. "Braggadocio" sounds authentically Italian, but it comes from a name which Edmund Spenser invented—"brag" plus an Italianate suffix—for a boastful character in his *Faerie Queene*. "Legerdemain" is a noun compounded of legitimate French elements (*léger*, "light," *de main*, "of hand"), but the French have never used such a word and it doesn't appear in French dictionaries. The word is strictly an English fabrication.

The languages which are the most prolific contributors to

others are often the busiest borrowers as well. To take French again as an example, it was appropriating bits of German as long ago as the fifth century; survivals in modern French include *auberge* ("inn," German *Herberge*) and *jardin* ("garden," German *Garten*). One of the things the Norman conquerors took with them to England in 1066 was their *rôti de boeuf*, and the Anglo-Saxon thane eventually learned to call his cooked ox "roast beef." Seven or eight hundred years later, the French, though they still had their *rôti de boeuf*, added to their culinary glossary that exotic English dish *rosbif*. And it seems that the Frenchman never had a word to describe the hinged fanlight above his front door until sometime in the last century, when a German tourist pointed to one and inquired, "*Was ist das?*" Evidently taking the question for a statement, the French have called the transom a *vasistas* ever since.

By the 1870s the English word "handicapper" was in common use at the Longchamps racetrack, English "flirtation" a common pastime at Maxim's, and French newspapers had substituted the English word "reporter" for their native *rapporteur*. In the 1920s *le coquetêle* ("cocktail") went to France, like other good Americans, to sit out Prohibition, and decided to stay. More recently, since World War II, France has seized on innumerable English expressions, most of them Americanisms—*le knockout*, Scotch *sur le rocks, gadget, le snack* (snack bar), *le self* (cafeteria), *le standing* (prestige, status), *le stripteuse* (masculine gender!), etc. The Academicians and purists raise hell about this "bastard Franglais" as they call it, and denounce the trend as a deliberate American fomentation calculated to "colonize" France.

But people only borrow what they want or think they need, and massive linguistic changes can seldom be accomplished by either fiat or fifth column. Quebec's recurrent threat to secede from the rest of Canada is impelled in large part by the desire to prevent further English-language inroads on its French culture. In southern India, where the speakers of numerous different Dravidian dialects have become accustomed to using English as a common tongue, scores of people died in riots in early 1965 protesting the government's move to convert them to the "official" Hindi.

As has been shown, a people will readily borrow foreign locutions to express things their own language can't. But in some cases a *little* borrowing is not enough. Take the Hopi tongue. While it has incorporated many English and Spanish elements, and is quite adequate for use in modern Hopi home life and tribal affairs, its basic structure just could not adapt

[44]

to the exigencies of "outside" civilization. The Hopi's negotiation of leases on their oil lands, for instance, would be next to impossible to discuss in a language lacking a conventional future tense. Only by adopting the white man's "language of commerce" entire—and with it much of the white man's way of thinking—were the Hopi able to join the modern-day world.

But then again, immoderate linguistic borrowing can have its drawbacks, as in Switzerland, which officially speaks nothing *but* borrowed languages. To mention just one area where the country finds this an impediment to efficiency: a military air force, of all things, ought to be guidable by instant and clear-cut commands. But the Swiss Air Force has to direct its pilots with orders issued simultaneously in French, German and Italian.

Of the languages in use in the world today, some 130 are considered "major" in that each is spoken by one million people or more. Most of the major languages and a great many of the lesser ones have contributed innumerable words and phrases to each other. But there is one hermit language—Basque—which, so far as can etymologically be proved (and unless "jingo" can be credited to that source), has donated just one solitary word to the rest of the world. In its English and French versions the word is "bizarre," and it came into circulation by a process that was—well, slightly bizarre.

The source word, *bizar*, means in Basque "a beard." The Spanish and Portuguese adopted it as *bizarro* and, apparently deeming hairiness an attribute of manliness, gave it the meaning of "gallant, bold." The Italians apparently judged a bold man to be one who could demand his own way, however whimsical, and so they took over the word (*bizzarro*) to mean "capricious." The French saw even more caprice in *bizarre* and defined it as "odd, queer." It came into English as "grotesque, fantastic" and that meaning has more or less eclipsed all the intermediate ones in the other languages.

Various other locutions have undergone even more surprising changes during their migration from one language to another. The otherwise undistinguished Vauxhall depot in London has been immortalized in Russian as *voksal*, the now-generic word for "railroad station." The noble English knight got his high-toned title from the low-born German *Knecht*, a servant or farmhand. Aspic, the chilled jelly used in salads, got both its chill and its name from a snake; specifically, from the French expression *froid comme un aspic,* "cold as an asp." The wonderfully descriptive English adjec-

tive "puny" represents a mild misunderstanding and mispronunciation of the French *puiné*, "younger." (The French
word for "puny" is *chétif*—not nearly so evocative of puni-
ness.)

The Latin *senior* ("older") became a title of respect in
most of the countries that once were part of the Roman
Empire—in England "sir" and "sire," in France *sieur, monsieur* and *seigneur*, in Spain *señor*, in Portugal *senhor* and in
Italy *signore*. The latter three gave the title a feminine ending to extend the same respect to married ladies (*señora,
senhora, signora*). Then, in a gesture of somewhat dubious
gallantry, they gave the feminine word a diminutive suffix to
make a title for unmarried maidens (*señorita, senhorita,
signorina*). The result is that the loveliest, liveliest lass in
Spain, Portugal or Italy is literally a "little elderly lady."

There are numerous words and expressions which are so
very much at home in their native tongues that other languages seem reluctant to adopt or adapt them. But they might
well benefit by doing so; some of these exotic locutions possess a utility, color or flavor that home-grown substitutes just
can't imitate.

The Chinese have what may be the world's most useful
term, *hao-bu-hao*, which means literally "good, not good," but
is colloquially employed to mean practically anything under
the sun. Used *in toto* as a question, it can ask, "How do you
do?"—and either *hao* or *bu-hao* can reply. It can ask, "Is
this O.K.?"—and answer it. It can ask, "Yes or no?"—and
answer it either "Yes," "No" or "Well, yes and no." Again
entire, *hao-bu-hao* can be put to all the noncommittal uses
of the English "so-so," the rural American "fair-to-middling,"
the French *comme ci, comme ça*, the Italian *cosi-cosi*, etc.—
and still not begin to exhaust its infinite variety of inscrutable equivocations.

Then there is the lovely Czech and Polish name for Novem-
ber, *listopad*, literally "the falling of the leaf." There is the
inspired Austrian name for Indian summer, *Bellermanswoch*,
or "the candle-snuffer-man's week." There is the German
Schadenfreude, which has no equivalent in any language I
know of; it means "a malicious joy at another's misfortune."

I also like the German *Pfiff*, as a nice change from "a
jiffy"; and as a replacement for "chauvinism" the magnificent German word *Hurrapatriotismus!* Then there's the Magyar *zsupsz!*, much more butterfingery than plain old "oops!"
There's the Scottish-Northumbrian *archilowe*, defined as "the
return which one who has been treated (to a drink) in an
inn sometimes considers himself honor-bound to make to the

company." There's the Portuguese *saudades*, literally untranslatable into any other tongue, but meaning a wealth of poignant and wistful things like homesickness, yearning and fatalism. There is the Mandarin Chinese *ho-ho*, which somehow manages to compress into itself "happiness and prosperity." And, for those unlucky ones of us who never get to enjoy *ho-ho*, and can't even afford to stand *archilowe*, there's always the Tahitian *aita peapea*—"ah, what the hell . . ."

Admittedly, not many other cultures could find use for the Arab's *six thousand* different words for the camel, its parts, characteristics, appurtenances, virtues and vices. And there is the Hawaiian word *humuhumunukunukuapuaa* (the name of a tiny reef fish) and the word *ô* (the name of a large deep-sea fish), neither of which, despite Hawaii's induction into the Union, has yet been welcomed into Webster's.

But there are other linguistic elements and even modes of punctuation, still little known outside their native languages, which do have qualifications for universal adoption. It seems to me that every language could benefit by adopting those two Spanish masterstrokes, the inverted question mark at the start of an interrogatory sentence, and the inverted exclamation point before an exclamation.

¿Quién mató a Cock Robin?
"¡Yo!" dijo el gorrión . . .

This would be a boon to readers-aloud, who often charge thundering into a sentence, only to find that it peters out into a pipsqueak query.

And every spoken language could likewise make use of the "oral question mark" as utilized by the Japanese (*ka*) and Chinese (*ma* or *ni*). A Japanese sentence like *Benjo-wa doko ni arimasu-ka?* ("Where is the men's room?") is unmistakably an urgent inquiry even when whispered through clenched teeth. For sheer, simple, instant comprehensibility, the *ka* construction is far superior to the Westerners' common makeshift of vocally tilting the end of a question upward.

Every so often, a philosopher, philologist or mere doodler will undertake to compile the ten (or dozen, or score) "most beautiful words in the language"—whatever his language happens to be—and newspapers use this for a filler for years afterward. There is usually a mild inconsistency in these compilations, as some of the words are obviously chosen for their sound alone ("murmur," "twilight" and "lullaby" recur frequently in English-language lists), while others rate for their semantic content or subliminal appeal ("mother" is probably on every such list in every language).

But if ever a list is compiled of the most beautiful words from *all* human languages, I have a nominee. It is *kharir,* the Arabic word for "splash." Those two softly-breathed syllables, besides being melodious to the ear, are a shining example of how a language can reflect its culture and milieu. In many Arab lands, water is a sometimes thing, so it has always been spoken of with loving reverence. A splash is simply a splash to us, but to the Arab—so I'm told by Saudi Arabia's consul in New York—*kharir* actually means "the sweet sound of water falling gently upon water."

> Perhaps of all the creations of man
> language is the most astonishing.
> —LYTTON STRACHEY

Oddities and Quiddities

NOBODY knows why the Sicilian waves "goodbye" with the beckoning gesture that almost everyone else employs to mean "come here." Nobody has ever been able to explain, to me at least, why the titles written vertically on book-jacket spines commonly read from bottom to top on British books and from top to bottom on American ones. Such customs are *just* customs, evidently begun at some antediluvian whim and made immutable by generations of usage.

Not everything unique about a language or its employments is necessarily fraught with significance or susceptible of analysis. A language can have trappings as useless as the human appendix and traits as trivial as hiccups. They're just *there,* and philologists dismiss them with a tolerant shrug. But I think some of them are interesting or entertaining enough to deserve mention—and the reader can decide for himself whether they say anything meaningful about either the languages or their speakers.

One aspect of language often ignored by professional linguists is what its own makers and users think about it. Individual attitudes have ranged from rabid partisanship to iconoclastic raillery. For example, in April of 1965, President de Gaulle flayed French scientists who "betray their language" by cravenly speaking English at international conventions. That same month, in a magazine article on the misuses of English, Charlton Ogburn, Jr., remarked with tongue in cheek, "The ugly suspicion insinuates itself that the only purity of speech is to be found in total silence, of which language is in its entirety a corruption."

In the main, though, each people's attitude toward language in general and their own in particular seems to be one of respect and reverence. Why else would they have concocted so many folktales to explain its magical or miraculous genesis?

One Chinese fable has it that writing was first shown to man in the markings of the turtle's carapace. Another story attributes the invention to the four-eyed dragon-god T'sang Kie. To Hindus, Brahma is the undisputed creator of the universe, but it was his wife Sarasvati who thought to contribute language to the grand scheme of things.

Evidently the Jewish Talmudists believe that language was created before there was anyone to speak or write it. According to philologist Noah Jacobs, the scholar Rabbi Akiba visualized the alphabet as already existing—somewhere in Chaos—before JHVH got around to creating the world. The letters of the alphabet, said Akiba, competed for the honor of being the first letter of the Book of Genesis. The letter *beth* was chosen because it was also to be the first letter of the benediction "Blessed is he who comes in the name of the Lord."

Perhaps the prettiest linguistic legend was concocted in Korea. One day in the year 1443, it is said, the wise King Se-jong decided that his country could be prosperous and powerful if only more of its people knew how to read and write. Korea already had the ideographic Chinese characters, but learning them was a hard, long process. What was needed, mused the king, was a simple alphabet which would phonetically transcribe the spoken language.

Se-jong sat down and worked one out, but he realized that he couldn't force its adoption; he would have to convince the people that this was a gift from heaven. Accordingly, that night he went into the palace garden with a writing brush and a pot of honey. On the leaves fallen from the plane trees he painted, with honey, the fourteen consonants and ten vowels he had invented, one to a leaf.

The next morning Se-jong invited the royal soothsayer for a stroll in the garden. During the night, as the king had foreseen, insects had eaten away the honeyed portion of the leaves. There lay twenty-four leaves each etched with one of the new letters. The soothsayer noticed, and gathered them up. "This is no accident," he told the king. "Perhaps the gods are trying to tell us something."

The soothsayer took the leaves up to his tower and spent some weeks puzzling over them, until at last realization dawned. He burst into the throne room with the breathless news: "They are an alphabet, sire! The gods have sent us an alphabet for writing our language!" King Se-jong expressed his astonishment, pleasure and admiration of the sage's acuity, and ordered that the alphabet (called *hangul*) be published for the use and benefit of all his people. They accepted it with alacrity, concludes the fable, and that was how Korea became the first nation to pioneer literacy for the masses.

There have even been legends concerning languages that never existed. Madame Helena Blavatsky, the flamboyant nineteenth-century spiritualist and founder of the Theosophical Society, disclosed to her awed followers that the "forgotten language" of lost Atlantis was called by the Atlantians *Senzar*. Emanuel Swedenborg, the eighteenth-century mystic and father of the Swedenborgian (New Jerusalem) Church, conversed with angels and the people of Venus, Mars and the moon. According to Swedenborg, the language of the Martians is "gentle, tender, zephyr-like . . . more perfect, purer and richer in thought, and nearer to the language of the angels than others." Of the moon people he wrote, "Their voice rolls like thunder, and the sound proceeds from the belly, because the moon is in quite a different atmosphere from the other planets."

Real languages, misinterpreted by outsiders, have contributed to beliefs in unreal peoples. Because the Finns called themselves *Qvoens*, early geographers assumed the existence of a northern matriarchy of amazons. Because the self-willed Turkoman tribesmen would never abide a leader, they referred to themselves as "a people without a head." This led Pliny to describe them as literally headless, having their faces situated, as a sort of bas-relief, on their chests.

Some other words, quite ordinary but misunderstood, misprinted or deliberately manipulated, have inspired tall tales and fanciful fakeries. The ancient seaport of Carthage was protected by a fortress called Bozra, which in Phoenician meant "hill city." Greek visitors confused the name with their word *bousa*, "oxhide," and from it made up their own story of Carthage's founding. According to this legend, handed down by Greek historians, the early traders who wanted to build a seaport at this site were opposed, for some reason, by the country's rulers. The traders could obtain only a niggling grant—the right to use as much land as a single ox-hide would encompass. But they cunningly took advantage of this limitation, by slicing their ox-hide into spaghetti-like strips and laying them end to end to encircle an expansively city-sized area.

On the Rhine River there once stood a bleak and derelict tower that had formerly been a customs house (*Mautthurm*).

As its original function was forgotten over the years, the riverboatmen came to mistake its name and refer to it as the *Mäuseturm* ("mouse tower"). This odd appellation required some accounting for, and the riverboatmen didn't mind fabricating a legend to fit. Eventually their passengers were being treated to the wonderfully Gothic tale of a wicked bishop who mulcted all the local farmers of their produce, hoarded it in his tower, refused to share it even in famine times, and was finally himself eaten—alive—by the rodents which swarmed to his rich granary.

The English town of Maidenhead, on the Thames, has endured several centuries of jokes about its name, but none of them has been as comic as the complicated legend of its origin. It is supposed to be the place where the severed head of one of eleven thousand martyred virgins is buried. And the notion that such a slaughter took place was founded on a mistaken transcription in the Roman Catholic Church calendar. It seems that there *was* once a virgin in Cologne, Germany, by the name of Undecemilla, and she *was* beheaded, which won her elevation to sainthood. But her "saint's day" in the church calendar, through a scribe's error, was labeled *Undecem milia Virg. Mart.*—shorthand Latin indicating that on that date "eleven thousands of virgins were martyred."

In relating this mythical atrocity as the basis for Maidenhead's name, no fabulist has ever explained why one of the supposed decapitated heads should have been shipped there all the way from Cologne. Anyhow, the true derivation of the town's name is much simpler. Maidenhead is merely a corruption of an older name, Maydenhythe, which meant a "dock midway" (between the towns of Marlow and Windsor).

Antwerp, Belgium, is another city which grew up "at the wharf" (Dutch *aan*, "at," *werf*, "wharf"), but the city's coat of arms and the citizens' favorite legend tell of a different derivation. According to the story, an ogre who once lived in the neighborhood used to cut off the right hand of any wayfarer who couldn't pay a toll, and throw the severed hand into the Scheldt River. Hence the name of the place, say the Antwerpers, from the Flemish *handt* plus *werpen*, "throwing."

But the true stories behind existing names, words, expressions and entire languages are often weirder and more wonderful than any bespoke legend could be. (Sometime, in a good English dictionary, look up the derivation of the simple word "rigmarole.") In the Lesser Antilles, at the time the white men first began to explore the Americas, the natives spoke two distinctly different tongues—the men spoke one, the women another. These islands had once been inhabited by the backward, indolent and peaceable Arawak Indians. Then the fiercer Caribs from the mainland of South America invaded the Antilles, massacred (and ate) the Arawak men and appropriated their women. For generations afterward, the Arawak widows commemorated their lost mates by refusing ever to speak their new masters' language. Until the slow erosion of interbreeding finally dissolved the old animosity, the women maintained their separate "female language," taught it to their daughters and brought them up in the same tradition of silence toward all males. The Carib men didn't seem to mind.

In certain societies, such as the aboriginal Arunta of central Australia and the Kiwanis of urban North America, where the males reserve unto themselves various activities, enterprises and entertainments, and make them taboo to the women, there is often a private "male language." Among the Aruntas, for example, boys at puberty undergo a rigorous ritual of fasting, flagellation and circumcision to fit them for manhood, and part of the initiation involves learning the age-old, for-men-only secret language.

There is a community in eastern Turkey known as Kuskoy, which means "bird village." The name is apt, because the people there do much of their talking in twitters and tweets. The village sprawls over two mountains on opposite sides of a deep river ravine and the area is often shrouded in dense fog. Ordinary voices could not communicate under these conditions, but the Kuskoyans have developed a piercing, variable whistle that can cut through fog and forests and be heard as far as five miles away.

The sound, produced by powerful lungs and tensely drawn lips, is like the signal blast of a steam locomotive, but the whistle language permits of sufficient modulation and nuance that Kuskoy men and women can converse, quarrel and even woo in whistles. The whistle-wooing is sometimes self-defeating. On occasions when a young couple have eloped, an angry father has been able to whistle a cease-and-desist order that is relayed with the speed of a telegraph by other whistlers throughout the mountains, until the elopers are nabbed and fetched home.

In the "click language" of the South African Khoi-Khoin, a majority of the consonantal sounds consist of abrupt, harsh, staccato clicks and clacks. This mode of vocalization is uncommon among spoken languages in that it is produced by breathing in rather than out. The noises are made by flicking the tongue during inhalation, as when we utter a reproving "tsk-tsk." The Khoi-Khoin's ticktock tongue is what inspired

[53]

the Boers to dub them Hottentots, from the Dutch *hateren en tateren,* "to stammer and stutter."

A curiosity among written languages is the *ogham* alphabet of the British Isles. Stone monuments in Ireland, Scotland and Wales, dating from as far back as the fifth century, were found to bear both an inscription in Latin and another, odder sort of engraving. Groups of straight and slanted little lines, unlike any writing known, ran along the corner edge of many such stones, some on one side of the edge, some on the other, and some rounding the corner from one side to the other. For a long time they were unintelligible, but eventually proved to be a kind of cipher—almost like the Morse dot-dash system— transliterating the Latin inscription.

The alphabet is written along a base line, usually the corner edge of a monument stone, with the letters represented by one to five scratches apiece; straight or diagonal; above, below or crossing the base line. It is a simple system to decipher if one knows the Latin of that era, and can easily be used for enciphering any other language. But although the writings themselves are no longer a mystery, the reason for the alphabet's development still is. Latin was already in use in Britain—the scribes who wrote the ogham obviously knew the Roman alphabet—why then the need for the auxiliary script?

The runic alphabet used by other northern Europeans was not an original invention, like the ogham, but a crude and debased version of Greek or Roman script. But both runic and ogham in their time basked in glamour and mystery. In those dark ages, anybody who could read and write *any*thing was esteemed as a sage and often feared as a sorcerer. Though more sophisticated systems of writing displaced the old, and literacy began to overcome ignorance, the ancient ogham and runic alphabets were never entirely forgotten, and continued to exude their miasma of pagan magic. It was supposed that one could put a curse upon an enemy by writing out the proper spell in runic and secreting it in his house or among his possessions. This procedure—called "casting the runes"— was believed in and dreaded right down to modern times.

Other superstitious beliefs have often affected human language. A fairly well known example is the "name taboo" existent in both primitive and civilized societies from prehistoric to recent times. In cultures as far apart as the ancient Chaldean and the modern Eskimo, it was taboo for an individual to reveal his true name, lest an enemy use the knowledge to exert a magical influence over him. In numerous other societies, including the Judaic, a deity's name was never to be spoken. And orthodox Jews still will not name a new baby after a living relative. The original reason for this was that, in sharing the same name, the two would have to share a single "life spirit" and both parties would be the weaker for it.

Another religious scruple, rather fanatically and foolishly applied, cost the Western world a good four centuries of possible progress. But for the Muslims' belief that the pig is an unclean animal, Europe could have been enjoying the enlightenment and enrichment afforded by mechanical printing at least four hundred years before Gutenberg and his contemporaries developed the process in the 1450s.

The Chinese technique of printing from carved blocks was already a commonplace in that country by about A.D. 1000; design and calligraphy were well advanced. Arab travelers and traders were already visiting China and bringing home new ideas and crafts. The one invention they refused to bring back to the West was that of printing. They considered it heathenish, a vile seduction contrived by the Devil. Why? Because the Chinese inked their printing forms with brushes—and the brushes were made of the unholy pig's bristles.

In the martial aspects of a language—for instance, a people's expression of *Hurrapatriotismus* in their national anthem—one would expect to see that nation's character plainly revealed. But the words of an anthem oftener constitute a flat contradiction: the smallest and feeblest nations squeak the most bellicose sentiments, while the huge and powerful ones rumble humble thanksgiving for their share of earth.

The newly independent but still abjectly dependent Senegal boasts (in the words written by its first president), "The red lion has roared, the tamer of the bush has with one leap rushed forward. . . ." In mitey Monaco, from his palace balcony Prince Rainier can pretty well survey all of which he is monarch (half a square mile), while his handful of subjects chant, "We shall die in his defense, / But after us our children will fight. . . ."

In their anthem *Hej Slovane!* ("Hey, you Slavs!"), the Slovaks of Czechoslovakia repudiate their country's history of having been trampled by one conqueror after another: "Death and Hell! Vain is your hate against us. . . ." Uruguay, the smallest republic in South America, trumpets, "Our country or the grave! / Freedom, or a glorious death!"—which has a rather hollow ring, considering that the Uruguayan army is largely composed of a foreign legion of hired mercenaries.

The professionally neutral Switzerland is nevertheless warlike enough to sing, "In danger never pale, / Meet death

[55]

without a wail. . . ." The equally pacific Andorra more real-istically lisps, "I was born a princess, a maiden neutral be-teen two nations. . . ." Poor little Laos bows its head and throws up its hands in the wistfully despairing anthem, "Once our Laotian race in Asia highly honored stood. . . ."

The big nations generally tend to refrain from flexing their muscles. Great Britain's official anthem is simply an invoca-tion of God's blessing on the reigning sovereign: "Thy choicest gifts in store, / On her be pleased to pour. . . ." The first verse of the United States anthem is a paean to Old Glory, and the rest of the song is pointedly omitted in public rendi-tions. The last stanza is particularly vulnerable to unfriendly interpretation: "Conquer we must, when our cause it is just. . . ." During its seasons of thaw, Russia tactfully sub-ordinates its militantly anticapitalistic "Internationale" to the blander "Anthem of the Soviet Union," which proposes "a bulwark of friendship for nations and men."

But anthems are only for pomp and parade, after all, and an army on the march is far likelier to step out to something less grandiose, like "You had a good home and you *left*, right, *left*. . . ." Nobody knows who composed that disenchanted chant, but every American infantryman knows more of its cadenced couplets than he does verses of "The Star-Spangled Banner."

This illustrates one thing that holds true for any language: the invented words, songs, slogans and expressions that be-come a lasting part of the popular vocabulary are seldom the solemn compositions enshrined there by edict. They are sim-ply the ones that catch the people's fancy; they generally come unbidden, and they may come from poet or peasant. No one can predict at the birth of a new word or expression whether it will find a place in the language but, if it does, one thing *is* certain. The man who fathered it—if he be known—may as well engrave it on his tombstone, because it will out-live him and outshine every other deed he ever did.

Some years ago, the *New York Times* ran two obituary no-tices within a week or so of each other. Presumably both of the men concerned had amassed respectable estates, sired fine families, engaged in good works and philanthropies, etc. But nothing of that nature was stressed in their obituaries. Instead, one man's biography extolled the fact that he had "invented halitosis." That is, early in his advertising career he had appropriated the medical term for "bad breath," made it the nonpareil gimmick that sold oceans of mouthwash, and put the word in John Q. Public's vocabulary. The second de-cedent had been a restaurateur in life, and his claim to immortality, according to the *Times*, was that he had "invented the cheeseburger."

Many a person has earned linguistic life everlasting by bequeathing his name to the dictionary—usually involuntarily and frequently in association with something even more demeaning than halitosis or cheeseburgers. The Germans esteem as a table delicacy curly chips of smoked fish, called *Schillerlocken* after the curly locks of the poet Schiller. The Norwegian Vidkun Quisling lives on as a synonym for "traitor." The executioner at Tyburn, England, in the early seventeenth century, Goodman Derrick, is still hanging things. Kindly Dr. Guillotin's name is no longer pronounced with affection, nor is General Henry Shrapnel's. Lord Raglan, Prince Albert and the Earl of Cardigan are mothballed together in the wardrobe, but on a somewhat higher shelf than Mrs. Amelia Bloomer. Dr. Thomas Bowdler, who wanted to prune and weed the English language, planted a new word in it instead.

The seventh-century abbess Etheldreda, or Audrey, was elected to be the patron saint of England's Isle of Ely, and medieval pilgrims visiting there could buy, for a souvenir, a slimsy lace necklet called "St. Audrey's chains." The name was gradually slurred to "tawdry" and comes down to us with the meaning of "cheap and showy." There is a color, a shade of brownish-yellow, known as "isabel," allegedly because it was the color of the underwear of the Infanta Isabella of Spain. She had vowed never to change or wash her unmentionables until her husband, Archduke Albert, took the city of Ostend by siege—and the city held out for three years.

Some other people have made more deliberate contributions to the dictionary. Among the innovators in the English language have been Jonathan Swift with "yahoo," Lewis Carroll with "chortle," Gelett Burgess with "blurb," H. L. Mencken with "ecdysiast," and scores of less celebrated contributors. About 1940 mathematician Edward Kasner was stumped for a single, short, easy word to designate the number "ten to the hundredth power" (10^{100}, or a figure 1 followed by one hundred zeros). He put the problem to his nine-year-old nephew, who promptly came up with "googol." It's in Webster's now.

But individuals have made only scant contribution compared with the multitude of linguistic novelties which the dictionary has acquired merely by eavesdropping on the *vox populi*. And many of these expressions are oddities in the sense that, though their derivation is known, there is no explanation of how the common people came to employ them. For example, in the old days in Edinburgh, a housewife preparing to empty her chamber pot out the bedroom window would call a warning to passersby below: "Gardyloo!" This is plainly derived from *gare l'eau* ("watch out for the water"), but what far-wandering Frenchman taught it to the Scots, and under what peculiar circumstances?

Other locutions deserve mention because they have so stanchly kept their original meaning through so many centuries and so many linguistic migrations. To cite one, the English language has cordially adopted the Creole *lagniappe*, from that pleasant New Orleans custom of "a little something extra" (e.g., the thirteenth bun in the baker's dozen). The Creole spelling is a French interpretation of *la ñapa*, appropriated from the earlier Spanish settlers in the New World. And the Spaniards originally got it, courtesy of Pizarro's conquistadors, from the Quechuan *yapa*, which the Incas had been using—with the very same meaning of "a little something extra"—since prehistoric times.

Among the oddest of linguistic oddities, however, are those words which have come into a language as a distortion or perversion of words in some other. The Dutch tongue has given two such expressions to English. "A forlorn hope" is only a minor warping of the original *verloren hoop*, "a lost band." But the English "nitwit" is a rude and scornful mimicking of the Dutchman's sincere *niet weet*, "I don't know."

The word "sardonic" has eerie associations. Ancient etymologies trace the word back through Latin and Greek to the name of a plant, *sardanē*, which grew on the island of Sardinia (and gave the island its name). According to some sources, this plant was so bitter that a taste of it contorted one's face. According to others, the plant contained a poison which made the taster laugh himself, humorlessly, to death. The term *risus sardonicus* is still used in medical terminology to describe an occasional corpse's "peculiar grin, as seen in tetanus, caused by acute spasm of facial muscles."

Every language also has words of its own which have in the course of time changed their meaning from odd to ordinary—or from ordinary to odd. Among English specimens, "naughty" originally meant "poor" (that is, "owning naught"). A "snob" was first a cobbler's errand boy, then a fawning toady, and only comparatively recently a self-styled superior being. A "rascal" was formerly one with a rash on his face—smallpox or syphilis—therefore unclean, therefore unfit company. Prior to October 4, 1957, the Russian word *sputnik* meant merely "a traveling companion." Now, in Russian and nearly every other language on this planet, it means "artificial earth satellite."

The word "cretin" comes from French, where it also means "an idiot." But the French *crétin* was derived from *chrétien,* "Christian," and the derivation constitutes a short horror story. Formerly, in the Alpine districts of France, what is now called cretinism was endemic among some villages. The villain was the natives' poor and scanty diet, which caused the thyroid condition known as myxedema. Many children, apparently normal at birth, grew to be monstrously deformed idiots. Though these unfortunates were as dumb and ugly as beasts, they had at any rate been baptized, and so had a hope of the Hereafter. In pity, their neighbors referred to them as *les chrétiens,* hence "human beings," as distinguished from the brutes they so hideously resembled. As the designation gained wider usage it gradually became today's disparagement.

The layman's attempt to explain exotic or esoteric terms by relating them to something familiar or plausible is called folk-etymology. The child's "flutterby" for "butterfly" is a good example. Sometimes this process has a folksy flavor indeed, as in the countrified "sparrow-grass" for "asparagus." Sometimes it can be fantastically far-fetched, as in the histories concocted for Antwerp, Bozra and Maidenhead. But in trying to bring alien words a little closer to his ken, the common man has come up with some wondrous inventions—as often through blissful ignorance as through bright imagination.

An English tavern named "The Bacchanals" became known to its habitués as "The Bag o' Nails." The British warship *Bellerophon* was called by its crew the "Bully Ruffian," and the *Hirondelle* the "Iron Devil," and the *Boreas* the "Bare Arse." American dock-wallopers renamed the Norwegian freighter *Björnstjerne Björnson* the "Be-Jesus Be-Johnson."

Many persons are confused by the assonance of "scallion" and "scullion" and forget which is which. But I have heard a gardener throw in an "onion" as well, and brag of his early spring crop of "scunnions." When the start of World War II cut off American imports of silk from Japan, coincidental with the first mass production of nylon, some Americans gleefully foresaw the collapse of the Japanese silk industry, and so decided that the new synthetic's name was an acronym of "Now You Lousy Old Nips."

Several individuals, both fictional and real, have doubly enriched their language—by their misuse of it, and by lending their names to describe the misusages. English provides some good examples. Malapropism, for instance, was the specialty of Mrs. Malaprop, a character in Sheridan's 1775 play, *The Rivals.* A specimen: "We will not anticipate the past . . .

our retrospection will be all to the future." Absent-minded metathesis is called spoonerism after the Rev. William Spooner of Oxford—e.g., his expulsion of a malingering student: "You have deliberately tasted two worms and you can leave Oxford by the town drain."

As far as I know, no one ever coined a word to describe the indescribable tortuosities tossed off by Father Divine during his heyday in the 1930s and 1940s. "Divinities" perhaps might fit such utterances as his "It is personifiably and repersonifiably metaphysicalzationally reporducible." (*Sic, sic, sic.*) About 1970, before he became notorious, Spiro Agnew briefly became famous for his lecture-platform addiction to such tormented epithets as "nattering nabobs of negativism." But he was actually serving as a mouthpiece for the vituperations of Richard Nixon, and those horrors were put in Agnew's mouth by White House speechwriter William Safire (who has since, like so many of his then colleagues, been born again whiter of fleece—in Safire's case, as a columnist-critic and arbiter of *other* people's use of the English language).

It is not the calculated and fabricated neologisms, but the accidental and inadvertent that usually best deserve admission to the dictionary. Novelist Anton Myrer relayed to me one he recently heard spoken innocently and artlessly— someone complaining of suffering from "cloisterphobia"— and we agreed that the word proclaims its meaning far more wonderfully than the right word does.

Of course, people everywhere are uttering similar marvels all the time. I heard a radio announcer in a Virginia city introduce a selection on a classical music program as "Bach's Toccata and Fug-you." The Rev. Dr. Billy Graham, in one of his inspirational books, advised his readers to "flee from paranoia as you would flee the plague." Think about that one for a minute. (Another oddity: why do such books never aspire to be "inspiring" instead of just "inspirational"?) I don't know what kind of descriptive term would best apply to a linguistic impropriety like the road sign I once saw in the hinterlands of North Carolina. It stood beside a road leading into a cemetery, and it said "Dead End."

But gaucheries of maladroit usage, abysmal ignorance and slovenly diction are not confined to hillbillies. In supposedly refined and cultivated San Francisco, the hostess of a radio program of classical music consistently refers to such keyboard artists as Eugene List and Philippe Entremont collectively as "great penis," and she recently recommended to her listeners a brand of stereo disk-player which features a "ten-genital tone arm." If I didn't already own one of those, I might never have realized she meant "tangential." Published authors are expected to have some acquaintance with the subjects they write about and the proper use of the language they write in. But the authoress of one of those Gothic romances described her heroine's climactic encounter with the supernatural like this: "I had come face to face with the unseen!" And the author of numerous popular adventure novels—on the jackets of which he is pictured wearing safari garb, presumably to betoken the "authenticity" of his writings—had one of his characters die in convulsions (and not of hilarity) after having been "bitten by a scorpion."

Some annoying abuses of language are perpetrated by people with pretensions to dime-store elegance. As one example of how the King's English is occasionally dethroned by fastidious ignorance, take the old, old adjective "tetchy," which means "irritable, testy, peevish." This is nowadays considered hick jargon of about the Dogpatch social level; the few who ever do use the word take care to pronounce it "correctly"—as "touchy"—and they are dead wrong. The word is nowise related to "touch." In Middle English it was *tecche,* "a bad habit," and earlier, in Old French, it was *teche,* "a blemish."

These same ultrarefined folk misspell the purely echoic "hiccup" as "hiccough." They also invariably use catsup—and pronounce it with utmost nicety, "cat-sup"—in preference to ketchup. This is presumably to dispel any suspicion of their having upjumped from a beanery background, but they're wrong again. "Ketchup" is closer to the source of the sauce, the Malayan *kechap,* in turn derived from the Chinese *ketsiap.*

When the *New York Times* quoted something or other from *Gulliver's Travels,* and scrupulously credited the author, "Dean Swift," a reader, more impetuous than erudite, immediately wrote in to correct the editors. Swift's first name, the correspondent said smugly, was not Dean, it was Jonathan. But the professional wordsmiths have their lapses, too. The once impeccable *New Yorker* magazine has succumbed to the mob's misuse of "over" for "more than" and no longer blue-pencils such jarring phrases as "over fifty people attended the opening." England's *Punch* magazine, which loves to pounce on American abuses of the English language, recently ran a cartoon caption revealing that *Punch* no longer knows the difference between "flaunt" and "flout." The publishers of *Bartlett's Familiar Quotations* have not yet retitled that tome to appeal to the loutish legions who now prefer to use verb for noun, but a newly published and competing compilation is unabashedly titled a "collection of quotes." Every news reporter nowadays seems to be ignorant of the fact that only a building or a territory can be "evacuated" (of its occupants). To evacuate the human occupants themselves could be done only by enema.

The most famous case of bungled plunder in the annals of philology was that involving Samuel Johnson, John Ash and the word "curmudgeon." Nobody, including Dr. Johnson, has ever ascertained the true derivation of that wonderful word. But when he was compiling his dictionary, an anonymous letter-writer suggested that "curmudgeon" might be an Anglicized fusion of the two French words *coeur* ("heart") and *méchant* ("wicked"). Johnson duly noted the suggestion in his dictionary, together with a credit line, thus: "*coeur méchant,* Fr. an unknown correspondent."

Johnson's dictionary was so popular that it inspired a flock of imitators eager to cash in on the public's sudden interest in lexicography. One of the imitators was John Ash, who borrowed liberally from Johnson's material. But he gave himself away, and revealed himself to be no linguist, when he copied Johnson's paragraph on "curmudgeon." It derived, said Ash's dictionary, "from the Fr. *coeur,* 'unknown' + *méchant,* 'correspondent.' "

No chapter on the oddities of language could be considered complete without some mention of the grotesquely sesquipedalian words so beloved of believe-it-or-not relevators. The most frequently aired specimen of this genre is the name of that Welsh town, Llanfairpwllgwyngyllgogergchwyrndrobwillantysiliogogogoch, 57 letters supposed to mean "St. Mary's Church in a hollow of white hazel close to a rapid whirlpool and St. Tysilio's Church, fronting the rocky isle of Gogo." But there is a longer one yet, a back-country whistle-stop in New Zealand called Taumatawhakatangihangakoauotamateaturipukakapipkimaunghoronukupokaiwhenualitanatahu—83 letters meaning I know not what.

For his *Ecclesiazusae,* Aristophanes coined what is probably the longest word in literature. Describing a buffet meal that apparently included every item on the Greek bill of fare, from oysters to *ouzo,* he compounded a single word which spans 77 syllables in Greek and requires 184 letters for a Roman-alphabet transliteration: *Lepadotemachoselachogaleokranio leipsanodrimhypotrimmatosilphiokarabomelitokatakechymenokichlepikossyphophattoperisteralektryonoptokephalliokingklopepeiolagoiosiraiobaphetraganopterygon.*

While a prodigy like this is deliberately contrived to amuse or amaze, there do exist in certain polysynthetic languages single words of breathless extent. Anthropologist Edward

Sapir mentions an auxiliary verb in the language of the Nootka Indians which translates "I have been accustomed to eat twenty apples a day while engaged in doing . . ." (whatever the speaker was wont to do at the same time; belch maybe). The Koryaks of northeastern Asia have one word which transliterates approximately as *Tyjamajin'ylautytkynajkyplyg'e* and means approximately "I'll hit you hard on the head."

Jawbreakers of this sort are not the expressions likely to become everyday commodities in any language. Most people prefer, for their clichés, proverbs and slogans, locutions of near baby-talk rhythm or rhyme. For example, the Italian *detto, fatto* ("no sooner said than done"), the Latin *dum spiro, spero* ("while I breathe, I hope"), the French *l'homme propose, et Dieu dispose* ("man proposes, God disposes"), the German *ohne Fleiss, kein Preis* ("nothing ventured, nothing gained"), the English "fair and square," "snug as a bug in a rug," "highways and byways" (and New York State has a marvelously horrid one in the "Thomas E. Dewey Thruway").

It is generally supposed that poetical figures of speech are to be encountered only in the more "civilized and sophisticated" societies. But even such rough-hewn unromantics as the American Indians have composed locutions of epigrammatic pith and striking imagery. In various Amerindian tongues occur such expressions as "person-push" (ambition), "heart-sunrise" (glad), "blanket-over-face" (ashamed). The rare albino Indian baby was, to the Algonquian tribes, a "moon child."

On the other hand, the haughty patricians of the most cultured societies have stooped to the breezy colloquialism of the man in the street, on occasions when stilted formal language simply would not do. A memento of one such borrowing, over two millenniums ago, can still evoke our smile of recognition, empathy and delight. Among the British Museum's collection of ancient Greek betrothal rings is a gold one hammered out about the fourth century B.C. Engraved inside it is the single Greek word *meli*—"honey."

To belong to the elect, the elite, the fortunate and the exclusive is as much a human craving as to be successful or loved. The object of desire may be a royal court, a gang of juvenile delinquents, a country club or the "in group" whose members are ever so important and knowing about quarter horses, bank mergers or contemporary art.

—ORVILLE PRESCOTT

Syzygy, Triakaidekaphobia and Other Everyday Words

I N any good-sized dictionary of any language there are many words which look to the layman like a misdeal at Scrabble. But to some they are everyday words, and unremarkable. They may even be such handy coinages that they transcend language barriers and are universally understood and used by speakers of many different tongues. The technical terms *syzygy* and *triakaidekaphobia*, for example, are of Greek derivation. But to an astronomer of whatever nationality, syzygy is a commonplace noun referring to opposing points on the orbit of a heavenly body. To an alienist in Vienna, New York, Johannesburg or anywhere else, triakaidekaphobia means an unreasoning fear of the number 13.

Every science, profession and trade has its specialized vocabulary and idiom. This kind of shop-talk is known to students of linguistics as "jargon"—perhaps not the happiest choice of designation, as that word is often used contemptuously to refer to gibberish or slang. Jargon and slang do indeed overlap here and there, but shop-talk which might *sound* like slang to an outsider would be perfectly correct and conventional usage to a worker in that particular shop.

And there are other jargons besides shop-talk. All people in the same walk of life, on the same social level, sharing the same interests, have an "in" language peculiar to their group.

Dancers, for example, talk a patois that would be unintelligible both to their audiences and to their musician accompanists. Bird-watchers employ a vocabulary incomprehensible to sponge-divers, and vice versa. Closely knit families have their own private frames of reference. Even twosomes can develop a jargon all their own—a husband-and-wife code, for instance, for signaling when to leave a party. Republicans and Democrats, city-dwellers and suburbanites, sportsmen and invalids, clerics and atheists, satyrs and inverts, policemen and convicts—any classification of human beings has and uses a jargon all its own.

Of all types of jargon, the shop-talk variety has been the most fertile in inventing and keeping alive specialized vocabularies. For that matter, there are jobs whose very titles would baffle an outsider: Pickled-Bellies Overhauler, Zig-Zag Inspector, Mudjacker, Hot Walker, Bosh Man, hundreds of others.*
But only a comparatively few of the trade jargon locutions are weird words like syzygy or centipedes like triakaidekaphobia. Most of them are short and ordinary, their oddity residing in the arcane meanings which have been assigned to them. For example, to an ordinary homebody, the term "baby bank" would most likely signify a little pink pottery pig with a slot in its back; to a financier it means a cooperative credit union.

On a ranch, a "bullpen" is a pen for bulls. In a lumber camp it's a barracks for the men. In baseball lingo it's the enclosure where relief pitchers warm up. In a commercial art studio "bullpen" refers to the roomful of underpaid apprentices and hacks who do the routine work of paste-ups, lettering, retouching and the like.

I remember how startled I was, as a very young and green apprentice in just such a studio, when I first heard the "bullpen manager" instruct a paste-up man to "trim off this guy's left arm and let him bleed in the gutter," and again when he told someone else to "kill this widow." I didn't exactly run for my hat and coat, but I did do considerable brooding before I dared ask the boss what he'd meant. In printing jargon, a

---

* *Pickled-Bellies Overhauler:* packs brine-treated meats in packing house.

Zig-Zag Inspector: examines stitching of parachute shroud lines.

Mudjacker: squirts mud under foundations of house to be moved.

Hot Walker: race-track apprentice who cools off horses after workouts.

Bosh Man: removes finished copper slabs from molds in casting mill.

"bleed" is a picture or design that runs right off the edge of a printed page, and the "gutter" is that edge of a page which is tucked into the binding. To "kill a widow" is to rewrite or reset a paragraph of type so as to eliminate a short line or single word dangling unattractively at the end.

Artists of the finer arts have a rather more precious jargon. They are inexpressibly pained to hear a patron mention that he is "sitting for an artist" to have his portrait painted. In the correct parlance, one sits *for* a portrait but sits *to* the artist. Again, it conjures up odd mental images when a painter modestly remarks, "I've been hung at the Wildenstein" or "Jackie Onassis is collecting me."

There are numerous other locutions, ordinary enough in their everyday context, which acquire esoteric significance when they're adopted into some jargon. For instance, there could be no more common and homely word than "toothpick," but in carpentry it has a highly specialized meaning: it specifies a massive 12″ × 12″ ridgepole timber. To the layman a "puffer" might be a cigar smoker, an advertising copywriter, an out-of-breath runner or what have you. To the professional auctioneer a "puffer" is a stooge planted in the audience to join in the bidding and so inflate the going prices.

Other terms are almost totally confined to the very limited occupation or society which begat them. A "squegging oscillator" must surely be unknown outside the milieu of electronics technicians. "Stinkstein" is peculiar to geology (where it describes a certain odoriferous sort of limestone). "Cutting to the girdle" is done by lapidaries. A "potsy" is what a policeman calls his badge, and a "hairbag" is an old-timer on the force. Plasterers are, one hopes, the only artisans who have to worry about "snots" in their work (lumps left in the finish). "Wayzgoose," in use since the seventeenth century, and literally meaning "field-goose," describes an annual picnic or party thrown by a printers' guild.

And while some jargon locutions freely waft across national and lingual borders, others do not. The practice of setting production quotas is common to industries on both sides of the Iron Curtain, but as yet workers in the Western world haven't felt impelled to coin anything like the Russian word *shturmovshchina*, which means the eleventh-hour, last-minute, frenzied flurry to fulfill one's production quota before deadline.

Some expressions are familiar to several different trades— even to the lay public—but have different meanings to all concerned. Take the "go-devil." It looks as if it ought to describe an exorcist's kit of bell, book and candle, but the priesthood appears to be about the only calling which *doesn't* use the term. To a plumber or an oil-field worker a go-devil is an instrument for scraping obstructions out of pipelines. To a logger it's a heavy hauling sled. To a construction worker it's a lightweight tractor. To a farmer it's a kind of plow. To a demolition expert it's a small explosive device. To a miner it's a gravity plane. To a railroad man it's a handcar.

"Buttons" can mean different things to those who make them, sew them, wear them, undo them, push them or eat them (button mushrooms), but to a hunter "buttons" are the feces of a hare. There are, of course, all sorts of well-known names for excrement, but the fastidious hunter classifies it according to the animal responsible: a bear drops "bruzzing," a deer drops "fewmets," a boar drops "fiants," an otter drops "spraints."

Though occupational jargons are spiced with whimsies, drolleries, *jeux d'esprit,* and even profanities and obscenities, most of their ingredients were whipped up for the sake of easy and precise communication. However, the fact that they are not usually easy for outsiders serves two further purposes. A trade jargon's incomprehensibility satisfies its speakers' very human urge to set themselves and their confraternity apart from (i.e., above) nonmembers, and it also enables them to speak freely yet secretly under the very noses of customers, clients and other such laymen. This *sub rosa* aspect of jargon is evident everywhere from hash-houses to whorehouses, but nowhere has it been refined to such perfection as in the fields of law, medicine and religion.

The theologians, dealing as they do with impalpable and indescribable matters, necessarily had to develop a language of infinite subtlety and infinitesimal ambiguities of meaning. The law, too, in its never-ending attempt to define the indefinable and limit the illimitable, had to develop a hair-splitting jargon of qualifiers, modifiers, mitigators, ifs, ands and buts. Medicine, for the sake of universal standardization and exactitude, has based its language on Latin and Greek derivatives which can be understood by physicians, surgeons and pharmacists of every Western nationality.

But ever since the days of witch doctors and priest-magicians, these dealers in light, law and life have found that they worked best when they maintained an aloof altitude above the common herd of their fellow men. In societies both primitive and civilized, it was the priest or the sorcerer who alone was allowed to speak the names of the spirits and exhort them to dispense grace, justice or panacea. This pretension to godhead on the part of the practicing sage was not entirely self-aggrandizement. It profited the common weal, too, in that the average man was more likely to obey a taboo, respect a judgment or respond favorably to a dose of calomel if it was accompanied by some ceremonial mumbo-jumbo.

He still is. And the modern medical man is well aware that any medication is made more potent by adding a minim of psychology. It is not just tradition that prevents a patient from reading the ingredients of his prescription. It is no accident that a hypochondriac's sugar pill is called a placebo (Latin: "I shall please"). And it is easily understandable that a patient will pay a doctor more readily and more liberally for treating his singultus spasms by inhibition over the cervical vertebrae than he will for—what it means—stopping his hiccups by squeezing the back of his neck.

Not all medical jargon, though, is sober-faced and classically oriented. When specialists go into consultation (a "hot-air round") at a patient's bedside, and agree on the cryptic diagnosis that he's suffering from "G.O.K.," it means simply "God only knows." A medical student memorizes the bones of the hand (navicular, lunate, triangular, pisiform, etc.) with the mnemonic key, "Never lower Tillie's panties, mother may come home." A hospital's psychopathic ward is the "flight deck." A gynecologist is familiarly known to his colleagues as a "fingersmith." Obstetricians refer to the placental membranes expelled in afterbirth as the "sad sac."

Legal jargon has awed and bewildered the common man at least since the day of the Magna Charta; significantly, that bill of rights for the underprivileged masses was written in a language known only to the privileged few. While the drumbeat rhetoric of the law ("do hereby give, bequeath, devise, grant and assign") is primarily intended to make statutes, judgments and contracts ironclad and leakproof, its considerable side effect is to buttress the law's solemn dignity by making it (and the lawyers) seem somehow something more than mortal. In Latin American countries, the lawyers have also appropriated the honorific "Doctor," e.g., Dr. Fidel Castro.

Legal jargon even admits of such suprahuman entities as an "artificial person" (an association of persons, such as a corporation, invested with the rights and obligations of a "natural person"). To a lawyer, the pristine Edenic state of nudity is to be despised; a "naked" agreement is one that's unenforceable because it omits some essential element. So as not to imperil the layman's high respect for the law, the slangier jocosities of its jargon are seldom aired in public. They include such terms as "apron-string tenure" (a man's rights in his wife's property) and "gospel title" (one that's absolutely incontestable). To the everlasting embarrassment of the legal fraternity, however, the jargon term "ambulance chaser" is one that escaped into public domain.

Religious jargon ranges from the rarefied abstractions of theology (of the "How many angels can dance on the head of a pin?" variety) downward through liturgical usages to the man-to-man vernacular of the determinedly reg'lar-feller priest or parson. Like doctors and lawyers, clergymen are inclined to keep their less rectitudinous expressions confined to the cloister. A Roman Catholic priest, in private, refers to an Irish-born priest as a "Turk," to his church confessional as "the box," and to a Protestant as a "southpaw." St. Patrick's Cathedral in New York City is called—by Protestants sarcastically and by Catholics affectionately—"the powerhouse." A Protestant clergyman speaks offhandedly of going to work at "the plant," meaning his church. He and his fellow preachers observe "the three B's" when composing their sermons; that is, "be brief, bright and brotherly." He refers to a Catholic priest as a "buck" (short for "buck nun"), and to *his* church as a "candle shop."

In that much of their content is deliberately intended to exclude the uninitiated from their mysteries, the jargons of law, medicine and religion are remotely akin to that of the underworld. The prestige professions discourage overfamiliarity; the criminal classes repel any familiarity at all. The most important word in the Mafia's glossary, for instance, is *omertà*. It can be translated as "keep quiet!" but it actually means much more. As Norman Lewis has written, *omertà* "takes in vows of silence, intransigence with the police, dedication to the laws of the vendetta, defiance of authority, and so on."

But many underworld expressions do sneak out into the daylight world, and shed their aura of secrecy and menace. "Big shot," for one, was evidently introduced into English by the Black Hand society, the American extension of the Mafia. It appears to be a figurative translation of the Sicilian *pezzu di novante* ("piece of ninety"), meaning a massive 90 mm. cannon of Garibaldi's time, which term became an admiring epithet for the upper-echelon *mafiosi*, the "big guns."

Such is the popularity of American gangdom, as represented in movies and private-eye novels, that much of its jargon has become an export commodity. In Hungary the ordinary word for ordinary "protection" is *pártfogás*, but the imported *protekció* means, there too, the Chicago-style extortion of tribute. And as long ago as 1942 a Scottish newspaper

[69]

was grumpily complaining that highland highwaymen no longer accosted their victims with the time-honored "Stand and deliver!" but now were commanding "Stick 'em up!"

But underworld lingo is flexible; by the time its jargon has become common property, a whole new and secret set of expressions has taken its place. The same adaptability is to be found in the jargon of Harlem and other black ghettos, which was evolved, consciously or not, as a private realm the white man couldn't muscle into. Blacks were using the word "ofay" for perhaps twenty years before the white man realized they were talking about *him*. But the black jargon does percolate into jazz argot and from there into the "hipster" world. To be "hip" is the highest social ambition of the "swinger," of the bohemian intellectual and of certain obtrusively liberal segments of the white middle class. Hip means "in" or "with it" or somewhere out in front of the *avant-garde*. The hipster thus allies himself with the embattled blacks and all the nonconformists, mavericks and visionaries who stand "somewhere" apart from "nowhere" society. But the black man, evidently disdaining these gratuitous fellow travelers, keeps changing his "in" idiom as fast as outsiders pick it up. As George Mikes has written, "It is often not easy to get out of the ghetto; but it is always much more difficult to get in." And so the hipster's proudly flaunted jargon is always rather stalely *arrière-garde*.

The blacks have deliberately and assertively put only one word into the language they share with the whites. That is the descriptive term by which they insist that they themselves be called, and, in fact, it has been one word after another. In 1910, when the National Association for the Advancement of Colored People was formed, "colored" was their preferred descriptive. In the 1965 edition of this book, I used "Negro" wherever I needed such a descriptive, *that* being then preferred. At various other periods, "Afro-American" has been in and out of vogue. But as of now, "black" is the requisite. I am, of course, speaking of American blacks; those in places like South Africa, and the commonalty even in black-governed African nations, have no voice in specifying terminology or in much of anything else.

Just as the blacks have cast about for an acceptable English-language alternative to such vile old terms as "nigger" and "darky," so has another, even more recently emancipated group, the homosexuals. Understandably, they would like to abolish the old insults—"queer," "fairy," "pansy," etc.—but they seem to dislike the textbook term "homosexual" as well.

(The "homo" in the word—this seems to require repeated pointing-out—is *not* from the Latin for "man," but from the Greek for "one and the same"; it would more properly be pronounced "hommo.") While female homosexuals seem content with the classically-derived "lesbian," the males prefer that the rest of the English-speaking world call them what they have long called themselves: "gay." Unfortunately, that is no contribution to the language, but a subtraction from it. A speaker or writer can no longer use the word in its old sense—to refer, say, to a "gay festivity"—without inviting a snicker from his audience.

Anent the gays, someone has remarked that "the love which once dared not speak its name will now never shut up." But, for all their volubility nowadays, the gays have made only scant contribution to the general vocabulary, simply because they never *had* a very copious group jargon. Most of what they did have has already slipped out into common usage: "straight" (heterosexual), "dyke" (lesbian), "AC/DC," "switch-hitter," etc. (bisexual), "rough trade," "camp," "drag," "cruising," "lipstick lesbian," "chicken hawk," some few other terms. The gays were never jealously protective of what jargon they spoke among themselves, but they are still secretly gleeful whenever some tough-guy novelist or screenwriter ignorantly uses "gunsel" to mean a gunslinger, or "punk" to mean simply no good, because both of those words (the first from Yiddish, the second from prison slang) mean specifically a catamite. The gays' most recent coinage is "homophobe," their epithet for anyone they accuse of being against them. But that is an error, too, since it would not translate as anti-homosexual but (see "homo" above) as "somebody fearing or disliking *himself.*"

Political jargon, featuring bombast and pomposity, is as old as civilization. Twenty-four centuries ago, in the Persia of King Darius, each minor governor of each little district took for his grandiose title "Protector of the Land"—*Shathrapavan*—and the derivative "satrap" is still among us, now with the meaning of "petty tyrant." Besides being ancient, the language of government and politics is probably the least private of private jargons; very few of its inventions have managed not to get into public usage.

A glossary of none but United States political terms would run to book length—starting from "no taxation without representation." Many of them have become permanent fixtures: filibuster, gerrymander, carpetbagger, brain trust, log-rolling, pork barrel, dark horse, etc. Others enjoyed a brief acceptance, then became obsolete; for example, the "grandfather clause" of Reconstruction days. It referred to the clause in the constitutions of several southern states limiting the vote to only those who had served in the Confederate or Union Army, and their descendants—the intention being to deny blacks the vote.

A "lobbyist" supposedly buttonholes legislators in the lobbies of their public buildings, but he was earlier called an "undertaker" (because he "undertook" to influence the lawmakers). More recently he has put the "wheeler-dealer" into the English language.

The Roosevelt administration flooded Washington and the press with what the New Deal's detractors called "alphabet soup"—a host of new agencies referred to by their initials: the NRA, the CCC, the OPA, etc.* During World War II, the *New York Times* defended this innovation as being at least a cut above the practice "in the unfree countries" of making *words* out of bureaucratic abbreviations: Nazi, Gestapo, Cominform, etc. The *Times* is being prudently silent on the subject nowadays, when every agency, private as well as governmental and military, has abandoned the mere monogram in favor of the punchy, pronounceable acronym: WAVES, SPARS, CARE, HIP, SAGE† and countless others.

In 1981 a mysterious new disease began to assume epidemic proportions in the United States. The affliction takes numerous forms, each of which is known to immunologists by a different and usually unwieldy name. So the news media seized on the general term under which all the ailments are lumped—despite its also being unwieldy: Acquired Immune Deficiency Syndrome—because that one could be made into an acronym easily pronounceable by newscasters, easily fittable into newspaper headlines: AIDS. (And, in so doing, they just about drove out of business a long-established and probably innocuous diet candy trade-named Ayds.) Even far-off foreigners, avid for celebrity in the West, even if only to be celebrated for their tactics of indiscriminate butchery, have learned to name themselves in a way that will provide an acronym writable and pronounceable in the English-

* The National Recovery Administration, the Civilian Conservation Corps, the Office of Price Administration.

† WAVES, the Women Appointed for Voluntary Emergency Service (in the U. S. Naval Reserve); SPARS, wrenched from S(*emper*) Par(*atus*), the women's branch of the U. S. Coast Guard; CARE, the Co-operative for American Relief Everywhere; HIP, Help for Incontinent People; SAGE, the Society for the Advancement of Good English, or Senior Action in a Gay Environment, take your pick.

language media—e.g., the detestable ASALA, the Armenian Secret Army for the Liberation of Armenia.

In the 1940s Congressman Maury Maverick endeavored to puncture the windbags of Capitol Hill by inventing a word to describe their bloated and gassy rhetoric: "gobbledygook." Ten years later, Milton Smith of the U.S. Chamber of Commerce introduced the equally apt "bafflegab," meaning the sort of gobbledygook that is spewed intentionally to confuse and becloud real issues. But the increasing heft of the *Congressional Record* and the mounting bulk of franked mail indicate that the politicians' prolixity is nowhere on the wane. The elective "ins" and "outs" alike rely on ghost speechwriters and even ghostlier phalanxes of advertising experts to add to their inventory of jargon.

During one of Eisenhower's campaigns for the Presidency, the employees of an advertising agency retained by the Republican Party were bidden to "brainstorm" slogans for (*a*) getting the voters to the polls and (*b*) getting them to vote for the general. One young copywriter's submission was a pat paraphrase of Luke. He was never sure whether the agency brass considered it levity, lese majesty or sacrilege, but it nearly got him fired. It said simply: "Go, and do thou Ikewise."

The students and critics of jargon have produced quite a jargon of their own. They refer to governmental speech and writing as "officialese," to lawyers' talk as "legalese," to professorial jargon as "pedagese" or "academese," and so on. But their own terminology is rather less precise than others'. For example, they can seldom agree as to where jargon, cant and slang are separate or where they overlap. They often describe pedagese in the same words they use to contemn officialese— viz., gobbledygook and bafflegab. But here, at least, there should be a clear definition. Gobbledygook and bafflegab are deliberately intended to impress or confound constituents or other outsiders. Pedagese more often seems an intragroup contest to see who can most effectively conceal quiddities in quibblings. No doctoral candidate seeking admission to the Grove would dare submit a thesis on the most trifling subject without smothering it in pedantry, polysyllables and footling footnotes. As one who in various capacities, and in torment for his crimes, has had to read too much of this dusty, desiccated and ivy-overgrown variety of language, I submit that the best epithet for it is probably "mumblefug."

Most jargons have contributed prodigally to the vocabulary of ordinary speech, and new locutions are coming into common usage all the time. In any newspaper one can find headlines and advertisements that would have been gibberish to a reader of a century ago—and probably one or two that would have been nonsense ten years ago.

The world's population today includes so many veterans of so many recent wars, and so many of their expressions have become common usage, that military jargon scarcely requires mentioning. The Vietnam conflict produced such novel combat concepts as "defoliation," "fortified hamlets" and "danger of escalation." The Korean War popularized "brainwashing" and "demilitarized zone." World War II introduced a host of terms which the dictionaries now seldom bother to snub as colloquial—GI, jeep, roger, blitz, gremlin, etc.

But some of the most common and seemingly contemporary military derivations date from much earlier wars. The "fifth column" came out of the Spanish Civil War. "Foxhole," "ace," "H-hour," "D-day," "scrounge"—all these are leftovers from World War I. The Philippine Insurrection contributed "gook"—then meaning a Filipino, but since applied to Nicaraguans (during the U.S. Marine occupation, 1927-33), Japanese and Koreans. The Spanish-American War is commemorated in "brass," referring to the officer ranks. The "grapevine" originated in the American Civil War, and "shavetail" (a mule or a second lieutenant) during the Mexican War.

Some military jargon, of course, has been too specialized in its application ever to gain much popular currency. A civilian hearing the phrase "Maggie's drawers" might envision all kinds of goings-on, but to the wartime GI it meant only the humiliating red flag that signaled a miserable miss on the firing range. And some of the most vivid wartime inventions were severely squelched at their first utterance. When a women's corps was assigned to each of the services, the Leathernecks accepted theirs with reluctance, and a high-ranking Marine officer sourly suggested an official name for the female branch; a name which, had it been circulated, would probably have careened the whole project. He suggested—instead of any oh-so-cute designation like the Navy's WAVES or the Coast Guard's SPARS—that the lady Marines be called "Leatherteats."

Military jargon has been avidly appropriated by the people of the workaday business world as a means of convincing themselves that they're involved in some more manly and praiseworthy occupation than mere huckstering and opportunism. Naval terms are particularly favored: the big boss's office is the "quarterdeck," the company keeps a "taut ship," each department is a "task force." But businessmen and industrialists have their own indigenous jargon as well. Some of the terms are still confined to the executive suites: "analytical projection," "time-sequence programing," "decentralization of authority." But others have spilled over into everyday speech: "red ink," "red tape," "know-how," "mass production," more recently "high-tech," "hands-on," "user friendly."

The business world's most noticeable contribution to popular language has been that of trademarks and brand names, many of which—to their copyright-owners' public dismay but private pride—have become generic terms. The Coca-Cola Company maintains a well-staffed watchdog department to protect the status of its trademarks, and the measliest weekly newspaper which spells Coke with a small *c* can expect to receive a letter of pained admonishment. The original makers of Cellophane and Celluloid, Zippers and Vaseline have pretty much surrendered to their trademarks' defection into the commonalty. And, despite the best efforts of the 3M Company, every competitive brand of transparent stickum stripping is now known to the public as Scotch Tape.

An interesting effect of the proliferation of brand names during the last sixty or seventy years is the far-futuristic look it has given to the world's languages. It would appear that George Eastman started a trend with his clipped, clicky, classical-Greek-looking "Kodak" in the 1880s. Eastman simply happened to like *k*'s and, contrary to the many lay and learned attempts at etymology (was the name a reversal of elements from "*accurate code?*"), his "Kodak" was a purely arbitrary fabrication. But it became a world-wide household word.

Subsequent entries in the photographic field followed Eastman's lead in syllabic sparsity, and many of the cameras still on the market bear terse names featuring click sounds: Exacta, Nikon, Technika, Leica, etc. The camera was the perfect and popular symbol of the burgeoning Scientific Age, and the mechanistic, unfrilly camera names seemed to express the essence of Modernity. So they may have been what inspired the makers of other products to coin the similarly curt, cryptic and "modernistic" trade names that are now at home in every language—Plexiglas, saran, nylon, Teflon, vinyl, Kotex, etc.

Those ancient words-of-tomorrow, "super" and "automatic," have suffered endless commercial mutations. For example, the few ma-and-pa grocery stores still defying the monster "supermarkets" now often boast the silly name of "superette." Kodak has the "Instamatic" camera. New York City's famous slot-machine Automat cafeterias inflicted a rash of things like "laundromats" and "tend-o-mats" (checking lockers). The "Futurama" spectacle at the 1939–40 New York World's

Fair spread a plague of "groceramas," "meat-o-ramas" and "burgeramas." From the Greek city of Marathon, and its tireless messenger boy of twenty-five hundred years ago, came the use of "marathon" and its misbegotten -*thon* offspring to mean anything enduring ("walkathon") or unendurable ("telethon").

The aim of the commercial world's twenty-first-century jargon is to appeal to the average man's itch to be first with the newest. Whether a man driving a car with Onboard Computer feels himself more in tune with tomorrow than his neighbor who drives one with Turbo Assist is unprovable, but it is true that the average person is eager to be ahead of the mob in seizing any new phenomenon—or at least enough of the jargon connected with it to seem *au courant*.

Science-fiction fans, who were talking space argot a good fifty years ago, and feeling superior about it, are discernibly disgruntled now that every housewife is familiar with the jargon. But the most prominent example of this urge to be in the vanguard is the way psychiatry and psychoanalysis gained instant popularity at their earliest introduction. This field contributed to everyday language more arcane jargon in less time than any other newly opened field has ever done. From the time of Freud's first renown, to this day, the argot of "headshrinking" has been a conversational shuttlecock second only to weather and gossip. People who couldn't tell Freud and Jung from the Smith Brothers have, sometimes in sheer self-defense, absorbed enough of the terminology to hold their own at cocktail parties and at intermissions of *The Cocktail Party*.

As in the Carib-Arawak communities of the Lesser Antilles, today's women—that is to say, those women not involved in women's liberation—maintain their areas of private language incomprehensible to their men. Part of it includes the park-bench parlance of child-raising, soap operas and "female complaints," but these can be translated into human language without too much difficulty. The one female tongue which the normal man can't fathom at all is that of fashion. He could no more make sense out of a *Vogue* editorial than he could out of one in the *Komsomolskaya Pravda*. He usually doesn't care to try, as he is inclined to be chary of familiarity with those fashion-world fops who possess only first names, like "Mr. Louis" and "Mr. Guy."

The fashion faddist feeds on a prose that's about as tasty and nourishing as marshmallow soup; for example, this photo caption from *Vogue*: "To sink into like a snowdrift, with all its glistening depths of dazzle: a coat of white ostrich feathers—swinging, weightless, wildly spectacular—for evenings when gala-levels are highest." Then there are all those too, too fashionable color names that call to mind no known hue except, possibly, that of a lavender copywriter—e.g., putty, bone, malt, passport, encore, tea-leaf, bisque, shell, hot sand, almond, lady-slipper, oatmeal.*

Husbands may be baffled by the jargon of their wives, but they both deplore the jargon of their teen-agers. On the one hand, it seems to connote congenital idiocy; on the other, its occasional inventiveness would seem to have required some intelligence to contrive. The fact is, though, that most of the teen-ager's jargon has been prefabricated for him by disk jockeys, rock festival promoters, the agents of recording groups, and others venally hoping to prompt profitable fads and fandom. (Excepted are the juvenile mobsters, who take most of their jargon from their elder idols in the underworld.) That the teen-ager parrots so much packaged patois is evidence only of his conformist need and desire to go along with the bunch. If teen-age language could be pruned of the exploiters' grafted-on inventions, it would probably be remarkable only for its calculated sloppiness and *Weltschmerz*.

Overheard outside a high school cafeteria:
"Jeat?"
"Yeah, jew?"
Two boys overheard on a New York street:
"Wunner what time it is."
"Argh, it's four-thirty 'r some shit like that."

But all the disparate levels, groups and cliques of society are alike in that the vocabulary common to us all (whatever national language we speak) is an amalgam of jargons appropriated from each of those levels, groups and cliques. Consider just American English and a minute sampling of its jargon contributors:

Adopting and adapting the lingo of the deep-sea sailor, we say that an honest man is "aboveboard." His opposite number talks "bilge" and should be given "a wide berth." In Lloyd's registry "A-1" originally designated the excellent condition of a ship's hull (A) and equipment (1). Fresh-water sailing has added rather little to everyday speech, but it did give America its most famous pen-name in "Mark Twain." Railroading gave us "asleep at the switch" and "to jump the track." From aviation came "nose dive" and "flying blind."

Baseball donated "southpaw," "rhubarb," "fungo" and scores of others. From boxing came "to take a dive," "knockout,"

* All of them beige.

"punch-drunk." Poker gave us "ante up," "misdeal" and "ace in the hole." Pool gave us "behind the eight ball." The golfer's "stymie," meaning to block an opposing putter's ball with one's own, now refers to any sort of hindrance or obstruction.

We even speak the jargons of vocations and avocations long extinct or, to say the least, uncommon. The ancient art of bell-ringing gave us the phrase "to ring changes on" something. Medieval armory gave us "plain as a pikestaff." The sport of cock-fighting gave us "crestfallen," "to crow over," "to show the white feather" (because a white feather in a gamecock's tail casts suspicion on his fighting pedigree). The opium addict gave us his "yen" (originally Beijing Chinese for "smoke").

But there are some jargons, not previously mentioned here, which are jealously and meanly guarded by their speakers. These are the secret locutions used by those who purvey goods or services to the public. For example, in the "friendly skies" advertised by the airlines, the passengers, whether first-class or budget-rate, are known to every airline employee from ticket clerk to flight crew as "the meat." Indeed, if the innocent paying customer knew how often he is being either despised, diddled or derided, he might resort to living in a cave, growing his own food and weaving his own clothes. The jargon is in commonest use among shady operators, and is generally deplored by reputable merchants (and commission salesmen) who, after all, have good reason to pretend respect for and cater to their customers. But it is often encountered among salaried menials—the perpetually disgruntled—even in the toniest boutiques.

Such sales clerks, in every branch of retailing, have two separate languages: one for pushing a sale and the other for referring to the transaction among themselves. The latter is again subdivided in two: one jargon damns the unskinnable customer and one expresses disdain for the pushover. The terms differ in different sorts of establishments but the customer (the "proposition") seems to be indistinguishably detested, whether he's a lunch-hour browser (a "J.L.," just looking) or a billionaire sultan (a "cream-puff") buying one of everything in the store for every wife in his harem.

The spiel used for pushing a sale includes asides generally not noticed by the shopper. If two clerks are waiting on a single party and one of them murmurs "thirty-four," it means for the other to get lost, he's queering the pitch. If the store manager says "thirty-three," it means that a particular salesman is getting nowhere with his customer and should turn him over to some other clerk who may have better luck. The customer may be exceptionally wary and sales-shy, in which case he's a "T.O."—to be "turned over" to the shop's ace sales-man, who is also known (by association) as "the T.O." and specializes in "T.O.ing" such tough cookies. If the customer finally does "crack wide open" and makes a purchase, then overhears his clerk describe the sale to another as a "P.M.," it means he has bought a "post mortem," also known as a "skig" or an "L.Y.," that is, a "last year's" or otherwise out-dated item. Or the customer may have been stuck with a "dog" (something nobody else would buy). If the customer overhears the whisper "O.C.," it means he's been overcharged. In other words, he has been "horned" and he is a "schnookle."

To the apathetic or splenetic sales clerk, customers en masse are "the dumb public." If a customer is impatient to be waited on he's a "C.U." (he wants to "see you"), and if he's really in a hurry he's a "blizzard." If he turns out to be readily sellable he's a "live one." If he's hard to satisfy or just downright nasty he's a "dog" or a "pig." If he's a cheapskate he's a "skank" or a "Mr. Griffin." If he's looking for something for nothing he's a "schnorrer." If he's on a buying spree he's a "palooka." If he doesn't buy at all he's a "lemon," a "float" or at best a possible "beback." If he brings along his wife or a friend to help him decide on a purchase, he's got a "lawyer" in tow. If he buys the first item he's shown, or pays a list price that he could have haggled down, he's a "wrap-up."

At his stockbroker's office he is a "lily." At a Las Vegas casino he's a "pigeon." At the carnival he's a "rube" or a "hiram." At his bookie's he is either a "piker" or a "plunger"—one term no more or less scornful than the other. The luxury hotel's obsequious bellboy who leads him to his suite privately refers to the quarters as "the kennel" and to the guest as a "McGee" (poor tipper) or a "sport" (big tipper)—one term no more or less scornful than the other.

The lady shopper who orders a brassiere because the ads described it as "enhancing, provocative and fulfilling" would be disillusioned if she could hear the counter girls refer to it disrespectfully—according to the customer's bra size—as a "teacup," a "grapefruit" or a "hammock." If she buys an in-expensive dress it's a "shroud," if she takes a large size it's a "tent." If her husband comes along to help her select an item, he's an "elmer." If she insists on squeezing a size 10 foot into a size 7 shoe, the clerk may surreptitiously mark her sales slip "T.S." (too small), for the store's rebuttal when she in-evitably comes back complaining.

When the lady goes to the beauty parlor she had better already be beautiful, or she's a "pickle" in the attendants' jargon. If she's the sort who pinches the tomatoes, her green-grocer knows her as a "lilac." And if and when she enters a hospital's maternity ward, *she* thinks of herself as embarking on woman's greatest adventure; the admitting nurse sees her merely as one more candidate for "the foundry."

Even at the wretched customer's very last paying stop on this earth he is an object of contempt. To Elmer's or Hiram's survivors, the undertaker unctuously speaks of him as "the departed" or "the loved one." Downstairs in the embalming room he is "the stiff."

There remains to mention one jargon which, in the 1965 edition of this book, was not touched on at all, and for good reason: it simply did not then exist. But, since about 1970, the linguistic contortions perpetrated by "women's liberation" have proliferated (in the English-speaking world) like some ghastly fungus. Having dared to write those last two words of the preceding sentence, I have no doubt that infuriated women everywhere are seizing pen and paper to start casti-gating me as a "male chauvinist pig" or some other one of their pet objurgations. They will not be deterred by my hon-estly averring that I am in total accord with their aim of achieving equal status, in all respects, with the male sex. (I am also in accord with the nineteenth-century French writer Mérimée: "If I were to define the difference between men and women, I should say 'que les hommes valent plus, mais que les femmes valent mieux'.") But, with equal honesty, I must deplore the feminists' violent manipulation of the English language in that cause—which practice has wittily been called by one of their own, Carol Travis, "the sound of one hand slapping."

Most other jargons have only gradually and sometimes re-luctantly seeped from their original user groups into common usage. To the contrary, the feminists concocted a jargon and immediately began foisting it—with tactics ranging from pretty-please persuasion through petty blackmail, coercion and intimidation—on all the rest of humanity (or what they could reach of it). Like every religion, which alone is the True Religion preaching the True Word, militant feminism insists that the whole world has been talking wrong all along, and demands that a "non-sexist" jargon be accepted and adopted as Gospel.

I am not the first to remark that the execrable invention "Ms." means nothing, is an abbreviation of nothing (if we except "manuscript" and "multiple sclerosis") and has none but an arbitrary and unmelodious pronunciation. Nor am I the first to point out that, like most perfervid linguistic innovators, the feminists have been ignorantly over-eager in demanding the adoption of such terms as "chairperson." The abominated final syllable in "chairman" has nothing to do with gender, but comes from the Latin *manus*—the "hand" that holds the gavel—as does the same syllable in manacle, manage, manhandle and manipulate.

Even when the feminists' coinages are acceptable, and their arguments worthwhile, these are often proclaimed in an English so sloppy as to lose them any claim to respect. Example: a female post-graduate in California, preparing her Ph.D. thesis on "sexist stereotypes in the comic strips"— (evidently doctorates are nowadays awarded for such endeavors)—has recently, repeatedly and loudly, declared on public radio that *"Beetle Bailey* is detrimental to both men and women." The woman may honestly hold the conviction that Mort Walker's good-humored cartoons are somehow a Bad Thing, in which case she should have said—certainly a Ph.D. candidate should be sufficiently educated to know this— that *Beetle Bailey* is "derogatory" or "denigrating." But a newspaper comic strip, unless it is printed in poison ink, can hardly be "detrimental" to anybody.

Any person has the right to choose what he or she shall be called—"black," "gay," even something as frightful as "Mzzz," and to request that others so address him or her—but not to insist that every other person likewise address anybody else. Any person has the right to speak any gibberish he or she cares to affect—but not to demand that everybody else do so. However, news and entertainment media, authors, speakers, even some usually-fastidious ones, nowadays routinely use "Ms.," "chairperson," all the other sexless and senseless coinages. They do so not from any noble motive, or amiable willingness, or even spineless acquiescence, but in cringing fear of losing audience, advertisers or customers (i.e., money) from among the "fifty percent of humankind" that the feminists claim to speak for.

The militant women ought not crow over such measly triumphs of their jargon, compelled from venality by the whip of boycott. A lot of news media, authors, etc., earlier and similarly truckled to the witch-hunting Joe McCarthy and the blacklisting Richard Nixon. Nevertheless, the feminists seem to feel that their having won some few toeholds on the linguistic beachheads has also won them the authority to pronounce on not just the "sexist" use of language, but also the "racist," "agist" (another horrific coinage), "environmentalist" and so on. I know of one female editorperson of a newspaper book-review section who approaches every newly-published work *first* to comment on how the author has represented women and attitudes-to-women in the book, then the book's acceptable-or-not representation of blacks, ethnic groups, gays, old folks, the poor, the handicapped, gun laws, tobacco smoking, endangered animal species, etc., before ever evaluating the book's content of entertainment, information or whatever it was that the miserable author mainly wished to convey.

A woman named Maj-Lis Loon, chairperson of something called a "Liberate Love" campaign in Sweden, recently proposed, for business offices and other public gathering places, what she would denominate as "erotic-free zones" where flirtation and "sexual innuendo" would be banned and punishable by law. Now, "sexual innuendo" is as impossible of precise definition as is "obscenity." It can be, like sin, anything the self-appointed sin-killer is personally averse to. Such a preposterous ban would be unenforceable, and no rational body of lawmakers is likely to consider the notion. Let us be glad of that. Men and women could eventually be deprived of *all* communication between them, were there any widespread adoption of anything like Ms. Loon's proposal.

I think such women's tactics are wrong, and not just because any unilateral shaping of language by fiat is indefensible. I think the women thereby do *themselves* a disservice. They claim that by such tactics as demanding—and getting—a new version of the Bible, in which (among other ungodly novelties) God is never referred to as He, they are "raising the consciousness" of all and sundry, so the world will recognize and lament and redress the inequalities women have endured ever since Eden. I am inclined to doubt that, just as I am inclined to be skeptical of the modern-day spate of "born again" Christians. Consciousness is not conscience, and it is a lot easier to pay lip-service—whether by muttering rote religious responses or by prating feminist jargon—than actually to strive toward an ideal. Sure, some writers of novels and scripts may now be pandering to the women's-rights movement by cranking out specious revisionist histories—writing stories of sultans overthrown by anachronistically butch harem maidens, or revising Catherine of Russia into a victim of lifelong gang rape, or rewriting the three Graeae into the earliest keen-eyed, sharp-toothed activists of the Sisterhood. But if the feminists can be thus persuaded by opportunists that history has been "improved," or that the future can be, then they are too easily mollified and they are pathetically gulled. Words can change things, yes, but merely changed words are not changed things.

Besides, the militant women do not, except physiologically,

represent "fifty percent of humankind." What impact the movement has had, in the way of infiltrating language, has been mainly in the United States and Canada, rather less in the other English-speaking countries and in Scandinavia, and only marginally in the rest of the Western world. French-women have not yet seen fit to wedge anything like "Ms." in between Mme. and Mlle. Most Europeans, female as well as male, regard the movement and its jargon only with bemused interest, as one of those curious Anglo-Yankee phenomena—like spiritualism or chain letters—that come along every now and then. As for the Latin lands south of the Rio Grande, the imperturbable Orient, the vast, grim territory of Islam, the stolid Soviet Union, darkest Africa—I can attest from personal observation that, wherever in those places the movement has even been heard of, it would be rabidly condemned if it were not so lustily laughed to scorn. Until the feminists truly can speak for (or at least to) all their polyglot female fifty percent of humankind, they cannot expect much applause for continuing to din only English-derived jargon at only the nearest and meekest of the male fifty percent.

The ancient Romans, who had some experience of militant females, coalesced the words *vir* and *virgo* to make the word *virago*, meaning a heroic woman, an estimable and admirable woman, a woman every bit as good as a man. But something— and it must have been the subsequent behavior of those *viragines* themselves—made the word pejorative, until it very soon came to mean what it still means today: a termagant, a harridan . . . and no Roman woman wanted any longer to be called a virago.

I hope the modern women's-rights movement achieves all its worthy goals. But in the meantime, as history has shown, people in general tend to turn a deaf ear to those who try to tamper with their language. I believe and expect that "Ms." and all the other feminist jargon terms will eventually go the way of virago—into obloquy, thence into hiding. I shall not be sorry. Neither should the women be. Better to lose the linguistic skirmish than to have it cost them the whole campaign.

Language is not an abstract construction of the learned, or of dictionary-makers, but is something arising out of the work, needs, ties, joys, affections, tastes, of long generations of humanity, and has its bases broad and low, close to the ground.
—WALT WHITMAN

Is Slang Bloody or O.K.?

I F an Englishman is reading this bloody sentence, he has just winced. Not because "bloody" is such a vile word— it has lost most of its shock power—but because he assumes he's in for another interminable analysis of just *why* "bloody" ever should have been anathema to the British. However, the analysis need not be lengthy, mainly because there *is* no accounting for the word's bloody reputation.

To most of the world, the idea of something being bloody may be less than pleasant to contemplate, but it has aroused nothing like the revulsion it caused in the British—for a while. The word was used as a slang intensive, but nothing more, as long ago as Swift's time. It wasn't considered really offensive until the Victorian era, but then it became tainted to the point of putridity. In 1887 Gilbert and Sullivan attempted a mild jape with their *Ruddygore*, but after only four performances they had to dilute the implied blood even further, to *Ruddigore*. Even the supposedly liberated and liberal followers of George Bernard Shaw were appalled when Eliza blurted the dread word in *Pygmalion* in 1912. But World War I, like every war, inured the soldiers to even worse profanities, and after that "bloody" became gradually enfeebled.

During its career as an abomination, however, "bloody" garnered some noteworthy accolades. It was euphemized into "ruddy," "bally" and "blurry." It put the word "bloody-mindedness" into the English vernacular, to mean a vile, nasty, cruel temperament. It even had songs written about it. One of them was called " '————,' the Great Australian Adjective," and was always printed in this manner (third stanza):

He rode up hill, down ——— dale,
The wind it blew a ——— gale,
   The creek was high and ——— floody.
Said he: The ——— horse must swim,
The same for me and ——— him
   Is somethin' ——— sicken',
      ———!

There have been many theories propounded as to why "bloody" should so shock the British or, if you prefer, why the British should be so vulnerably shockable by "bloody." Some see the word as a contraction of "by our Lady!" or as a reference to the horror of the Crucifixion. But there have been many other, similar ejaculations which never bore the obloquy of "bloody"—for example, "Zounds!" (God's wounds), "'Sblood!" (God's blood), "Gadzooks!" (God's hooks: the nails of the cross), "Odds bodkins!" (God's needles), "Marry!" (by the Virgin Mary) and "Drat it!" (God rot it).

Etymologist Eric Partridge perceives in the word the loathsome "violence and viscosity of blood," but that seems a weak explanation for its detestation, considering the upper-class Briton's devotion to blood sports like fox-hunting and otter-baiting. Other scholars suggest that "bloody" is an oblique reference to the female menses. It is true that the woman's monthly discomfiture is a phenomenon feared and dreaded by the males of some primitive societies. But why should the sophisticated Briton share the taboo of a superstitious savage?

Inasmuch as the connotations of "bloody" are inexplicable, etymologists are doubtless gratified by its fading from eminence. No other slang locution in human language has ever engendered so much conjecture and debate—except the American term "O.K."

This is unquestionably the single most universally used and useful of human utterances, profane or sacred, slang or otherwise. It knows no boundaries, from pole to equator, from submarines to space craft. It is not unlikely that one of the landers still sitting on the moon has an "O.K." stenciled, stamped or chalked somewhere on some one of its components. The atlas declares that there is a community named Okay in Oklahoma, and there is probably no community in the whole United States which doesn't contain at least one company trading under the name of "O.K." or some variant of it. The Manhattan telephone directory lists twenty-five of them, dealing in everything from stockbrokerage to "kosher seals." As recently as 1956 the Nicholson-Fowler *Dictionary of American-English Usage* peckishly dismissed "O.K." as "a U.S. national disease." But by that time the term was being freely used by staid Prime Ministers and the even more hide-bound *London Times*. London also has the Okay Building Supplies Co. Paris has its O. K. Bag-Fastener Co. Every camp-town crowding the gates of every American military post overseas has its "O.K." bars and brothels.

"O.K." is variously spelled (okay, okeh), compressed (oke) and elaborated (okey-dokey), but an attempt to give it an antonym (nokay) has not had much acceptance. "O.K.'s" popularity is not hard to understand; it is brief, breezy, in-stantly comprehensible, unmistakable in meaning, and can function as almost any part of speech: noun, verb, adjective, adverb or interjection. The only thing unsimple and unclear about "O.K." is the matter of its origin.

Where did it come from? Some say we picked it up from the Powhatan Indian *oke,* meaning an idol doll or amulet. Some say it came from the words *Aux Cayes* branded on barrels of rum imported from the Haiti seaport of that name. (Today a French manufactory uses the brand name *Aux Cayes* on its products as a phonetic rendition of "O.K.") Some claim that Andrew Jackson inadvertently invented it; that he approved documents by scribbling on them "O.K." as an abbreviation of his alleged illiterate "orl korrect" for "all correct." Some believe it came from the early telegraphers' signal that the line is clear: the Morse dots and dashes for O and K. But the philologist who made the most exhaustive study of "O.K." was H. L. Mencken; he finally satisfied him-self as to the term's provenance, and his conclusion is now accepted by most dictionaries.

After citing in his *The American Language* the numerous claimants to "O.K.'s" paternity, Mencken settled on an 1840 appearance of it as the likeliest first. In that year Martin Van Buren, nicknamed "Old Kinderhook" after his New York State hometown, was running for President. His supporters orga-nized the "Democratic O.K. Club," a campaign march was called "The O.K. Quick Step," and "O.K." gradually became the Democrats' slogan. There is, of course, the possibility that the campaigners were making a word-play on some previously popular use of "O.K." But until an earlier source is estab-lished, "Old Kinderhook" appears to have the firmest claim.

Between them, "bloody" and "O.K." pretty well bracket the extent of slang. At the one end, slang's ejaculations and vul-garities coarsen into the plain "dirty words." At the other, its brisk utilitarianism blends into jargon and idiom. In any lan-guage, the area between these extremes is a wide, fertile field for imagination and invention.

Slang has inspired both calumny and eulogy. Lexicographers Samuel Johnson and Noah Webster considered it low, crude and despicable. But Hayakawa has called it "the poetry of everyday life," and Emerson wrote, "Cut these words and they would bleed; they are vascular and alive; they walk and run." The French call slang *la langue verte*, "the green language." Professor Charlton Laird makes the measured judgment that "slang is never respectable; when it becomes respectable, it is no longer slang."

Because of slang's scope and variety, it is hard to define exactly; a loving mother's baby talk is just as truly slang as is a drill sergeant's profanest fulmination. To cite examples only from English (and American), slang boldly extends or telescopes or combines word meanings for its effects: "to chisel," "to rib" (from rib-tickle, presumably), "brunch," "rubberneck," "pussyfoot." It includes abbreviations: "VIP," "BMOC," "IOU"; and curtailments: "natch," "terrif," "feeb"; and metaphors: "she's a peach," "he's a cold fish"; and synecdoche: "threads" for clothes, "wheels" for automobile; and similes both direct and oblique: "drunk as a lord," "happy as a clam," "dead as a doornail"; and enantiosis: fat people are nicknamed "Tiny," anything admirable or enjoyable is "crazy."

It uses antonomasia: "Shylock" for a usurer, "Milquetoast" for a timid soul, "Scrooge" for a miser; and onomatopoeia: "razz," "gooey," "yack"; and metonymy: "you can't fight City Hall," "Uncle Sam wants you"; and mispronunciation, intentional or not: "sweet patootie," "Wipers" (for Ypres, in World War I), "she's got a big bazoom"; and hyperbole: "blockbuster," "smash hit show," "fantabulous" (Partridge has drily remarked that in America "sensational" means "mildly surprising"). Slang appropriates from other languages: "vamoose," "kibitz," "presto"; and makes up inventions of its own: "pizazz," "gutbucket," "screaming meemies," "flapdoodle."

The English language leads the rest of the world's tongues in slang content, with the American variety somewhat ahead of the British. There are an estimated half-million words in formal English today; probably closer to three-quarters of a million, if we include all the scientific and technical terms. But slang—American slang alone—numbers an additional 100,000 words. Of course, not all of these are in common use. Slang, like trade jargon and formal language as well, is infinitely compartmented—into underworld slang, jazz slang, sports slang, etc. And the various slang lexicons are hatching new locutions all the time, but that 100,000 figure remains fairly constant, because the mortality is just as high as the birth rate. Very few slang expressions become permanent fixtures in a language, and by the time they do, as Laird has pointed out, they have attained at least the semirespectability of colloquialism.

"Sweater," for example, was a rather uncouth word as recently as the 1880s. Certainly no lady's woollen wrapper bore such a name; a lady might get "bedewed," but she didn't sweat. Today no one thinks twice about the name, and in some circles "sweater girl" is a term of high admiration. In the seventeenth century, "miss" was an epithet applied only to prostitutes, while "mistress" meant a sweetheart or fiancée. Until just about sixty years ago, "sophisticated" meant "falsified, corrupt, impure." "Quaker" is no longer the derisive catcall it was when first applied to members of the Society of Friends. (Founder George Fox had preached that men should "quake at the word of the Lord.") And even the German Baptist Brethren themselves now use the name "Dunkards," though it was originally a slighting reference to their baptismal dunking. Dr. Johnson deplored "frisky," "gambler" and "conundrum" (but he used "bubbies" for bosom). Such words as "wherewithal," "kidnap," "workmanship," "quiz," "broadcast," "blizzard," "slum," "smog" and "furthermore" were all slang terms which had to fight their way into formal English.

"O.K." has been with us for a century and a half, but during that time countless thousands of other terms have caught fire only to fizzle. Consider just this small sampling, dating from the 1970s back to the turn of the century—"like wow," "keep on truckin'," "hep," "hubba-hubba," "ish kabibble," "the berries," "the cat's pajamas," "banana oil," "it," "lounge lizard," "twenty-three skiddoo," "yea, bo!" They are as laughably archaic, and very nearly as incomprehensible, as the "odd-come-shortly," "in Lob's pound" and "showing the way to Redding" of two and three hundred years ago.*

Yet there are slang expressions far older than "O.K." still in common use, and others which once flourished, died and then were reintroduced. James Thomson used "smooth" in the slang sense of "crafty" in 1748. "Out of sorts" was another eighteenth-century term, originally a printer's complaint that he was short of "sorts," type characters of a particular font. "Elbow grease" dates from the 1600s, and so does "sap" for "fool." Shakespeare used "O boy!" "beat it," "not so hot" and "lily-livered." A good-looking woman was already a "broad" in the sixteenth century, and had been a "piece" since the fourteenth. Today "frying" is prison slang

---

* *Odd-come-shortly:* sometime soon.
In Lob's pound: in difficulty.
Showing the way to Redding: showing off to attract attention.

for what happens in the electric chair, but Spenser used it identically, four hundred years ago, to describe the tortures of the damned. "To mooch," in the fifteenth century, was to pretend poverty. Chaucer used "gab" in the fourteenth century just as it is used today. And Aristophanes described a loony as "cracked" in 400 B.C.

Rather oddly, some English expressions have tended away from once-correct usage toward a sort of slangy second childhood. "Coolth" was formerly the formal and very useful antonym of "warmth"; today's lexicographers mark it "jocose." "Dizzy" has the formal meaning of "affected with vertigo," but is oftener used to mean "scatterbrained"; yet that, too, was once accepted usage even in the Bible. In a ninth-century translation of the New Testament parable of the ten virgins, Jesus was quoted as remarking that five of them were wise but "five of them were dizzy. . . ."

The now mild and empty interjection "by George!" was once as solemn an oath as an Englishman could swear; that is, on the name of his country's patron saint. "A pox on you," when it is heard at all, is now humorously bestowed, but these were once fighting words, "pox" having meant syphilis. The Doxology ("Praise God from whom all blessings flow . . .") was generally the most popular, loudest-sung and often the closing hymn of the nineteenth-century church service, so the stately word was hauled into the slang vocabulary and hooked up to "sock" to provide "sockdolager," meaning a knockout punch or untoppable phenomenon.

Slang is generally right in step with the times. The mentally afflicted person who used to be a "crackpot" is, in this Age of Analysis and Technology, a "psychoceramic." An earlier, more leisurely era delighted in big words and mouth-filling phrases, but the slang trend today is to the curt and telegraphic. A one-time "flibbertigibbet" is now a "kook." To make a hurried departure was once to "absquatulate," then to "skedaddle"; now it is to "scram." An error was once "putting the saddle on the wrong horse"; today it is a "booboo." In England, "aggro" (short for "aggravation," misused to mean "irritation" or "troublesomeness") even gets into the usually elegant writings of *Punch* gourmet columnist Clement Freud, M.P.

A slang word can undergo a complete change in its meaning without graduating out of the slang class. "Fairy," in its slang context, now means a homosexual or effeminate male; less than a hundred years ago it meant a depraved and hideous old woman. In the early decades of this century the word "nut" meant a person odd in dress or behavior; today it means someone totally addled. And there are various words (like "bloody") which mean quite different things in different places.

Rapariga means simply "girl" in Portugal, but in the Portuguese of Brazil it means a kind of girl that one doesn't mention in polite company. The wife of the Spanish ambassador to a certain South American country once remarked, on leaving a tea party, that she was going "to catch" (*coger*) a bus. "*¡Qué bárbaro!*" her hostess gasped in shock—or possibly admiration. In South America *coger* means "to have sexual relations with."

To "knock up" an American girl is to get her with child; to "knock up" an English girl is merely to rap on her door. People who wouldn't dream of saying "damn" will utter seemingly gentle ejaculations like "dear me" and "poppycock," unaware that they're really being blasphemous or vulgar. "Dear me" is simply a phonetic variant of the Italian *Dio mio*, "my God," and "poppycock" comes from the Danish *pappekak*, "dung" (to be precise, *soft* dung). A once-popular school of jazz, and the dance it inspired, got the name "boogie-woogie" from a southern black term for the secondary (or twitchy) stage of syphilis.

The most distinctive and long-enduring form of slang ever bestowed—or foisted—on the English language is the rhyming slang created by the London Cockneys. It was first heard as long ago as the seventeenth century, but hit its heyday in the 1840s and shortly afterward infected the rest of the English-speaking world. It enjoyed only a brief vogue in America, where it was welcomed mainly by prison inmates as a "secret jargon," but it was long popular among all classes in Australia. Rhyming slang appeared to be on its way to extinction about the time of World War II, but it has recently had a resurgence among England's juveniles, and bids fair to live at least until the teen-agers drop it for some other fad.

Rhyming slang began by substituting such locutions as "needle and pin" for gin, "bees and honey" for money, "storm and strife" for wife, "Gawd forbids" for kids, "gay and frisky" for whiskey. But this was too easy for outsiders to decode, so the speakers garbled their language even more, by using only the nonrhyming elements of the locutions. This resulted in such terms as "china" for mate (from "china plate") and "bacon" for legs (from "bacon and eggs"). There are probably Londoners today saying "loaf" for head (from "loaf of bread") who've never heard the full expression and have no idea it has anything to do with a rhyme.

The self-appointed curators of a language, being always

uncomfortable about the existence of slang, like to believe
that it is an ailment endemic only among the lower classes,
or a virus that somehow slipped through quarantine from the
benighted colonies. Thus English purists have futilely tried to
prove that rhyming slang was really an Australia-born freak.
And they have tried to blame America for unloading much
other slang on the mother country. This attempt has led some
lexicographers into preposterous mistakes; one English glossary of American slang defined "heck" as "familiar for Hec-
uba, a New England deity."

But the upper classes and the old guard are just as much
given to slang as any spiv or swagman or muleskinner. The
only difference is that the aristocratic argot is flaccid and
juiceless compared to the earthy, racy locutions from below-
stairs. It was the *oligoi*, the favored few in ancient Greece,
who invested with disdain the term for "the masses," *hoi pol-
loi*. The Roman *patricii* were similarly supercilious toward
the *plebs*. In England and America, it was the upper class
which invented the term "upper class" and slangier cultural
distinctions like "U" and "non-U"; "highbrow," "middlebrow"
and "lowbrow"; "blue-bloods" and "the great unwashed." It
was not the vulgar tabloids but elegant periodicals like *Vogue*
and *Town & Country* which invented the "jet set" and "the
beautiful people," i.e., those well-born or well-heeled enough
to spend all their time doing "fun things." It was the uppity
"white-collar" office worker who smugly dubbed the drudge in
the machine shop a "blue collar." It is only the members of
"cafe society" who can discern their set's superiority to common "pub-crawlers."

The philologist can perceive only one instance where slang
expressions might be divided into sheep and goats. And that
would be to acknowledge that slang-makers of an earlier day
were rather wittier and more imaginative than our own (and
that they could take for granted a similar acuity in the people to whom they addressed their slang). For instance, an
eighteenth-century lexicographer listed "Athanasian wench"
as one slang term for a promiscuous female. He did not
bother to explain its etymology, obviously assuming that his
readers would spot the allusion to the Athanasian Creed, the
first words of which are "Whosoever desires. . . ." Early in
this century, the English businessman or shopkeeper referred
to a bad credit risk as a "mavourneen." This wouldn't make
much sense to anyone who didn't know that the old song
"Kathleen Mavourneen" includes the line "It may be for
years, and it may be for ever. . . ."

One reason why the American slang vocabulary has always

[91]

bulked larger than the British is the greater opportunity it has had for absorbing words from the languages of immigrants. In metropolitan areas, Yiddish has contributed heavily: *kosher* to mean "fitting, proper, legal, O.K."; *goy,* a Gentile; *shiksa,* a Gentile girl. The useful word *chutzpah* designates an outrageous kind of gall or impudence for which English has no word. It is illustrated by the story of the man who murdered both his parents, then asked the court for mercy on the ground that he was an orphan. Both *schlemihl* and *schmendrik* mean a dope or a dupe, but with a distinction. It was once explained to me that a house-painter who stupidly drops a paint bucket from his scaffold is a *schlemihl;* the dunce who strolls underneath and gets it on his head is a *schmendrik.*

The Italian Bologna sausage arrived here to be simultaneously mispronounced, confused with the gypsy *pelone* ("testicles") and converted into a euphemism for the interjection "balls!" A similar euphemism, "bushwa" for "bullshit," is a western American corruption of the French *bois-de-vache,* dried buffalo dung used by the voyageurs as campfire fuel. The Romany language of the gypsies contributed, via underworld slang, the words "pal," "shiv" and "stir" (from *staripen,* "prison").

Army veterans of the Japanese occupation still use *honcho* to mean a "big shot" (evidently it derived from Honshu, the name of Japan's biggest island), but the term never became too common. Neither did the expression "numbah ten," which came into GI slang during the Korean War. In the Japanese-Korean-American pidgin, things were rated numerically from good to bad; a very good thing was *ichi ban* (Japanese) or *che il* (Korean) or "numbah one"; less good was "numbah two" and so on down the scale. There was nothing worse than "numbah ten" except the unspeakable; that was "numbah hava no."

Various nationalities have become inextricably identified with their favorite slang words. English explorers, colonists and tourists have been known all over the world, by both civilized and primitive folk, as the "goddems." The French have similarly been referred to as the "deedonks," from their insistent *dis donc*—which is the same as the English attention-getter, "say!" (and both of which, when you think about it, really mean "listen!"). Turn-of-the-century Italian immigrants in the United States called their American neighbors and co-workers *gli sanemagognas* (the "son-of-a-guns"). No derogation was intended; that was what the Americans called each other.

Britain and America have freely shared their wealth of slang with less well-endowed countries, and frequently formal English words too have become the slang of other nationalities. Many of the migrant words have already been mentioned—*le knockout, biznis*, etc.—and of course "Yankee" is internationally employed, quite often in an uncomplimentary sense. "Gangster" has gone into the French language unchanged, and so has "partner" into Hungarian. Four other Hungarian slang words would appear to have come from the States: *jany* ("girl"), *korista* ("chorus girl"), *sztriptíz* and *jassz* (though in Hungary this means a rowdy or hoodlum).

English slang is most firmly rooted abroad in those places where American troops have been stationed for any length of time. "Hamburger" has gone back to its homeland to replace *Fleischpflänzchen*. German workers on American posts are "ge-hired" and "ge-fired." Italians who used to incline to *dolce far niente* now *tegedizi* ("take it easy"). The Japanese *chiine-ijya* (teen-ager) is addicted to the *jyukubaksu* (juke-box) and the *disuku jokii* (disk jockey). And everywhere in the world, a land-based American serviceman, whatever his branch and whatever his rank, from buck private to company-grade officer, is democratically and invariably hailed as "GI."

In American slang, the three topics which have engendered the greatest number of expressions, whether admiring or disparaging, are drinking, love and money—in that order. But in any language, slang terms of ridicule, denunciation and vituperation far outnumber the expressions of praise or affection. And the slang terms used by one ethnic group to refer to another may be the single most striking and instructive aspect of a language's personality.

When syphilis first made its appearance in the Old World, its victims blamed whichever distant or neighboring foreigners they happened to detest most. The Germans called it the "French disease," the French called it the "Neapolitan disease," the mainland Greeks called it the "Corinthian disease," the English called it—depending on what war was going on at the time—the "French pox," the "Spanish gout," etc.

An Englishman or American, confounded by some unintelligible piece of writing or speech, dismisses it with the words, "It's Greek to me." Other nationalities do the same, but no two agree on what *is* the most damnably incomprehensible language. The French say, "That's Hebrew to me." The Germans say, "That's Spanish to me." The Russians say, "That's Chinese to me." And the Poles say, "I'm hearing a Turkish sermon."

The French refer to a dirty trick as a "Chinese trick," and to intolerable red tape as *chinoiserie*. The Spaniard, when wronged, complains that he's been victimized by a "Basque trick," the Dutchman by a "German trick." In both Spain and Romania, a "German joke" is a stale and unfunny one. The Germans refer to sloppy management as "Polish economy." The Romanians refer to inept statesmanship as "Bulgarian diplomacy."

Britain's slang has bequeathed to American numerous slanderous terms that date from the seventeenth century, when British and Dutch seamen were vying for ocean supremacy. Thus we have the belligerent drunk's "Dutch courage"; the cheapskate's "Dutch treat," which is no treat at all; the expression "in Dutch," to be in trouble; and the self-righteous "Dutch uncle." These terms, too, have correlatives in other languages. What is to us "Dutch courage" is to a Frenchman "German happiness." Our "going Dutch treat" is in France "going Swiss."

English and American soldiers refer to a buddy who has gone over the hill as being on "French leave." The French call the same dereliction *filer à l'anglaise* (which my French-English dictionary translates delightfully as "to take French leave"). Americans, when they want to do something unobserved, wait until "the coast is clear." Spaniards, apparently still rankling from the Moorish occupation of five hundred years ago, use the more explicit expression, *Ya no hay moros en la costa*, or "The coast is clear of Moors." An amusement park roller-coaster, called in most European languages "the Russian mountains," is called in Russian "the English mountains."

The United States "dollar diplomacy" and "Coca-Cola culture" have been fleered in many lands, and in Denmark even Detroit's proudest products were derided, their chromium grilles described as "dollar grins." Canadians (who are technically also Americans, but hate to be told so) call the U. S. flag the "gridiron," and blacks "unbleached Americans."

Most of the slang common to any nation is just so much gibberish to one who doesn't speak the national language, and speak it fluently. According to S. Stephenson Smith, the American locution "know-how" would require forty-three words for an adequate French translation. (The French word *expertise*, so eagerly and ubiquitously but ignorantly adopted into English in recent years, does *not* mean know-how, expertness, savvy, capability or anything of the sort. "Know-how" does.)

Like the English variety, other people's slang depends on figures of speech peculiar to that language, or makes plays

[94]

on the formal words of that language, or includes outright inventions as hard to etymologize as the American "O.K." But some foreign slang does evoke images which can be appreciated by an outsider. For example, every society uses the real or fancied characteristics of various animals to describe various sorts of persons.

English-speakers refer to a dolt as an "ass," to an eccentric as a "queer duck," to a scoundrel as a "skunk," "rat" or "louse," and so on. To be called a "turtle" by a Chinese is the vilest of insults; the belief in China is that the turtle commonly practices incest. The French call a miscreant a "camel," a pimp a "mackerel" and a whore a "hen." An "April fool" in France is an "April fish." The Germans call a villain a "pig-dog" (*Schweinehund*). Botanical metaphors are also universally employed. English slang includes "pansy," "seedy," "wall-flower," etc. The Spaniard calls a policeman a "hot pepper." To the French a dunce is a "sauerkraut-head." The jilted Frenchman accuses his inconstant mistress of having an "artichoke heart" (easily peelable, one assumes).

Himmelkreuzdonnerwetterpotztausendnocheinmal! gives a good idea of the German's rolling, rumbling, thunder-weather cuss-words. (Though it must be admitted that to a non-German even an innocuous substantive like *Überschwemmungskatastrophe* looks and sounds equally fearsome.*) Kipling once said that Arabic was made to swear in, but few Arabic imprecations carry their full import in translation. Only a person to whom pork is anathema can truly shudder at the curse, "May your mouth be full of pig's flesh!" Perhaps the Arab's direst insult is the abrupt "Your religion!" The insultee is expected to understand the implication—"Your religion be damned!"

Blasphemy is, of course, the basis for much invective. The Oriental's ancestor worship is impugned in the Chinese curse, "May the wild asses browse on your grandfather's grave!" And the Parsee invokes demons when he wishes on another, "May your daughter be wedded to a *jinni* and give birth to three-headed serpents!" In his book *The Lost Art of Profanity*, Burges Johnson cites a wonderful irreverence overheard at a Havana baseball game. When a certain batter struck out, he flung his cap on the ground, jumped up and down on it for a while, finally shook both his fists at heaven and bellowed, "I spit on the twenty-four feet of the twelve Apostles!"

In India, one of the most scurrilous insults is to call a man "brother-in-law." The intimation is that you have been inde-

---

* All it means is "a flood."

corously familiar with his sister. In old China, where mental torpor was as much despised as moral turpitude, a hair-curling fulmination was "Drink ink!" meaning that the one addressed was ignorant and should study more.

In addition to the profanities and blasphemies which pull no punches, every language has at least one alternate set of expletives and intensives which mean the same thing but are euphemized for the use of younger, more polite or timid speakers. In America, for example, a big-league baseball team may play "a hell of a game," but Little Leaguers play "a whale of a game." "Hell" has another kid brother in "heck," and "damn" has its "darn." Popular legend has it that Mark Twain invented these to tone down his riverboat profanity out of deference to his sensitive wife, Livy. Actually "heck" came from Lancashire dialect centuries before, and "darn" is a curtailment of "tarnation," which in turn was a blend of "damnation" and "by the 'tarnal" (eternal), a favorite oath of American Revolutionary days. Other tongues use similar evasions to avoid provoking the reigning deity. Italians exclaim, *Per Bacco!* calling on a god (Bacchus) who has been extinct for some twenty centuries. Spaniards "swear on the spirit"—*Voto a brios!* (instead of *dios*, "God"). The French say "by the blue!"—*Parbleu!* (instead of *dieu*).

Civilization and culture are not necessarily prerequisites to profanity; slang in all its variety has been present even in those primitive societies which, having no writing, were not particularly committed to a "formal" language. The Maori cannibals gleefully referred to human meat as "long pig." The Plains Indians of North America called the white man's railroad train "many wagon, no horse." The Algonquian Indians thought the white man's trousers effeminate, and among the Pamunkeys one white trader, whose sartorial singularity was a pair of trousers held up by one suspender, was called by his Indian customers *Kish-kish Tarakshe*, which can best be translated as "Him-with-his-arse-in-a-sling."

> If any word or expression is of such a nature that
> the first impression it excites is an impression of
> obscenity, that word ought not to be spoken nor
> written or printed; and, if printed, it ought to be
> erased.
>
> —DR. THOMAS BOWDLER

Those Four-Legged Words

EVERY language has a split personality. Behind the fa-
çade it shows the world, it secretly cossets a skeleton-
closetful of words considered unfit to parade in public.
These are commonly known as "obscenities" (*obscénités, Zo-
ten, oscenitàs, etc.*), but in the English-speaking milieu somehow even "obscenity" is regarded as vaguely obscene, and so
the euphemism "four-letter words" has been substituted. In
America even *that* delicate phrase has incredibly been found
tainted.

Cole Porter's song "Anything Goes,"* as originally written,
contained the wry remark that ". . . Good authors too / Who
once used better words / Now only use four-letter words . . ."
This pained some Mrs. Grundy somewhere, and so in radio
and television broadcast versions the blameless lines are now
often rendered: ". . . Good authors too / Who once used better words / Now only use three-letter words . . . ," whatever
that is supposed to mean.

The expression "four-letter words" is actually a simplistic
misnomer. A tabulation of English "obscenities" reveals that
only a minute fraction of them consist of just four letters. Of
the words generally deemed unspeakable and unprintable,
there are really only eight in common use which do not have
other, innocent definitions. The eight are all cloacal; one refers to that butt of jokes, the "arse"; five pertain to excretory
functions: "shit," "crap," "turd," "piss" and "fart"; and two

* "Anything Goes," copyright 1934 by Harms, Inc. Used by permission.

[97]

deal with sexual matters: "cunt" and "fuck." All but the last one of these have attained to inclusion in *Webster's Third New International* unabridged; most of them can be found even in desk-size dictionaries; and all without exception can cite centuries of literary history and tradition as precedent for their usage.

Among the oldest of them, "shit" came into Anglo-Saxon (*shite*) from the Old Norse (*skīta*), and had a noteworthy champion in Chaucer (". . . did most foully beshitte himself . . ."). "Crap," from the Middle Dutch word for "chaff," was quite respectable as a synonym for "dregs" until the mid-nineteenth century, when it began to be used as a euphemism for "shit," and gradually inherited much of the opprobrium of the older word. "Turd" derived, through the Old French, from the Latin *torquere* ("to twist"); Shakespeare used it in the modern sense of "a piece of dung" in his *Merry Wives of Windsor*. "Piss" was a socially acceptable word in Middle English; the King James translators of the Bible saw no harm in using it (and its elegant variant "pisseth") seven times in all. "Fart" is as old in English as "shit," and has apparent cognates that go all the way back to Sanskrit (*pardate*, "he breaks wind"). "Arse" is not a dialect pronunciation of "ass," but came from Old Norse, and has a relative in the Greek *orrhos*, "buttocks." In fact, the animal, the ass, was hauled in as an attempt at euphemizing "arse." But when, as always happens, the word "ass" began also to sound naughty to tender ears, the word "donkey" was coined (about 1780) as a more polite name for the poor put-upon beast.

"Cunt" came into Middle English (*cunte*) as a bequest from the Latin *cunnus*, and has an abundance of cognates in the Indo-European family of languages: the Spanish *coño*, Dutch *kunte*, French *con*, Scandinavian *kunta*, Persian *kun*, etc. "Fuck" also has numerous cousins of other nationalities: the German *ficken*, the Italian *fottere*—and had its earliest beginnings in the Latin *futuere*, "to have sexual intercourse with a woman" (the Romans had other verbs relating to intercourse with other sorts of partners).

There are various other four-letter words which are equally reprehended—"frig," "coos," "twat," "poon," etc.—but they are less widely used, and might even slip by in a spoken or written passage, unnoticed by the innocent. There are also innumerable four-letter words of otherwise innocuous meaning which have secondary definitions that are decidedly indecorous. "To know," for instance, is the biblical euphemism for "to have sexual intercourse." Many other simple words— "hard," "make," "bang," "feel," "blow," "jerk," etc.—have specialized off-color meanings. As for the taboo words of more than four letters, just to list them would pretty nearly fill this chapter.

But even the eight words first mentioned, though they have no other applications, formal or acceptable, to justify their existence, do have synonyms which can be mentioned without paralyzing polite company—"buttocks," "defecate," "stools," "micturate," "flatus," "pudendum," "copulate" and others. As Isaac Goldberg has remarked, "There is nothing so disagreeable in the matters of sex or digestion that cannot be said in English—provided you make generous use of Greek or Latin derivatives." Thus, even the most prudish must concede that the things or acts referred to are natural ones common to the entire human race; indeed, to the whole animal kingdom; that they are not perversions or monstrosities or crimes against nature. Obviously it is only the words describing these things or acts which are nasty—and only certain of the words, at that.

But the notion that a word can *be* anything is utter nonsense. Every word in the human vocabulary is of human invention, and no word can lead an existence apart from the concept to which it applies. Yet there is no denying that even modern, civilized, supposedly enlightened people will connect a word to its referent phenomenon, and will thereafter consider the word, like its referent, either a gladsome or a gruesome one. In the fall of 1963 a popular mystery novelist was at work on the first of a projected series of novels to feature a detective hero named Dallas. But then occurred the assassination of President Kennedy in the city of the same name, and the novelist hastily changed his protagonist's name to Travis. The writer was afraid—and rightly so—that a hero called Dallas would be a less "sympathetic character" now that Dallas had become a "dirty word."

But those who see a word as an entity independent of its referent, who invest it with any innate quality of goodness or badness, are intellectually as crippled as the Stone Age savage who believed that the name of a thing possessed the "life spirit" of the thing itself. These are the same people who say "pass on" for "die"—in the belief, conscious or instinctive, that to mention a dire thing is to risk invoking it.

Semanticists have suggested, however, that the shock power of "obscene" words is not entirely in their reflection of primitive superstition but in their ability to evoke empathic identification. That is, any person can hear the word "copulate" without a blush; it is dry, technical, devoid of any striking imagery. But the word "fuck" seems to call to mind the act itself, complete with all the attendant psychosexual repression-tensions which the act inspires in the individual—feelings of desire, repugnance, enjoyment, shame or whatever. It may be that the person really repelled by "obscene" words is the person most susceptible to the tumefacient images and emotions they evoke. This is not necessarily to imply that the puritan is the paradigm of prurience, and certainly there are many who shun such words simply because they're in "bad taste." But there is reason to believe that the person who is truly shocked by a four-letter utterance, and who is truly vehement in his loathing of it, is probably less stable emotionally than one to whom the word is no more than an impolite word.

There are intelligent people who will grant that the "obscene" terms are no more than arbitrary labels, inoffensive in that sense, and who object to them solely on the ground that they are "ugly." But ugliness is in the eye or ear of the beholder. Is "fuck" less pretty or less euphonious than "luck" or "folk" or the coy "oh, fudge"?

There are only a very few words whose look or sound command the same response from people of different tongues. These are the purely echoic words. "Babble," as earlier noted, has recognizable correlatives in numerous languages, and the sibilant sound of a bladder being voided is everywhere the same. So, although the cultured Roman's verb for the act was *urinare,* the common man called it something like *pissiare,* and the echoism fitted so well that it has served for that common man's descendants in many lands. In Italian the word is *pisciare,* in French *pisser,* in English "to piss." And other peoples seem to have derived similar echoisms independently, e.g., the Hungarian *pisalni* ("piss") and the Hittite *pisan* ("water pot").

But others of the "obscene" English words do not inspire any universal revulsion by their mere sound; quite bland and virtuous homophones are to be found in many languages. In Arabic *kun't* means only "you were." The German *Fahrt* means "journey." In Hungarian *fuccs* is a slang word, but its meaning is just "gone to seed." The Perrier company plasters posters all over France to advertise its carbonated beverages, and these posters proclaim Perrier's lively effervescence by boldly bellowing the one word *PSCHITT!* I remember how, in high school Latin class, we insufferable adolescents used to snicker at words like *fac* and *fucus,* but to the Roman the former was merely the imperative "do!" and the latter only "a purple dye."

When American bombers raided a number of North Vietnam seaports in the summer of 1964, newscasters in the

States carefully refrained from mentioning which ports they were—not out of any consideration of military security, but because one of them was named Phuc Loi.

The obscenities and vulgarities of other languages are just as ancient and tradition-steeped as those of English. To take French for example, the word *merde* ("shit") was entrenched in literature by Rabelais in the sixteenth century. The word for "rod" or "wand" (*verge*) has been used as slang for "penis" for so long that it is now considered acceptable by all levels of society. The word *pétard*, "detonation," has served for "fart" since about the fourteenth century (it also means, *a posteriori*, "bean").

The French word *bougre*, originally a "Bulgarian" and now a "heretic," has since the eleventh century had the vulgar meaning of "one who practices sodomy." This fragment of obscenity was invented with the approval of the Church, to discredit several sects of religious dissenters, reputedly outcast from Bulgaria and at that time resident in the South of France. The trumped-up libel was that their revolting rites included anal coitus; the result was that the godly French ousted or exterminated them, and made the name "Bulgarian" henceforth a dirty word.

Languages occasionally swap obscenities back and forth as readily as they do other bits of slang. The American GI has sown his favorite four-letter word—"fuck" plus its numerous compounds—wherever he has traveled. From the French *bougre*, English has made "bugger." Originally this had the same vile meaning in the English-speaking countries that it still does in France, but lately it seems to have lost much of its opprobrium. Male friends now greet each other with "you old bugger" as often as with "you old son-of-a-gun." Another taboo Gallicism, *soixante-neuf* or *six-à-neuf*, meaning a slightly contortive sexual diversion, came into English as "sixty-nine."

Considered simply as straightforward nouns and verbs, most "four-letter words" are no more than short and pithy synonyms for longer locutions, and there is no real reason—except the artificial aesthetic ones—why the short words should be abjured in favor of the long ones. But there is another aspect to these words, a less defensible one, and that is their employment as coarse interjections and intensives, lewd descriptives and invectives.

The words might have retained their one-time usefulness if they hadn't been debased to gutterisms, but no doubt it was their monosyllabic bluntness that so endeared them to the rabble. The words early became the linguistic standbys of mental bankrupts incapable of originality, and of inarticulates who found them easy to grunt. And so, in the limited vocabulary of the streets, the basic Anglo-Saxonisms came to do multiple duty as all parts of speech and with arbitrary variations of meaning.

For example, "fuck," as a verb, maintains its meaning of "to copulate," but has also become a noun for the act and, derogatorily, for a person ("he's a stupid fuck"). Again as a verb, it can mean to cheat or dupe ("he fucked me out of a dollar"). It can be employed adverbially ("get the fuck out of here!"). With auxiliaries it can mean to malinger ("to fuck off") or to bungle a job ("to fuck up") or to trifle ("to fuck around") or to meddle ("to fuck with"). Most of these have their nominal forms, too; a despicable person may be a "fucker," a "fuck-off" or a "fuck-up." The participle is an ambivalent intensive ("a fucking good time" vs. "a fucking bore").

"Fuck" will doubtless be the last of the four-letter words ever to be reaccepted in polite company, but in street speech it long ago became so commonplace that it occasionally requires an intensifier itself to serve as a really scurrilous insult. One such compounding produces that hideous execration generally elided to "muh-fugger."

Having consigned (or surrendered) the "four-letter words" to the gutter, the higher classes determined to leave them there, and through the ensuing centuries have invented substitutes for them, and then successive substitutes for the substitutes. These have ranged from baby-talk words like "wee-wee" for "piss" to replacements hardly more acceptable than the originals. The Yiddish *futz* for "fuck" and *scheiss* for "shit" seem little improvement; even the learned "pudenda" for "genitals" comes smirkingly from the Latin for "shame." Oftener than not, each new euphemism, however neat and clean at its introduction, soon took on the odor and odium of whatever it was replacing; e.g., "crap" for "shit."

A story told during Harry Truman's tenure as President relates how he addressed an Illinois Grange meeting one time when his wife Bess and a lady friend were in the audience. "I grew up on a farm," the President told the Grangers, "and one thing I'm sure about—farming means manure, manure and more manure."

"For goodness' sake, Bess," the friend whispered to her, down in the auditorium, "Why can't you teach Harry to say *fertilizer*?"

Mrs. Truman replied with a sigh, "Good Lord, Helen, it's taken me thirty years to get him to say *manure*."

Apocryphal of course, but it illustrates the progressive degeneration of euphemism. Today's "fertilizer" was "manure" yesterday and "meadow dressing" the day before. All the way back through "horse apples," "cowpats," "prairie chips," "muck," "dung," etc., to the Middle English *slyppe*, every one of them inevitably began to smell of "shit." (And "fertilizer" is already on its way out; the latest attempt at deodorization is "organic plant food.")

As for prettying up the verbs "to piss" and "to shit," the dainty have tried everything from baby talk ("doing number one" and "number two") to a locution so imbecilic that its popularity is astonishing: "going to the bathroom." A bathroom, by definition, is a room to take a bath in, not a leak or a crap, unless the bathroom also has toilet facilities, in which case one would be "going to the toilet." But so ubiquitous has the former phrase become that a 1983 California statute mandated the provision of "bathrooms" in supermarkets for the convenience of the elderly and incontinent or impatient. And I have even seen, in print, this absurdity: "My little doggie went outdoors to go to the bathroom."

The penis and testicles have gone by numerous names during the course of history, but the majority of them were and are considered uniformly bawdy—e.g., "cock," "pecker," "dick," "whang," "balls," "pudding," "family jewels"—and none ever competed with the Latin derivatives as being acceptable for polite usage. But of all the various "unmentionable" parts of the body, the humble buttocks have been most heavily festooned with euphemisms in the continuing search for *something* that area could be called without offensiveness.

When the Anglo-Saxon "arse" was deemed too vulgar, "ass" was substituted. Nowadays, people who wouldn't say "ass" will occasionally deign to say "arse" in the mistaken belief that they're humorizing and prettifying the naughty word by "talking Cockney" or something. Other names for the buttocks have ranged from the childish "bum" and "fanny" through "prat," "can," "tail," "cheeks," "caboose," etc., to the archaic "fundament," the pedantic *glutei maximi* and the arch Americanisms "sitting-down place" and "the part that goes over the fence last." The word "keester," considered harmlessly schoolboyish, is actually derived from underworld slang: a "keyster" being a trunk, hence a hiding-place for valuables, hence the anus, where packets of dope or jewels have sometimes been concealed.

While euphemisms are generally doomed to the same fate as their referents, an occasional once-ribald word has achieved enough usage to be smoothed and polished into acceptability.

"John," as a nickname for the toilet, was earlier considered either vulgar or puerile, but lately it has come into use in otherwise scrupulous circles. (It is a wonder to me that any parent can still name a boy child John, Peter or Dick.) "Prat" is still *non grata*, but the stage comedians' "pratfall" now appears in the most solemn theatrical reviews. "Screw," as an alternate to "fuck," is quite taboo, but "screwed-up" is widely used by all classes to mean muddled, entangled, disordered.

Today many of the most civil-tongued civilians freely use the World War II acronym "snafu" (there was even a movie by that name), and if asked to translate it would evasively reply, "situation normal: all fouled up." But everyone knows that the Army word was and is "fuck," not "foul." While most Army cuss-words have had little wit or originality to recommend them, there was a delightfully mordant humor to "snafu" and its wry variants denoting increasing desperation—"susfu" (situation unchanged: still fucked up), "tarfu" (things are really fucked up), "fubar" (fucked up beyond all recognition) and "sapfu" (surpasses all previous fuck-ups).

Another American Armyism, "crud," has come into popular use as a euphemism for "shit" or anything else horrible, but the etymology of the word is something of a mystery. "Curd" and "crudd" were interchangeable in Middle English for the coagulated solids of milk; Shakespeare once mentioned "dull and crudy vapors"; Charles Lamb once referred to some repulsive dish of food as "crug"; but it is unlikely that the GIs pirated any of these sources. "Crud" probably came into being because anything curdled is rather awful, and because slovenly speakers often say "cruddle" for "curdle."

Any attempt to classify the expressions which are and are not obscene, blasphemous or profane must take into account myriad factors of time, place and *chacun à son goût*. Frank Harris, in *My Life and Loves*, freely flaunted every other four-letter word in several languages, but consistently wrote "d - - n" and "h - - l." To snarl "Berk!" at a Mayfair Londoner would probably provoke no reaction whatever, but in the East End it would be recognized as a deadly insult. (It is another example of clipped rhyming slang: from "Berkeley Hunt" for "bloody cunt.") A hundred years ago, women walked on "limbs" and were so liable to swoon at the thought of a "leg" that they even adorned the legs of pianos with frilled little panties. About that same time, haycocks were becoming "haystacks," cockroaches were becoming "roaches," barnyard cocks were being emasculated into "roosters," and bulls were enduring truly ridiculous transformations into "cow-critters," "gentleman-cows" and, unkindest cut of all, "preacher-cows."

But preposterous prissiness is not wholly a thing of the naïve and distant past. When *Esquire* magazine was having a court squabble with the U. S. Post Office in 1943, regarding its moral qualifications for mailing privileges, one witness for the prosecution could think of only a single "obscenity" in that magazine which had distressed him: the rude reference to a female's buttocks as "her behind." Mencken related how the *Los Angeles Times*, in 1933, referring to a table staple of the poor, could not bring itself to print "sow-belly" but invented "sow-bosom" instead. It's too bad that Mencken wasn't around to jeer when, thirty-one years later, the same newspaper refused to print an advertisement showing a shapely, bikini-clad girl—until an airbrush artist obliterated her navel. Jessica Mitford has reported, in *The American Way of Death*, that Massachusetts not too long ago was mulling over legislation that would make it a criminal offense to "use profane, indecent or obscene language in the presence of a dead body."

Most newspapers today assume their readers to be sufficiently mature to accept the word "rape," but some American ones still prefer the less horrendous "attack" or "molest," and British ones incline to the ultra-fastidious "interfere with." This old-maidish prudery often results in such witless reportage as: "The girl had been beaten, stabbed and viciously mutilated before being strangled to death, but an examination disclosed that she had not been molested." In an English account, she wouldn't even have been interfered with.

Victims of sexual misadventures have always tended to dismiss them with insouciance or drollery—not so much, it would seem, to humor other people's sensibilities as to mitigate their own misery. A college girl who discovers herself untimely pregnant tries to soften the reality by calling her condition preciously "preggers." A venereal infection is evidently less awful when offhandedly referred to as "a dose" or "the clap"—in the 1700s it was "Cupid's itch." A favorite story among Army medics is the one about the hillbilly rookie overheard confiding to a buddy, "The clap ain't no worse'n a bad cold, and the syph, they can cure that now, too—but man, what they tell me y'gotta watch out fer is that-there veedee."

The subject of obscenity is bound up with that of pornography, but this too is an indefinably amorphous and relative term. As D. H. Lawrence wrote, "What is pornography to one man is the laughter of genius to another." Modern-day archaeologists have been shocked by some of the paintings they've unearthed in ancient Egyptian tombs. But the Egyptians hadn't seen anything shameful in providing pictorial

erotica to entertain the tomb's occupant while he was awaiting Ra's ferry to the promised land. The pictogram of an erect
penis was an accepted hieroglyph for "strength," and certainly no one would have boggled at the word *qe-fen-t*
("cunt"). On the other hand, certain parts of certain bodies
were inviolable. An Egyptian could count on blanching all bystanders if he swore the fearsome oath, "By the foot of the
Pharaoh!"

Explorer-writer Sir Richard Burton recounted with awe and
amusement an incident which occurred during his travels in
Arabia. An Arab woman fell from her perch on a camel,
landed upside down and all asprawl, her robes up around her
neck and her uncovered privates displayed to everyone in the
caravan. But her husband was instantly loud with praise of
her unblemished modesty; during all the agitation of her accident, he pointed out proudly, she had managed to keep her
yashmak secured across her face.

In certain parts of Polynesia, before the white man civilized
them, every sex act from masturbation to "sixty-nine" was indulged in whenever and wherever the urge inspired, be it bed-
stead or roadside. But what *was* taboo was being seen eating
in public, except at specified communal feasts. (Incidentally,
the white man brought with him one practice which these
primitives thought novel. They had copied their standard co-
ital position from the animals, so they referred to the white
man's innovation as "missionary position." The term is now
to be found, without quotation marks or any need for ex-
planatory diagrams, in sex manuals both solemn and frivo-
lous.)

Autre temps, autre moeurs, but the differing opinions of
what constitutes pornography and/or obscenity are by no
means delimited by epochs or ethnic boundaries. At this moment, a New York theater audience is probably being bored
to distraction by an "art" movie which Virginians consider
too indecent to be shown.

However, it is possible to write the most libidinous pornography or to hurl the foulest invective without using a single
"bad word." The snarl "up yours!" says nothing but means
much. The insult "you mother!" would not offend anyone
who didn't know the implied suffixion. Contrariwise, it is possible to declaim a whole string of sexual obscenities without
causing the slightest sexual excitation in a listener—quite
the opposite, most likely. Yet the general tendency is to see
obscenity and pornography as inseparable; and anyone who
dares to speak or write a "four-letter word" is automatically
presumed antagonistic to virtue and morality.

For the moment, let us compact the whole range of obscenity, blasphemy, profanity and invective into the catch-all term "cuss-words." The nature of cuss-words is to tread where angels fear to. A man riled to the point of uttering a cuss-word wants it to express the whole of his emotion, whether he feels outer-directed loathing of some person or some thing, or inner-directed exasperation, indignation or frustration. No feeble word will do. It must proclaim that the man has been tried beyond all endurance, that he is at the point where he dares to offend God and man, to defy piety, prudery and smuggery.

He says it.

That is a cuss-word. Whatever noise he chooses to utter, it is a cuss-word, whether it be a deacon's "oh, me" or a dockhand's most ear-searing, skin-blistering, blood-curdling eruption of unprintables. An American, a Spaniard and a German may separately revile each other with "son of a bitch!" *hijo de la puta!* and *Hurensohn!* and no one of the three will know he's being insulted; but each speaker knows what *he* is saying, and it gratifies him.

Even little children, innocent of both virtue and the loss of it, have their little cuss-words. A boy's worst-intentioned insult is to say of another that "he pees sitting down." Little girls dare the thunderbolt with "son-of-a-Beechnut-gum."

The trouble with cussing is that it grows by feeding on itself. The deacon can explode with "oh, me" just so many times before it loses its tang and savor, its apocalyptic dreadfulness. He must in time step up (or down) to "Heaven help us" and even more sordid depravities. The guttersnipe does exactly the same thing, though he usually starts from a level that the deacon probably will never reach. But the gradual debasement is not merely a matter of individual retrogradation. To be effective, cussing must be distinctive; in a society which has attained only to "darn," the man who says "damn" stands out, but when everybody around him starts to say "damn," he must introduce something more gross and grandiose.

It was only a comparatively few years ago that "damn" and "hell" were forbidden utterance from America's movie and television screens. Then the movies, later television, began admitting those words and also such one-time indecencies as "bitch" and "bastard"—then venturing an occasional muttered "crap"—then "piss" and "shit" and even "God damn!" I think the 1970 movie *M*A*S*H* was the first to say "fuck." I saw that film in Mexico City, and the "fuck" was one English word that required no subtitle translation; the Mexican audi-

ence roared in concerted surprise, shock, appreciation, out-
rage and hilarity. It is probably only a matter of time before
late-night television makes *all* the four-legged words acceptable parlor parlance. And so, as the old expressions shed
their chest- and pubic-hairiness, and turn into clean-shaven
clichés, the man bent on cussing must dig deeper into the
sewer to find a word to fit his mood.

In the English-speaking countries, the "four-letter words"
have had innumerable ups and downs of permissibility and
proscription. The table talk of Elizabethan days would peel
the varnish off any table of our present day, and the language of the streets back then is indescribable. A sort of last-
ditch profession for mustered-out soldiers who couldn't find
honest employment was to take up "ruffling," that is, putting
up for hire their parade-ground voices and barrack-room invective. Any citizen who possessed both an enemy and a few
coppers could hire one of these ruffians to dog that enemy's
footsteps all over town—for an hour or for the rest of his
life—bellowing the most ungodly vilification at him.

Of all the English written works which have suffered the
slings and arrows of outraged bluenoses down through the
years, the foremost example is not *Fanny Hill* or *Ulysses,* but
the Bible. When the King James version appeared in 1611, it
did indeed represent quite an overthrow of inhibition—for
one instance, in having Adam and Eve perform a sort of
striptease. In the King James rendition of Genesis, the couple cover their nakedness with fig-leaf "aprons." In the earlier
Geneva Bible they had somehow contrived more modest fig-
leaf "breeches."

A Quaker Bible of 1828 excerpted all the passages "unsuit-
able for a mixed audience" and printed them in italics apart
from the rest of the text. Noah Webster was one of several individuals who have taken it upon themselves to whitewash
the Scriptures. His 1833 Bible made such substitutions as
"breast" for "teat," "to nourish" for "to give suck," and "peculiar members" for "stones" (which itself was the King
James euphemism for "testicles"). In 1895 a Kansas man
was convicted of disseminating obscenity through the U.S.
mails; what he had posted was a list of quotations from the
Bible. In 1910 a Boston busybody stirred up quite a furor
when he tried to get a court injunction to prevent the Gideon
Society from distributing Bibles in hotel rooms "on the ground
that it is an obscene and immoral publication."

All down the ages, otherwise righteous and rectitudinous
writers have delighted in busting loose once in a while and
really letting rip with the indecencies. Why, they reasoned,

should an entire vocabulary of highly expressive expressions be marooned among morons and yahoos, and denied to the artists who could make constructive use of them? The roster of writers who have done so includes some of the classic masters, and others who are remembered *only* because they tried their hand at obscenity or pornography.

John Cleland wrote plays and works of philology, but his fame rests on the two books of pornography he ground out to save himself from debtors' prison: *Fanny Hill* and *Memoirs of a Coxcomb.* Benjamin Franklin, while uplifting the masses with his Poor Richard aphorisms, penned rather wittier and wickeder advice for his intimates—for example, his *Reasons for Preferring an Elderly Mistress,* with its wonderful "8th and lastly They are so grateful!!"

Mark Twain wrote *1601* in an access of whimsy, and then prudently hid it away. His friends and heirs conspired to keep it hidden after his death, so as not to sully his memory, and until just recently it was little more than a rumor to Twain's public. Now procurable in unexpurgated printings, *1601* reveals itself to be no horrid stain on Twain's name—though it doesn't add much gloss either. The account of an imagined conversation among Elizabethan courtiers, it is an adroit re-creation of the bawdry of the time. But what humor there is depends on the laying of a strong, silent-type fart by one of the company and, as for nastiness, no reader will find in it any word he or she did not already know.

When Twain and Rudyard Kipling became friends, they engaged in a sort of competition to see who could write the hairiest obscenity. It is said that one of Kipling's sketches (which began, " 'Shit!' said the Queen . . .") was somehow brought to Victoria's attention. She was not amused. And that, allegedly, is why Britain's most British poet never was honored with knighthood, and why the laureateship went to Alfred Austin.

George Washington was likewise disinclined to tolerate bad language—in others, at any rate; he himself was not averse to grinding an occasional gritty oath between his wooden dentures. But he took time out from preparations for the Battle of Long Island to issue this pronunciamento to his troops in July 1776:

The General is sorry to be informed that the foolish and wicked practice of profane cursing and swearing, a vice heretofore little known in an American army, is growing into fashion. He hopes the officers will, by example as well as influence, endeavor to check it, and that both they and the men will reflect that we can have little hope of the blessing of Heaven on our arms if we insult it by our impiety and folly. . . .

This passage may have more than antiquarian interest; it may be a revelation. If at that time cussing was "little known in an American army" then that army was something marvelously unique in human history. But evidently it wasn't; the general had to issue several more such ukases at intervals during the Revolution.

Another futile attempt at soaping the military mouth was the quaint and ephemeral Silent League. This society was organized among U. S. Navy men by Chaplain Carroll Q. Wright in 1903. It was to be "composed of men who solemnly agree to discourage Profanity and Obscenity everywhere so long as they live." I know of no sailor today who ever heard of the Silent League, but I know several who are walking evidence that Profanity and Obscenity have outlived it.

In 1922 the League of Nations paused in its task of picking up the pieces after World War I to consider legislation against obscenity; specifically "the production and distribution of articles intended merely to gratify the passions of depraved persons or to spread corruption among others, especially the young of both sexes." But here, as in so many more urgent matters, the League was unable to come to any agreement. In this case, the project foundered before it was even launched, as the members immediately despaired of ever framing "an international definition of the word 'obscene.' "

Today, in the English-speaking countries, language is nearly as free of restraints as it was in the time of that other Elizabeth. This fact is gratifying to most people of enlightenment and reason, but others are outraged and incensed. Some of them feel that "too much" freedom of speech is a symptom of our rapidly decaying morality. Others go even further and denounce it as a direct *cause* of the same. In any case, the modern trend toward linguistic liberalism is a sometimes thing; even the nonvocal majority's attitude toward obscenity is still many-faceted and fuzzy.

On the one hand, this multivalent attitude has caused the censure or censorship of much worthwhile literature; on the other, it has made best-sellers of trash. President Truman's unbridled use of invective made him many friends who admired his "talking straight from the shoulder"—and many enemies who deplored his "vulgarity."

The everyday language used by most actors, backstage or on the movie lot, is what might be described as Basic Longshoreman. But a well-known actress shocked her colleagues and nearly scuttled her career when, at an awards banquet, she replied to an emcee's fulsome introduction with a deprecatory laugh and the comment, "Shit." The sailor's lingo is traditionally the saltiest there is, but the U. S. Navy has gingerly dropped "coxswain" from its glossary of occupational titles, just because of the way it sounds. Sweet little old ladies can now procure, from the corner lending library, books that they couldn't have bought—when they were sweet little young ladies—from under the counter in a Yokohama smut shop. But if they buy one of the more recent vernacular translations of the Bible, they'll find that words like "ass" and "cock" have been bowdlerized into "donkey" and "rooster." If they buy a *very* recent one, the feminist version, they'll find that even God has been emasculated.

No Englishman seeking sensation is likely to look for it in a 970-page, three-pound, fine-print tome of etymology like Eric Partridge's *Origins*. But in it the author was forced to apologize for a couple of instances of typographical syncope, thus: "F**k shares with c**t two distinctions: they are the only two Standard English words excluded from all general and etymological dictionaries since the 18th century and . . . outside of medical and other official or semi-official and learned papers, still cannot be printed in full anywhere within the British Commonwealth of Nations."*

When Webster's Third was published in 1961, it caused a great outcry from purists because, for the first time, "ain't" was listed without the patronizing *Colloq*. As far as I know, there was no tumult at all over the fact that this dictionary also provides instructive definitions of such terms as "hard on," "feel up" and "jerk off." Nor was there much of a fuss when Harold Wentworth and Stuart Berg Flexner published their *Dictionary of American Slang* in 1960. It got good reviews from both scholarly and lay publications; even the *Christian Science Monitor* found it worthwhile; and so for more than a year it led a peaceful and useful existence on library reference shelves. But then, in the spring of 1963, it came to the attention of a California politician, and all h - - l broke loose. His denunciations of the book as "pure filth and obscenity" and "a practicing handbook of sexual perversion" were soon ringing up and down the state.

California, the citadel of every sort of eccentric cult, seems always to have been peculiarly prone to fanaticism. Certainly

* That edition of *Origins* was published in 1959. Within three years, the two words were cautiously appearing in print in Britain. By now, they are commonplace everywhere from etymological library shelves to street-corner newsstands.

in this case a large and hysterical segment of the population rose up in arms. Marchers carrying placards ("Ban the Book") demonstrated in numerous cities. Organized groups mimeographed lists of the "dirty words" contained in the dictionary, and distributed thousands of copies on streetcorners. Other groups motored through the state in chartered buses to spread the excitement around. Some citizens even demanded the dismissal of a junior-college instructor because he dared to defend the book.

At any time during the brouhaha, anyone seriously concerned about the book's toxicity could have invoked the State Penal Code to have the book legally judged. But that would not have created such a satisfying uproar and so much free publicity for so many self-seekers.

The net result of all this ruction: the various politicians who jumped aboard the ban-wagon got a lot of publicity both in California and outside it. Numerous California schools and libraries were forced to consider banning the book, but only a scattering actually did so. Some hundreds of marchers enjoyed some open-air exercise. Newspapers had an "issue" to enliven the summer doldrums. But the *Dictionary of American Slang* is still legally for sale in the state.

There are other book-banning campaigns still in full operation which are better organized and less perfervid, but for all their sobriety they are pursued with no less zeal. The Roman Catholic Church maintains several watchdog tribunals, from the internationally powerful Index Congregation (officially disbanded in 1967, with much publicity about "new liberality," but really only subsumed into the Congregation of the Holy Office) down to purely local vigilantes such as the minions of the National Organization for Decent Literature. These last, in many American communities, have strong-armed booksellers into removing "offensive" titles from their shelves on threat of a boycott by their Catholic customers.

While the Mother Church's now ostensibly abolished *Index Librorum Prohibitorum* is primarily concerned with quashing works of heresy and heterodoxy, the grass-roots groups are engaged in preventing the "moral corruption" of Catholic readers. This corruption they seem to assume would be the inevitable result of readers' exposure to stories of love sans marriage, sex sans impregnation, or even to a frankness of language untrussed by dogma. The obvious parallel to totalitarian thought-control has already been drawn, and by one of the Catholic antivice groups themselves. According to *Harper's* magazine a Connecticut Catholic War Veterans post once went on record with, "We have to hand it to the Communists . . . who have launched a nationwide campaign against pornographic trash. . . . Should not this example provoke a similar literary clean-up in our land where the morality of our actions is gauged by service to God and not to an atheistic state?"

There are several less-than-altruistic reasons why a person will cry havoc and go to do battle against obscenity. There is plain self-aggrandizement, as in the California case, where any issue would have served, where a book of "dirty words" just happened to come handy, and where there was a ruck of sheep to be stampeded. Then there is outright prurience; it goes without saying that to become an energetic officer of a vice-suppression society is the best way to get a good leer at pornography without having to skulk to do it. There are other, less hypocritical motives, too, of interest mainly to psychopathologists. But the typical crusader for decency is—as Richard Hanser described Dr. Bowdler—"the quivering moralist who is certain in his soul that others will be contaminated by what he himself reads with impunity."

The kind of people who heed such self-elected censors are likewise various. They range from the mildly irrational to the cringingly timid, from the superstitious who see actual malignity in "bad words" to the insecure status seekers who pretend refinement by putting on odiously fastidious airs. The one thing which all these sin-shunners have in common is a pitiful ignorance—of varying degree, to be sure, but invariably evident.

In his play *The Best Man*, Gore Vidal mentioned a politician who lost an election in the South because the whisper went around among the yokels that his wife had once been a "thespian." Fictional perhaps, but fact can top it. It is amazing how many people abhor the word "intercourse," unaware that it has any but the limited meaning of "copulation." (A hundred years ago "congress" was similarly supposed specific and similarly avoided.) Words like "masticate," "cunctator" and "formication" seldom come up in conversation, but when they do they make many an ignorant listener flinch or snigger. Incredibly, there are people who are made uncomfortable by terms like "penal code," "crapulent," "houri," or a mechanic's reference to a "male plug" or a "female coupling." People who shrink from lewd words frequently won't use "lewd" either, it sounds so absolutely oozing with nastiness; but all it originally meant was "lay" in the sense of "ordinary," as in "lay reader."

[113]

Ludicrously ignorant of which words are *not* obscenities, such people are usually equally dim about which ones *are*. I have heard a respectable female TV commentator blithely use the term "bollixed up," evidently unknowing that the word is a "dirty" one ("bollix is a version of "bollocks," an Elizabethan synonym for "balls"). All manner of people say "you jerk," believing it a comparatively harmless epithet like "you ninny." But in alley parlance a "jerk" is one whose brain has been addled by excessive masturbation (i.e., "jerking off"). "Jazz" has long had the demirep meaning of "fuck," and "juke," as in "juke-box" or "juke-joint," came from "juke-house," a Gullah term for "brothel." A hymn-singer would reject as blasphemous the information that his "hymn" is a cognate of "hymen," and that a "hymn" was originally a nuptial chant sung to celebrate the defloration of a bride.

Sly wags occasionally take advantage of the public's dependable obtuseness to put over little "in" jokes, as when Dylan Thomas created the fictional Welsh village of Llareggub for his radio play *Under Milk Wood*. The name looks and sounds so authentically Welsh that the censors never thought to try spelling Llareggub backward. The writers of the 1964 movie *Dr. Strangelove* named one character (the President of the United States) Merkin Muffley. "Muff" is an old, old word for the female genitalia or, specifically, the hair around it. A "merkin" is a sort of little wig for that same pubic area. But, to my knowledge, no reviewer of that film caught the ribaldry.

Considering the many contradictions and contrarieties in the obscenity issue, the most charitable conclusion might be that a great many people have dulled their good sense by too assiduously honing their sensibilities. One can only marvel that people of such questionable discernment, taste and knowledge can presume to set the standards of linguistic propriety for anyone else, let alone *everyone* else.

For one whole calendar year, 1982, the state of Texas managed, in effect, to deprive its every schoolhouse of the *entire* dictionary of the English language. It happened like this. Texas has a special committee which each year selects, from among all reference and textbooks published, those it recommends for bulk purchase by the State School Board. At the start of 1982, that committee selected, in addition to its other recommended purchases, three or four newly published English dictionaries, and left it to the convened Board to choose one of those for statewide use. The School Board members were "scandalized" to find "seven dirty words" (*which* seven words, unspecified) in every one of the candidate dictionaries. The Board rejected all of them and, bound by the system, could not start seeking anew to find an "un-dirty" dictionary acceptable that year. So it bought none at all, giving Texas a distinction dubious even by Bible Belt bigot standards—that of being the only sovereign American state in which every student has been forbidden access, as it were, to the whole of the English language

It ought to be unnecessary to remark that nothing in this chapter is meant to recommend that everybody should go around continually and publicly exclaiming "shit!"—any more than that everybody should go around publicly *doing* it. A libertine use of such language is just as vapid as a too-genteel horror of it. But there will be those—the militant Comstocks and the meaching Bowdlers—who will read into this essay a blatant call to universal licentiousness and turpitude. No attempt at reasoned argument is likely to broaden their peep-hole perspective; every clear-headed thinker from Milton to Mencken has tried. But the everlasting pity is that these people had to grow up not quite to an intelligent maturity, but just far enough to have forgotten that wise old childhood chant, one version of which went:

> Sticks and stones
> May break my bones,
> But words can never hurt me.

> The ancient Athenians used to cover up the ugliness of things with auspicious and kindly terms, giving them polite and endearing names. Thus they called harlots "companions," taxes "contributions," and the prison a "chamber."
>
> —PLUTARCH

Nice Nellies and Fancy Dans

THE "four-letter words" are not, by a long shot, the only ones that are repudiated and euphemized. In all societies and all eras, the human tendency has been to substitute an inoffensive expression for any that is remotely distasteful. And just about any word in any language can be interpreted by *somebody* as distasteful; the innocent word "you" has been forsworn by the Quakers from the seventeenth century to the present day.

At the time the Quaker sect was founded, the English language used alternative second-person pronouns: "you" was formal and employed when addressing superiors, "thou" and "thee" were informal, addressed to familiars and inferiors. This pronominal inequity grated on Quaker sensibilities because it appeared to deny the equality of humankind. They decided to use only one pronoun for everybody, and chose the humbler one. In time the rest of the English also settled for a single form—but chose the "classier" one.

A similar sensitivity in the matter of equality impelled the French, after their eighteenth-century revolution, and the Russians, after their twentieth-century one, to toss out of their language every honorific that distinguished among classes or ranks. In France everyone became a *citoyen,* in Russia a *tovarishch.* But even proletarian "citizens" and "comrades" can tire of an artificially imposed sameness of stature. The French soon went back to addressing each other respectfully as *monsieur* and *madame,* and lately the Russians have been hankering to do the same. There is a quiet agitation going on in the Soviet Union now for a return to the use of the tsarist-era addresses *sudar* and *sudarynya* (equivalent to *monsieur* and *madame*).

As one other example of how the simplest word can sometimes demand substitutes and circumlocutions: in the Romance countries during the Middle Ages the very word "word" became a problem. It came to mean so distinctly and specifically "the Word of God" that finally, in order not to affront the Almighty, the Spanish, French, Portuguese and Italians had to develop parabolical euphemisms for use when they wanted to indicate an ordinary, unsanctified "word."

A close cousin to euphemism is euphuism. It means artificial and high-flown elegance of language, and the word comes from *Euphues,* a sixteenth-century romance by John Lyly, who wrote in just that gilt-and-tinsel fashion. But the style is far older than the name; both euphuism and euphemism have been characteristics of language as far back as we can trace language itself. During all of history, whenever euphemism has failed to prettify the "bad things" in the world, euphuism has tried to hide them in a lavender smokescreen of verbiage. The best examples of outright euphuism in English today can be found in the *Congressional Record*—gobbledygook harangues full of flowery rhetoric and flashy filigree. But in everyday language, euphuism is commonly coupled with euphemism; Fancy Dans and Nice Nellies working hand in glove to round-off the honest rough edges of everything in life and to oil every interesting squeak.

The two isms have their prominent place in the personality of language because of four traits in the personality of people—squeamishness, vanity, fear and cupidity—each of which is opposed to calling a spade a spade.

Man's squeamish reluctance to admit the harshnesses of reality was recognized and satirized some three and a half centuries ago by the "Spanish Shakespeare," Lope de Vega: "The blind we say are one-eyed, the cross-eyed merely squint . . . the bald deserve respect, admit the ass is graceful . . . the pettifogger is called diligent; malcontents, philosophers . . . the impudent grow witty, the taciturn sit pretty, all hail the Idiot!"

As for the use of edulcoration to shore up one's own vanity, or to butter up another's, Ovid recommended two thousand years ago that "you must disguise every defect under the name of its nearest quality."

Fear is manifest in the superstition that soft words can turn away wrath and ruin. The Greeks of old feared the Furies, their personification of the spirits of vengeance, but snivelingly referred to them as *Eumenides,* "the gracious ones." In medieval Europe, the common folk believed themselves constantly beset by supernatural pests, but took care never to risk offending them with a bad name. In Scotland, for instance, they were always *daoine sithe*, "the little men of peace," and in Spain *las estantiguas*, "the venerable ones." In India to this day the native fiends and imps are called *punya-janas*, "the good people."

Lastly, cupidity encourages euphemism and euphuism in that opportunists employ such sweet talk to batten on the squeamishness, vanity or fear in those with whom they deal. For example, it is only good salesmanship to give the name of "life insurance" to what is patently a provision for death.

Euphemism's evasiveness and euphuism's camouflage are most often used for the ostensible sake of politeness, but they can also serve for the extremes of self-deception and deliberate lying. However they are used, though, one or another of those four human traits is almost always the underlying motivation—and sometimes several of them simultaneously. It was moral squeamishness that made the Quakers abandon the word "you" for "thee," and vanity that made the rest of the English-speaking world do just the reverse.

Most of the equivocations used by the ordinary person are trivial and inconsiderable, mere slipcovers on the sleazy fabric of life; as when Mom serves stew and calls it *ragoût*, or describes her weak-chinned scion as having "a sensitive mouth." But as tools of the tastemakers, the motivators and the professional persuaders, euphemism and euphuism can be subtle, sinister and often devastating in their effects. Consider the calamitous reverberations of that quiet-sounding term *die Endlösung*, "the Final Solution"—Nazi Germany's laconic euphemism for the program which eventually exterminated six million European Jews, gypsies and other undesirables.

George Orwell said of political language that it is "designed to make lies sound truthful and murder respectable, and to give an appearance of solidity to pure wind." Some striking examples can be culled from books of ancient history as well as from this morning's newspapers. "Spontaneous demonstration" is considered a modern euphemism for a prearranged and strictly organized show of obediently simulated "public feeling" pro or contra this or that. But there is nothing new about either the phenomenon or the name for it. Nearly two thousand years ago the Emperor Augustus ordered Romans and colonials to stage "spontaneous demonstrations of gratitude [to himself] throughout the Empire."

Queen Elizabeth I pardoned pirates and elevated them to "privateers" when they agreed to focus their piratical attentions on the shipping of enemy and rival nations. At least one textbook history of the American Revolution lauds the French troops who fought under Washington as "friends of the cause of freedom," but sneers hatefully at Howe's "Hessian hirelings." Today, in American estimation, a Pole who takes over an airliner at gunpoint is "bravely seeking political asylum"; a Cuban who does the same thing is a "criminal hijacker." Our bomb throwers are "activists"; anybody else's are "terrorists."

Hitler "liquidated undesirable elements"; Stalin "eliminated counterrevolutionary tendencies"; both did it with mass executions. When Italy surrendered in the middle of World War II, it was obviously impossible for her to become an "Ally" overnight, but it was important to the Allies that their homefront populations cease to detest her as an "Axis enemy," so the word "co-belligerent" was invented to proclaim her new status. In 1947 the U.S. Department of War was abolished forevermore; in 1949 it was quietly resurrected as the U.S. Department of Defense. In the Soviet Union today, a government department devoted to planting false and troublesome rumors in foreign countries is blandly designated the Ministry of *Dis*-information.

Each nation that has gone Communist since World War II has named itself a "People's Republic" or a "Democratic Republic" or even, rather redundantly, a "People's Democratic Republic"—every such name being totally refuted by the police-state form of government which it actually maintains. The Western countries call themselves collectively the "Free World," a term which could justifiably be challenged by such of its inhabitants as the Haitians enslaved by "Baby Doc" Duvalier, the Indians and mestizos downtrodden by Ecuador's flagrant feudalism. (The term *has* been challenged by blacks in the United States.)

The vacillations of the Third World's "nonaligned nations" are of great concern to both East and West. As real or potential allies of either side, many such countries will never be anything but parasites, but they must not be "lost to the cause" of either side. And so neither Moscow nor Washington ever refers to those nations as "backward," lest they take umbrage and snuggle up to the opposite bloc. Instead, such countries—no matter how barbarian, bankrupt, and benighted—are invariably euphemized as "emergent" or at worst "undeveloped" nations.

Moscow and Washington are also alike in their semantic dealings with issues inside their borders. In the Soviet Union, a "free election" is one that's uncontested, i.e., free of controversy, demagoguery, and any necessity for decision. In America, "mail cover" is the U.S. Postal Service's euphemism for its clandestine scrutiny of the mail of Americans who correspond with Communist countries. In the Soviet Union, every economic crisis, shortage and famine is swept under the semantic rug of another "glorious five-year plan" or "reclamation of the virgin lands" or whatever. In America, no politician would ever dare propose a "tax increase," though some few of his constituents are probably fooled when he calls it "revenue enhancement."

The prettying-up of ugly realities, the substitution of pleasing falsehoods for unpleasant truths, these are not limited to ideologists and heads of state. They are practiced on every level of society—by pressure groups, commercial interests, editorial writers, ax-grinders, confidence men, even husbands sneaking home late. People of all climes and all times have used such sugar-coated language, but the ones most inclined to it—and most exploited by it—are the Americans of today. Some observers say it is because Americans have become effete and spiritually flabby, but there are at least three other contributing reasons.

One is that America has been imbued and obsessed, ever since its colonial days, with optimism even unto boosterism ("where seldom is heard a discouraging word"). Another is the influence of advertising and its offshoots, press-agentry and public relations; most of their techniques were invented in America, whetted and honed on Americans. And third, Americans are bombarded more than any other people by the media of mass communications: from television and telephones to billboards, bullhorns and bumper stickers.

The result is that Americans live in an all-pervasive, inextinguishable, rose-colored floodlight. Nothing is so bad that it can't be prevented or cured, everything good is improvable, anything better is perfectible, and whatever is perfect is eternizable. The individual may occasionally grumble, fret, worry or even entertain the idea of hermitage, but the mass of people seem to visualize themselves ideally as they are pictured in *The American Home*'s glossy-paper stereotypes of Mom, Dad and the Kiddies all smiling in happy concert at their gleaming dishwasher.

(I have known a New York corporation executive to wax apoplectic because his advertising agency proposed, for a magazine spread, an "American boy" model who did *not* have red hair, freckles and a photogenic gap in his teeth. When the agency art director pointed out that the ad they were casting called for a fourteen-year-old, and that the majority of boys of that age have mouse-colored hair, their full second set of teeth and generally more pimples than freckles, the client muttered grave things about the art director's "un-American attitude." This client was a purveyor of plumbing fixtures, and so could be presumed an expert on Americanism.)

Any discussion of the euphemisms and euphuisms—written, spoken or pictured—which infest the American language has to put advertising high on the list of contributors. Its contributions are, in fact, far too numerous to catalogue. One of its most notable successes in this area was the invention (*ca.* 1922) of "halitosis." A contemporary expression was "B.O." for bad smell, i.e., "body odor." About the same time, ringworm of the feet became "athlete's foot." There is "irregularity" instead of constipation, and "problem days" for the menses. Anything from incontinence to bromidrosis is now merely "wetness." The smallest tube of toothpaste you can buy is the "large size." "Discomfort" can signify anything from itchy scalp to terminal cancer, and "protection" is the promise of everything from theft insurance to foot powder. A "personalized" Christmas card is an expensive one on which the sender's name is printed in cold, impersonal type. Used cars are no longer second- (or sixth-) hand, they are "previously owned." Probably the most insidious of all advertising's euphemisms is "*free!*," it being merely the price of whatever is offered, as translated into collateral obligations.

While many businessmen hawk their wares in "world of tomorrow" jargon, others have to perpetuate deliberate archaisms. This is especially necessary in the food field, where synthetics must be made to sound like natural-born victuals. However, it is doubtful that there are many consumers who still believe that those rubberoid yellow blocks of "processed cheese food" are cheese, or that "chocolate dairy drink" is chocolate milk.

To the ad men, ever since the late 1800s, there has been no such thing as a fat woman. Back then, she was called "Junoesque," "statuesque" or "plethoric." (I've seen one old-time ad that referred to "the feminine Falstaff," if that could be taken as euphemistically complimentary.) Today she is "the full-figured woman." Also, she sits on her "hips" rather than her buttocks—or, if she can pronounce it, she sits on her *derrière*. Her abdomen is her "tummy." Her underwear is "lingerie" (almost invariably mispronounced, even in TV commercials, "lon-jer-ay"). A very tender spot is her bosom, and especially to be avoided is any reference to the cubic measure of it. Hence brassieres are advertised as sized for women of "minus," "average" or "plus" bosoms. The minus type of creature used to resort to "falsies," but now her bra comes with "added development" or "enhanced contouring." Incidentally, "brassiere" itself is some sort of euphemism, as it comes from the French word for "arm." The manufacturers of such articles refer to them as "booby-traps" or "bust-buckets."

Even the makers of diet foods, who must naturally expect their customers to be somewhat big, don't risk offending them by calling them fat. Their ads are addressed to "weight watchers" and "calorie counters." And those magazine articles telling Mom how to minimize Junior's bloat always seem to be entitled "The Chubby Child," the identical euphemism used by the makers of children's clothes in the more voluminous size ranges.

Another noncommittal euphemism is "the older woman," a tactful admission that she is no nymph but a tacit denial that she is anywhere near being "elderly." Still, there are some old people. And because they live longer nowadays, still functioning as consumers and voters, they too must be handled with euphemistic kid gloves. They are addressed as "senior citizens" and congratulated on their attainment of the "golden years."

One of the features of a recent World's Fair was a "Dynamic Maturity Pavilion." But its purpose was rather less than dynamic; it was mainly a garden full of benches where the oldsters could collapse once in a while to rest and wheeze. In the mealymouthed United States, old folks' homes and retirement communities have meretricious names like Sun City and Golden Heritage. When I go, I intend to go to that one I once saw in realistic, no-nonsense Mexico. Its entrance gates were topped by an arch on which was boldly graven "Senilia."

It is a truism that women will endure almost any indignity, so long as it promises Youth, Beauty or Popularity, and so long as it wears a stylish name. Not a woman alive would be caught dead in a *déclassé* torture device like a corset, though she may be half-perishing in the clutch of a "foundation garment." She would not knowingly smear her face with sheep grease, but she will if it's called "lanolin." She would not expect a dose of horse urine to erase her wrinkles, enliven her gonads and enrich her social life, but she will if it's sold as "estrogenic hormones." It is increasingly hard to find a woman wearing the color hair she was born with; it is equally hard to find one who'll admit that she is not. She "mutates" or "adapts" or "color-corrects" her hair with rinses, beauty baths, tints, hues or retouching. Never say dye.

Lest the males smirk too smugly at these *recherché* little coynesses, it should be pointed out that the men too are push-overs for euphemism and euphuism. Brand names like "Boiler-maker" and "Sweatshirt" for shaving lotions and hair oils may not be effeminate, but they're just as affected as a woman's "Priss" and "Poof," and just as cunningly calculated to cozen men into buying. (Or *usually* cunningly; the name giver who dubbed a men's cologne "Chaps" can never have smelled a working cowboy.)

As has been amply demonstrated, any sampling of euphe-mism and euphuism must necessarily range from the formi-dable to the paltry, from execrable to silly. But some of the most ridiculous examples may be masks for culpable igno-rance and irrationality. Certainly it says something about the squeamishness of Americans that a syndicated newspaper astrologer dropped from his daily horoscopes all mention of the venerable sign of the Crab—because it bears the dread name "Cancer"—and substituted for it a category of his own invention: "Moon Children."

The same fearfulness and fastidiousness about unpleasant words extends to just about every other disease and deficiency that flesh is heir to. According to *Today's Health* magazine, we now have "the terms *educable*, corresponding to moron, and *trainable*, corresponding to imbecile." An idiot, we are informed, is now a "totally dependent." A violently insane person is "assaultive." The blind are now "sight-deprived," as if to refute any suspicion that they got that way voluntarily. Any cripple from a harelip to a basket case is merely "handi-capped." A "troubled child" may be anything from a bed-wetter to a prospective John Hinckley. The illiterate no longer are, though it would seem unlikely that they could be offended by a word they can't read; they're now "verbally deficient." Anyone who abjectly fails at anything is only an "under-achiever."

The poor undertakers have for generations been trying to wash the smell of grave-mold out of their calling, and to up-grade themselves to something more estimable than ghouls. They turned their funeral parlors into "mortuary chapels," named their laying-out chamber the "reposing room," exalted their embalming schools into "colleges of mortuary science" and designated themselves "morticians." This neologism was patterned on the prestigious "physician," but both titles were considerably diminished by the sprouting of vulgar "beauti-cians," "cosmeticians," etc. The most recent occupational eu-phemisms to be tried by the undertakers are "funeral service practitioner" and—*splendide mendax*—"grief therapist." In

Britain the undertaker is a "funeral furnisher." In France, Spain and Italy he is grandly an "impresario of funeral pomp." Only in Germany is he satisfied to be known for what he really is. There his title is either *Leichenbesorger* or *Leichenbestatter*—either "corpse-looker-after" or "corpse-putter-away."

In America today the "image" or the "posture" is the all. It matters less what a man is or does than what guise he "projects" to others. The politician seeks to project the image of a statesman, opportunists project a posture of altruism, industrial monopolies pose as public servants, undertakers try to shed the gravedigger image for one of nobility and unction. And workers in other fields are just as eager as the undertakers to glorify their occupations. Though they usually have less dismal and demeaning associations to slough off, they do have the compulsion to assert that their role in life is an important and praiseworthy one. Vanity again, coupled with the fairy-tale delusion that the right word can transform the toad into Prince Charming.

Thus hotel dicks and night watchmen are now "security officers," garbage collectors are "sanitation engineers," a barber is a "hairdresser" and a hairdresser is a "coiffeur," housewives are "homemakers," a shipping clerk is a "traffic expediter," a ditch digger is an "excavation technician," a switchboard girl is a "communications monitor," a floorwalker is a "department supervisor," a salesman is a "manufacturer's representative." I don't believe there used to be *any* job title for the kid who ran my automobile through the carwash. Today, I am told, he is a "corrosion control specialist."

The job title "janitor" was originally a euphemism, intended to set him above mere floor-sweepers and furnace-stokers. But "janitor" too came into disfavor and has been supplanted by "custodian." In at least one case, this required a university's distinguished Custodian of the Research Library to change *his* title to Director, so he wouldn't be confused with the janitor of the building.

Such wistful whimsies might seem to be the cold comfort merely of the lower classes, but nowadays even such higher orders as educators prefer the added syllables and prestige of "educationalists." And although the Americans may have carried this trend to the farthest limits of absurdity, their cousins abroad have been no laggards. Garbage men in Britain have long been "cleansing personnel." John Moore reports, in his book *You English Words,* that a chimneysweep there advertised himself as a "flueologist." English clubwomen evidently haven't felt any need of upgrading themselves, but charwomen now insist on being called "charladies."

The occupational euphemisms in which the Romance people indulge tend to be somewhat more poetical than those of the Americans and English. In Spain, for example, a night watchman is one who works "under the stars." In France the streetcorner vendor of hot roasted chestnuts is *l'hirondelle d'hiver*, "the swallow of the winter." In Italy, what used to be a "maid of all work" is now a *collaboratrice familiare*, a "family collaborator," and so common has that euphemism become that it is usually abbreviated to *colf*.

In India a street-sweeper is a *mehtar*, or "prince." In Japan, metropolitan railroads employ *kyaku atsukai yoin*, or "passengers' service workers," but the unhappy passengers they serve refer to them less euphemistically as *Oshiya-san* ("Mr. Pusher") because that's the service they perform—packing passengers like sardines into the commuter trains during *rasshu awa* ("rush hour"). At the other end of the line another passengers' service worker, *Hagitoriya-san* ("Mr. Puller") unpacks them again.

In America that fine old cultural institution, the rummage sale, came to sound too poor-folksy; churches and charity bazaars now hold "mutual exchange sales." Airlines no longer entreat their passengers to fasten their safety belts—danger must not even be hinted at—the stewardess now calls them plain "seat belts." And the vomit bag she provides for airsick passengers is now a "comfort container." Educational terminology uses the euphemism "exceptional child" to refer to either the budding genius or the vegetable dullard. No student ever gets expelled any more, though he may suffer "academic dismissal." Farmers can still unflinchingly talk of castrating their animals, but pet-owners "alter" theirs. Of course, some euphemisms have always been so transparent—such as the gossip columnists' smirking usage of "long-time companion" to mean "illicit lover"—that we nowadays automatically supply our own translation when *People* magazine refers to "a flamboyant financier" (a crooked one), "a temperamental actor" (habitually drunk) or "a controversial work of art" (a dirty picture).

In America even the children, normally the most clear-eyed, plain-spoken and unsentimental of creatures, are fitted with rose-colored glasses from babyhood. An authoress of my acquaintance used to specialize in rewriting for today's tots some of the classic fairy tales and nursery rhymes, deleting or euphemizing their "harmful" elements. Jack and Jill no longer fracture their skulls, the Black Dwarf is no longer discriminated against, Tom the Piper's Son is cured of his kleptomania, stepmothers are kind, and the witches, ogres and dragons eventually see the error of their ways and are re-habilitated into model citizens.

Persons whose ways of life used to be damned as unnat-ural or unsavory or debauched or downright taboo or just plain ridiculous are now tolerated, legitimized, even cham-pioned, by their former revilers—not because the mavericks have changed their ways, but because those ways are now euphemized as "alternative life-styles." You never even *hear* the word "taboo" any more. Once upon a time, when I was reduced to living for a year or so on Skid Row, I did not much bridle at being called a "bum." How could I? There I was, one among all the other bums, derelicts, drunks, and drifters, living from hand to mouth, sleeping in flophouses, on park benches, occasionally in jail. It would have been laughable for any of us, when we seldom indulged in a bath or a change of underwear, to have indulged in tetchy hauteur. But if I had abided on Skid Row until now, I would be called a "street per-son" and—purely in consequence of the nicer name—have all sorts of social workers worried about my subsistence, my uplift, and my redemption. Sweden recently tried to dignify its welfare dole recipients by calling them "paid consumers," but the new name got lost in the resulting national roar of ridiculing laughter.

Euphemism is particularly exercised these days as a means of soothing the sensibilities of minority groups. But "minority group" is often itself a catch-all euphemism. Inasmuch as a minority can consist of as few as one, it is possible for eccen-trics, cranks and self-seekers to militate for or against almost any proposition under the sun, and in the prevailing climate of "offend nobody, please everybody" they have every chance of being heard, heeded, placated and catered to. The sponsor of a television program can afford to ignore the unanimous an-guish of critics who decry it as a new low in banality. But let him receive one postcard from one viewer complaining, say, that last night's show contained a slighting remark about button-collectors. The sponsor will investigate, discover that there does exist a National Button Society and that its mem-bership consists of 1,516 potential customers—and he'll have his program producer on the carpet.

So entertainers, script-writers, editors, commentators, ad-vertisers, columnists, all speak softly and carry a big blue pencil. The consequent spate of euphemisms may not all be motivated by hypocrisy or venality. But even the honest ones are so obvious and affected that you'd think they would be as embarrassing to their subjects as an equal amount of slurs and slights. This linguistic bending-over-backward has been best satirized by Peter De Vries; in one of his novels an incorrigibly correct character refers to Brazil nuts as "Negrotoe nuts" and to Joseph Conrad's classic as *"The Negro of the Narcissus."* I was once warned by a literary agent that a certain magazine editor was "terribly niggardly—or is it negroidly?—anyway, he's a cheap son of a bitch."

In the musical *My Fair Lady* the nearest thing to a villain is Zoltan Karpathy, a bearded Hungarian referred to in the lyrics as a "hairy hound from Budapest." *My Fair Lady* opened on Broadway in March, 1956; in October of that year, the people of Hungary exploded their dramatic revolt against the Soviet-dominated regime. Such was American sympathy for the rebels that *My Fair Lady*'s producers hurriedly revoked their villain's Hungarian citizenship. For whatever aid and comfort it gave to the embattled heroes of Budapest, Zoltan Karpathy was transpatriated into a "hairy hound from Bucharest." Whether *this* offended Romanians, I don't know, but in the movie version of the musical Karpathy was once again a Hungarian.

There was good reason for pressuring comedians to cut out the old-time jokes that derided national or racial characteristics and dialects. But the minorities' undestandable aversion to being unfairly belittled has often been pumped up into a demand for dignification that is out of all reason. Away back in the 1930s, Franklin P. Adams bemoaned the minority-forced decline of topical humor, when he complained that eventually a humorist wouldn't be able to twit "anything but the man-eating shark."

During World War II, Chinese-Americans protested because Hollywood was using Chinese actors to portray Japanese villains. But the actors themselves didn't mind; they delighted in making the Japanese appear as vicious and vile as possible. The protest might better have come from Japanese-Americans, but they were in no position to air their objections, most of them being interned at the time in "relocation camps" (an interesting American euphemism). Every U.S. postage stamp commemorating some action of the Civil War has to be *exactly* half gray and half blue, or complaints pour in from the slighted side of the Mason-Dixon line. Not long ago an Indian uprising demanded that the television networks portray only noble-type red men on their Western shows. Italo-American groups have insisted that television's black-handed Mafia villains sport non-Italian names. There is no longer any such thing as a half-breed, mestizo, mulatto or mongrel person; he or she is now "of mingled ethnicity."

In their fight for their due rights, the minorities run the

risk of losing others' sympathy and support, when the extremists among them insist on being respected *retroactively*. They seem merely peckish and picayune when they attempt to rewrite history and censor classical literature to expunge every indignity their forebears ever suffered. Or, as the feminists would like, to tidy up every allegedly "sexist" reference to the whole female fifty percent of humankind.

Jewish organizations succeeded in preventing New Yorkers from seeing the English motion picture *Oliver Twist*, and they are aggrieved because *The Merchant of Venice* and *Ivanhoe* are allowed to remain in the high school English curriculum. Black groups object because children still read *Huckleberry Finn*, and toddlers are not forbidden *Little Black Sambo* (everyone seems to have forgotten that Sambo was never an African or an Afro-American; he's an East Indian boy). It is useless to try to point out to the would-be censors that neither Dickens nor Shakespeare was anti-Semitic, that Mark Twain was an avowed friend and admirer of the black people, that Rebecca is the heroine and by far the most appealing character in *Ivanhoe*.

The day may yet come when the only allowable villain or butt of slapstick will be the Wasp: the "White Anglo-Saxon Protestant"—and only the male Wasp at that. When *that* group rebels—and I, for one, could protest that all my way-back Saxon forefathers are maligned in *Ivanhoe* as "churls" and "vassals"—then the only licit entertainment and literature available to Americans may be science-fiction stories about purple Arcturians with names like CSX-12.

But to repeat, although modern America may be most prone to prettification and falsification, it has no monopoly on them. To judge from their prevalence in every language and every culture, extinct or extant, these tendencies are both universal and perpetual. Twenty centuries ago Plutarch disparaged the mincing words of the ancient Athenians, and twenty centuries later philosopher Herbert Spencer was still saying much the same thing:

"The ultimate result of shielding men from the effects of folly is to fill the world with fools."

> In Homeric times people and things had two names: the one given them by men and the one given by the gods. I wonder what God calls me.
>
> —MIGUEL DE UNAMUNO

Our Shining Names Are Told

DEAR ANN LANDERS: Our family name is Hooker. . . . It is a noble name. All the Hookers who are members of our family tree are fine people. The problem is that our name has become a synonym for "prostitute." Our children are made fun of in school and we get obscene phone calls. We have discontinued watching all TV shows that abuse our name in this manner. We have written to the editor of our paper and threatened to cancel our subscription if he does not stop using our name when he means "prostitute." Will you help us in our crusade, Ann?

The foregoing is excerpted from an actual, agonized and lengthy letter which appeared in that syndicated newspaper column in 1984, signed "Respectable Hookers."

A person's name can be many things: label, badge, epithet, medallion or millstone, plume or plummet. But first and always, a name is a word. And like every other kind of word, personal names have both contributed to and evolved from the vagarious personalities of language. In the names we wear today are traces of every factor that has ever gone into the making of speech and writing—from the earliest echoing of natural sounds to the later leaning toward euphemism.

Echoism, for example, is represented by the name Barbara, cognate with "barbarian," both of them derived from the Greek word mocking the "babble" of foreigners. Instances of euphemism are to be found in the actors' names on just about any movie marquee.

It is conceivable that names—or distinguishing grunts—were the very first words spoken. At any rate, language could not have been long under way before men began to find it necessary to identify themselves and to indicate precisely to whom or of whom they were speaking. The obvious distinction would have been according to some individual physical characteristic, so the earliest names were undoubtedly the equivalents of Peewee, Limpy, Slim, Fatso and so on. But while Fatsos might have been at a premium in a foraging Stone Age tribe, there would be Slims and Limpies aplenty, and so more subtle distinctions had to be made. In time men must have discerned individual traits of personality, too, and from them fashioned names like Grumpy, Happy, Dopey, etc. Or when a person made a hero or an ass of himself, that fugacious eminence could also give him a name, on the order of He-Who-Killed-the-Bear or He-Who-Sat-Down-on-a-Scorpion. A man's family would have been considered merely his appendages and, if they were mentioned at all, would have been simply Woman-of-Peewee or Son-of-Bear-Killer.

When eventually the nomad hunters began to settle down and domesticate their environment, their numbers increased and required still more variety of names. By now it was possible to denominate a man according to where he'd planted his homestead, e.g., He-Who-Lives-in-the-Field. And as communal society encouraged a gradual division of labors, a man might also be known by his occupational specialty, e.g., He-Who-Makes-Wheels.

There was nothing permanent about those early names; a change in a man's circumstances could mean a change in his name. He might be known as Blacky or Smiley or Fisher, until he lost a leg in an accident, and afterwards be called Hopalong. A Wheeler's son might choose a different trade and become a Potter. Infield's son might move to the seashore and become a Bays. The nearest thing to a permanent name in early times was the sharing of a group designation, for instance the name a tribe gave itself, or the name of the totem of a clan, or the name of the deity a particular people worshiped. Many societies called themselves simply and smugly The People; thus an individual Gael might have been known as Cramer Mac Leod, literally a Shop-keeper-of-The-People. An Occaneechee Indian might have been Attonce Kemotte Ohawai, literally an Archer-of-the-Crow-Clan. A Teuton villager might have been Smid von Zeernebooch, a Smith-of-the-Worshipers-of-the-Dark-God.

In contrast to the businesslike, classifying name by which he was known to the outside world, the names a man gave to himself, his friends and family—especially the ones he bestowed on his children—were likely to have more personality and warmth. A baby might be named to commemorate a circumstance coincident with its birth (e.g., Yuki, Japanese for "snow") or to curry divine favor (Yohanan, Hebrew for "God is gracious") or as a flattering descriptive (Margaron, Greek for "pearl") or as a hopeful augury (Shu-sai-chong, Chinese for "happy all his life long"). Though most people inclined to give their children "nice" names, others considered it prudent to do just the opposite, on the theory that evil spirits would not bother to bedevil a child named "filth" or "wretch." Such names are still given in parts of India and China, generally when the parents' previous child has died.

The invention of writing brought a tendency to stabilize personal names, at least through an individual's lifetime. The complexities of civilization came to depend heavily on paperwork, and this demanded some constancy. Hitherto, there had been nothing to prevent a citizen's being named Heaven-blest at birth, apprenticed as Freckles, serving in the army as Bowman, signing the marriage register as Handsome, being entered on land rolls as Underwood, paying his taxes as Weaver, and being buried at last as Oldfellow. Now, though he might still pursue this chameleon career in private life, he had to have an unchanging "public" name for clerical purposes. But even this measure of regimentation had no influence on what that name might *be*. (*Domesday Book* lists one landholder as Roger God-Save-the-Ladies.) The invention and bestowal of personal names was still very much a spontaneous affair, unbound by tradition and conformity; and continued to be so for centuries.

What first began to diminish the wealth and welter of given names in the Western world was the coming of Christianity. Baptism combined the rites of naming a child and enrolling it in the Church. The solemn occasion discouraged any frivolity or plain-spokenness in the name-giving, and encouraged the bestowal of an auspicious and high-sounding appellation. So the Europeans began to abandon their former pagan whimsies and adopt the Hebraic names from the Scriptures: those of the Holy Family, the Apostles, and the prophets and heroes of the Old Testament. Later, as native-born saints multipled and were allotted "days" in the Church calendar, it became an alternative practice to name a child after the saint on whose day it was born. This preserved at least a few home-grown European given names.

The result of the Christian enthusiasm was twofold. The literal meaning of a name was ignored and forgotten; even where the meaning was obvious it seldom had any discernible reference to the person wearing it. For example, the name Mary had been rather unprophetically applied even by the parents of the Virgin Mary—inasmuch as it means "rebellion" in the original Hebrew (Maryam)—and now it was haphazardly given to hundreds of thousands of females who could not *all* have been either rebellious or virginal their whole life long.

Secondly, the quantity of "acceptable" names, formerly as copious as human imagination could devise, was now more and more confined to the biblical cast of characters and the Christian roster of saints. The Hebrew name Yohanan became—as John and its many variants—the most popular name for males in every country of the West. (It still is.) This necessitated maintaining an additional descriptive (or byname) in order to minimize confusion. An English village might swarm with Johns, so they had to be differentiated as Little John, Jolly John, John's son, John-the-Barber, John-of-the-Gatehouse, etc.

But still none of these bynames was handed down from generation to generation. The notion of instituting hereditary names was a long time in taking hold. Here and there in ancient days, hereditary rulers had maintained a family name, e.g., in the second millennium B.C., the dynasties of Shang in China and Hyksos in Egypt. In the sixth century B.C. the Etruscans had family names, even among their middle class, and passed the custom along to the Romans. But none of the peoples conquered by Rome took up the practice, and it died out with the fall of the Empire, not to reappear until midway in the Middle Ages. Then it was again the royalty who revived it, calling their "houses" after the byname of an illustrious predecessor or making a new byname out of the name of their demesne.

Human vanity, no respecter of rank's privileges, soon proliferated the practice. The nobility imitated the royalty, usually taking for surname the name of their estate, viscounty, marquisate or whatever. Next, the middle classes aped the nobility, and finally the lower classes followed suit. The ordinary folk, having no ancestral manor or title from which to derive a family name, settled for eternizing the byname attached to one of its members.

Naturally enough, a family generally chose to perpetuate the most flattering byname to which it was entitled, and only scant attention was paid to the likelihood of its continuing to be appropriate. Even when it fitted the paterfamilias who decreed its new permanence, it seldom suited his descendants of two or three generations down the line. If any Fletchers are still earning a living by gluing feathers on arrow shafts today, it is one almighty coincidence. And how many Russells are either red-headed, ruddy of complexion or fiery of temper? Those were the various reasons for the original bestowal of the byname.

Not every country of the Western world adopted hereditary names simultaneously, nor propagated them in the same manner. Some backwater districts of Wales and Scotland did not take up the practice until well into the nineteenth century. Various other nationalities tried different methods of handing down a family name, to distinguish between generations or to acknowledge the maternal branches of the family tree. But by now, today, most Western peoples have settled for a system whereby a name descends through the male line, unchanging along the way.

Modern folk who undertake to backtrack their lineage are often surprised to find that family names are such a comparatively recent innovation in Europe. While some ancestor-hunters may claim, with plausible evidence, to trace their pedigrees clear to the Crusades, this is still a skimpy stretch compared to the foregoing thousands of years and thousands of begettings. Except in the case of well-documented royalty or nobility, most genealogical researches are doomed to peter out in impenetrable fog just a few hundred years back—no more than a score or so of generations, in the case of most Anglo-Saxon names. Beyond that, all the way back to the dawn of time, our ancestors lurk anonymous in the obscurity of arbitrary and discontinuous bynames.

However, many of those old-time bynames are fossilized in the family names of today. Almost any name of almost any nationality can be traced to a given name, byname or nickname originally bestowed on the basis of something peculiar to its first bearer. There is the name denoting parentage, the name derived from occupation, the name descriptive of either physique or personality, the name derived from residence, and the name commemorating an incident or exploit.

Some of them are obvious. Names ending in -*son*, for instance, patently belong in the "parentage" category, and there are several other affixes indicating kinship or connection. The English -*s* ending on a name may be a contraction of -*son* or of the possessive "his." Thus Peters may originally have been— like Peterson—Peter-his-son, or else someone belonging to Peter, like Peter-his-valet. The ending -*man* almost always indicates that the first bearer was someone's servant, serf or slave. The ending -*ing* or -*ings* indicates a belonging to or descent from, and so does the prefix *Fitz*-. This was borrowed from the Normans, who used it to designate the bastard son of a prince (e.g., Fitzroy).

The patronymic affix exists in most languages. In Swedish it's -*sson*, in Danish -*sen* and in Norwegian -*ssen*. In Armenian it's -*ian*, in Finnish -*nen*, in Polish -*wiecz* or -*ski*, in Spanish -*ez*. The Greek "son" transliterates as -*poulos*, the Russian as -*ov* or -*ev*. In the Semitic languages "son of" stands alone as a separate word, transliterated *Ben*. In Welsh it was also a separate word, *ap*, but this has tended to meld into the surname, e.g., ap Richard into Pritchard, ap Evan into Bevan. The Scottish and Irish *Mac* (of which the *Mc* is just a contraction) also used to stand alone. The Irish *O*, meaning "grandson of," originally took no apostrophe, as it does now in O'Brien, but stood separate (Sean O Brien) or abutted the surname's capital initial (Sean OBrien). The Irish also had the word *ni* to signify "daughter of," e.g., Katharine ni Houlihan.

The use of -*sson*, -*ssen* and -*sen* in Scandinavia was for a long time the only method of handing down a name. In Sweden, for example, if a man named Swen Johansson had a son named Erik, the boy would be not Erik Johansson but Erik Swensson. His son Gunnar, in turn, would be Gunnar Eriksson. If Gunnar had a son Knut and a daughter Helga, the boy would be Knut Gunnarsson, but the girl would be Helga Gunnarsdotter. Folks would have thought it ridiculous to call a female a "son." But eventually these shifting patronymics began to petrify—though not until the nineteenth century in Sweden—and a surname was handed down without change. Scandinavian girls are no longer mortified to bear names like Harriet Andersson.

The ubiquitous John and his multitudinous sons have given the most surnames to the Western world. The English have Johns, Johnson, Janes, Jaynes, Jenks, Jenkins (son of Jenkin, "little John"), Jenner, Jennings, Jennison and compounds like Littlejohn. (The omission of Jacks, Jackson and Jaxon from this list is no oversight. Jack was originally derived from Jacques as a nickname for Jacob or James, and only comparatively recently became a popular substitute for John.)

The Welsh have Jones, Jonas and Upjohn (a corruption of ap John). The Scots have Ianson. The Irish have McCain, McKeon, Shane and McShane (from Eoin and Sean). The French have Jean and various compounds of it. The Italians have Giannini, Giovanni and Giovanetti. The Greeks have Gianopoulos. The Russians have Ivanov. The Swedes have Jahn, Jansson and Johansson. The Danes have Jensen and Jessen. The Norwegians have Jenssen. The Dutch have Jantzen and Yanke. The Germans have Janicke, Yonan, Johannes and Henning (from Hans). The Czechs have Janda and

Jeschke. The Poles have Janik, Janowski and Janowicz. The Lithuanians have Janis and Jonikas. The Hungarians have Janosfi. And there are many, many more.

John and company are rivaled in profusion only by Smith and his equivalents. This is the most common "occupational" name, because Smith was originally applicable to so many trades. It meant anyone who worked with metal, from a blacksmith to a locksmith. In France the same name is Lefevre, in Italy Ferrari, in Spain Herrero. In Russia it's Kuznetzov, in Poland Kowalski, in Denmark Smed. In Germany it's Schmied, Schmid, Schmidt or Schmitt. In Bulgaria it's Kovac, in Hungary Kovacs, in Czechoslovakia Kovar. In Syria it's Haddad and in Ireland Magoon.

The occupational origin of many British names is easy to perceive: Butler, Taylor, Thatcher, Hunter. Others are a trifle less obvious: Wainwright for wagon-maker, Baxter for baker, Webster for weaver, Brewster for brewer, Hayward for a keeper of the fences (literally "hayfield-warden"), Chapman for peddler, Faulkner for falconer, Scully for scholar. Still other names are almost inscrutable, because of changes in the language or extinction of the occupation itself: Dempster for judge (cognate with "deem"), Chaucer for cobbler (from the Old French), Latimer for interpreter (the word being originally "Latiner"), Lardner for a keeper of the cupboard (from Norman French, cognate with "larder"), Stewart for a keeper of pig-sties (literally "sty-warden"), Talbot for wood-cutter (from the Norman Taillebois), Mailman for a tenant, especially a tenant-farmer (from Scottish dialect "mail," meaning rent or tribute—as in "blackmail").

It is the same with occupational names of other nationalities. A few of the continental ones are easy even for a nonlinguist to spot: the German Müller for miller and Buchbinder for bookbinder, the French Tourneur for turner and Boucher for butcher, the Italian Farina for miller, the Danish Praest for cleric. Others can be interpreted with the simplest pocket dictionary: the Spanish Calderón was obviously either a maker or user of caldrons, the German Zuckermann was a confectioner ("sugarman"), the Italian Balsamo and Profumo were engaged in the perfume trade, while Lazzara was a beggar. The Hungarian Molnar was another miller. Some names require more digging, and even then don't always explain themselves. The Hebrew Cohen was a priest, the Polish Bednarski a cooper, the Hungarian Asztalos a carpenter, and the Dutch Koopman a merchant. But exactly what relation the Pole named Placek bore to a pancake, or the Ukrainian Maslanka to buttermilk, can only be guessed.

[135]

The category of descriptive names has similar gradations ranging from obvious (Longfellow, Crookshank) to obscure (the English Drinkwater and French Boileau; at a guess, they were notorious teetotalers). Many such names, though easy to translate, are ambiguous. There is no telling which of the Blacks, for instance, were black-haired, dark of complexion or gloomy of temperament, but they abound: the Scottish Duff and Irish Duffy, the German Schwarz, the Polish Czarny and Czechoslovakian Cerny, the Spanish Negron and Moreno, the Portuguese Prêto and Italian Nero, the Malayan Hitam, Japanese Kuroi and Hebrew Pinkus.

The Scottish Campbell, "crooked mouth," may have referred to a facial distortion, a speech impediment or a penchant for nasty remarks. The Italian Malatesta may have meant either an ugly head or a dirty mind. Or consider the many descriptives derived from animal names. Presumably the English Finch, its German equivalent Fink, and the Czech Hrdlicka ("dove") all signified a birdlike voice. But the Italian Leone, Welsh Llewellyn, Dutch Leeuwenhoek and Norman-English Leonard; were they "lionlike" in ferocity or merely shaggy-maned? There are some names in this category that actually belie what they seem to mean at first glance. The English Best originally meant "beast," the Hungarian Kiss means "small man" and the German Funk means "lively." Onomatologist Elsdon C. Smith claims that the name Belcher came from the French *belle* and *cher,* that is, "beautiful and beloved." While this is disputable, it must gratify the Belchers.

Other descriptive names defy any accurate exegesis, e.g., the English Evilchild, Prettilove, Foulfish and Strangeways. And only a comparative few are bluntly unequivocal; among them the Celtic Goff, "a fool," the Latin-derived Calvin, "bald," the Italian Alegretti and Czech Blaha, both "happy," and the marvelous Polish Babiarz, "one who likes women." Of course, any similarity between the descriptive and the descendant wearing it has to be coincidental. In 1822 a London woman was arrested and fined for giving short measure in her shop; her name was Virtue Innocent. But there used to be a waiter in a Hawaiian restaurant in New York City whose name was Willie Monnao Kelani, or "Sweet Fat of Heaven," and Willie weighed 250 pounds.

There are myriads of "residential" names, memorializing the birthplaces or homesites of long-ago ancestors. It is safe to assume that some one of Mr. Wood's English forebears lived in, at or near a wood, and his neighbors could well have included the Messrs. Grove, Park, Greenwood, Birch, Beech, Alder, etc. Other forest dwellers were the German Holz, Baum and Wald, the Swedish Skoog, the Polish Bizozowski, the Dutch Boom, the Czech Strom, the Finnish Puuronen, the Italian Bosco and the Japanese Hayashi.

It should be mentioned that almost any of the original Woods, of whatever nationality, might well have been called something like Son-of-John-Who-Lives-in-the-Stone-House-Outside-the-City-Gates-at-the-Wood. He could be the primogenitor of any number of family lines, depending on whether his immediate descendants chose to call themselves, say, Johnson, Stone, Outergate or Atwood.

The earliest names were often unwieldy, especially those specifying a place of residence. In Britain the later generations have tended to pare them down to essentials, and so there are only a few prepositional indicators (Underwood, Bywater) left in their names. But on the Continent the inclination has been to hang on to the preposition and often the article as well. France has such names as Duchamps ("of the field") and de la Fontaine ("of the fountain"). Spain has del Monte ("of the mountain") and de la Torre ("of the tower"). Holland has Vandermeer and Italy has di Mare (both "of the sea"). In Germany the *von* of names like von Riesenfelder ("of the vast estates") is presumed the prerogative of those descended from the former nobility.

Like other names, those of residence are often indistinct to the unaided eye. Doolittle, for instance, looks as if it must have been first applied to some village ne'er-do-well, but it's really a corruption of the French de l'Hôtel, or "dweller in the mansion." Longbottom looks ribald. (Robert Graves mentions the wonderfully punning epitaph on a Longbottom who died untimely young: *"Ars longa, vita brevis."*) But it and all the other *-bottom* names merely refer to dwellers in the riverside bottomlands.

The smallest category of personal names, and often the hardest to etymologize, is the one indicative of an event, exploit or incident. Most of the people first bynamed Christmas and Noël we can assume to have been born at that time of year, and the name Astor was originally Easter. Probably the German Maier and the Italian di Maggio were born in May, and the English Greenleaf must have arrived about the same season. But it's chancier to assume that Frost and Snow celebrated a winter birthday; the original bearers may merely have been tow-headed.

The Italian names Esposito, "exposed," and Anonimo, "anonymous," are frank enough admissions of their origin, each being a name originally given to foundling infants. Not quite so apparent are the other Italian names Benedetti, de

Angelo, della Chiesa ("of the church") and della Croce ("of the cross"). These too were bestowed on babies abandoned at church and convent doors. Though the good priests and nuns evidently intended to give such children a boost by thus blessing them with pietistic names, the actual effect was to brand them bastards throughout their lives—and to leave their present-day descendants forefatherless.

The name Palmer, Rameau, Palma, Palmera or Ramos was given to a person entitled to "wear the palm," that is, the palm-leaf badge signifying that he had made the arduous pilgrimage to the Holy Land. The Irish name Mahon comes from the Celtic *mathghamhain,* meaning "bear"; but did the first Mahon win celebrity by killing one, or by being outstandingly burly, hairy or irascible? As for such a curiosity as the French Meurdesoif, we can only wonder what melodramatic event must have impelled the bestowal of a name that means "dying of thirst."

Wherever names have multipled in variety they have contributed to the orderliness and smooth-running organization of a society. But wherever their variety has been constricted, confusion has resulted. Because of the Scandinavian practice of handing down a comparatively few given names, and eventually freezing them into an equally few surnames, Denmark found itself in trouble by the turn of the twentieth century. One out of ten Danish families was named Hansen ("John's son" again), and Sorensens and Petersens were close runners-up. In one commune there were only twenty different surnames, shared by twenty thousand inhabitants. Presumably in every commune the record clerks were going crazy, so in 1903 the government passed the first Danish law legalizing (and tacitly encouraging) a change of surname.

An even worse situation still exists in China. Although the Communist government is attempting to deal with the insufficiency of names, along with various other linguistic reforms, there were still at last estimate only 150 to 400 different family names among the one billion Chinese, a quarter of the human race. According to legend, all Chinese names derived from a poem called *Pe-Kia-Sin,* or "The Families of a Hundred Houses." The poem was written by the "Model Emperor" Yao, of indeterminate place in prehistory, who decreed that each of his subjects should select his family name from its contents. Since the poem was only 408 words long, says the story, the people had few choices, hence the still-limited variety of names.

The roster of Korean surnames is similarly meager, with Kim by far predominating. A story popular among the GIs during the Korean War related that once, when the enemy launched a particularly heavy attack on a position held by combined American and Korean troops, an American sergeant turned to a Korean buddy and said, "Let's get the hell out of here, Kim"—and immediately two-thirds of the line dissolved in retreat.

All of the few Chickahominy Indians still existing in Virginia are surnamed Bradley. This commemorates either the popularity or the fecundity of an early English colonist, a runaway indentured servant, who joined and married into the tribe. In highland Scotland every family took as surname the name of its clan. This resulted in a paucity of family names and made each one of them an unmistakable indicator of the bearer's relation to other families, clans and interclan alliances. Therefore, in the old days, when warrior chiefs confronted each other in battle, they purposely kept from identifying themselves lest their names reveal some distant kinship or ancient fellowship that would prevent their enjoying the fight.

It is a common notion that all the American blacks' names were appropriated from the white owners of their slave forebears. But it must be assumed that many slaves would have felt sufficient antipathy, even hatred, toward an owner to abhor any further connection with him. And still more of them, on the large plantations, barely knew their owner except as a distant and unapproachable figure. It is likely that most blacks, on emancipation, assumed the name of some kindly former overseer, or some name that happened to be common in the area, or a name unconnected with any white man they knew, but that they'd happened to hear and took a fancy to. One white man who *was* much admired by the better-informed blacks was General Oliver Howard, commissioner of the Freedmen's Bureau after the Civil War. The first black university was named for him, and so many ex-slaves adopted his name that their descendants today constitute an estimated one-third of all the Howards in the United States.

Personal names have been affected, as has every other aspect of language, by passing fads and fashions. For example, in an earlier and less delicate society, bluntly descriptive names were considered no great horror. William the Conqueror, in one of his first proclamations to his new English subjects, announced himself as "I, William, surnamed the Bastard. . . ." A king of Denmark was known familiarly as Harold Bluetooth (Harald Blaatand).

In the eighteenth and nineteenth centuries, serious actresses, especially tragediennes, billed themselves simply as Mrs. Siddons, Mrs. Fiske, etc.—often even when unmarried—in an attempt to impart respectability to a profession then considered only a cut above street-walking. It has long been the fashion for lady authors to go by three names. A byline like Sarah Smith Jones is presumably a double-barreled brag intended to turn all her old school chums green. Sally Smith has not only written a book, see, she has landed herself the Jones boy.

Though it is customary in most parts of the world for a personal name to consist of given name first and surname last, with any extra names or patronymics somewhere in between, several societies still prefer other arrangements. The Chinese and Koreans put the family name first, and so do the Hungarians. In Spain and Portugal a man's name takes this order: given name or names, then father's surname, then mother's surname (usually separated from the others by "and": *y* in Spanish, *e* in Portuguese). A Spaniard named Herman Begega y Suarez would use the full name only on the most formal occasions; in everyday life he goes by the paternal name Herman Begega. However, there is no deterrent to his using the maternal name if he prefers, or if that side of his family is the more distinguished; Pablo Picasso did.

Personal names come in all varieties from short and simple (Primo Carnera's brother was Secundo) to long and complex (Pablo Diego José Francisco de Paula Juan Nefomunceno Crispín de la Santissima Trinidad Ruíz y Picasso). Among European nobility it was usual to lump every favored and illustrious member of the family into a new child's name. This often resulted in a mélange of both masculine and feminine appellations regardless of the child's sex; Lafayette's first name was Marie. In one district of France, it was for ages the custom to give the youngest child in a family its mother's maiden name as a new and permanent surname. In America today it seems to be increasingly the fashion to give a child its mother's maiden name as a middle name.

Names have gone through numerous mutations depending on who was spelling or pronouncing them. When writing was in its infancy the spelling of any word at all was at the mercy of the scribe, priest or clerk putting it down. If a common man's name was rendered nine or ten different ways by the various clerks he encountered during his lifetime it didn't matter much, so long as it remained fairly recognizable. Even when the commoners began to learn to write for themselves, they were pretty slipshod about consistency. Shakespeare never could make up his mind how he liked his name best; he seems to have tried it all kinds of ways, including Shaxper. So the various modern renditions of names—e.g., Smith,

Smyth, Smythe—may be the result either of a long-ago illiteracy or of a whim or a desire to stand out from the mob. One Smith, an Essex baronet, took to writing it Smijth when he thought he saw it spelled that way in an old document. He was unaware that *y* was sometimes written in medieval times with two dots above it, and what he had seen was simply Smyth.

The initial double-*f* of some names, like Ffrench and Ffolliott (sometimes still written ffrench and ffolliott), is nowadays only an affectation, left over from an obsolete style of writing *ff* for the capital *F*. Another nominal eccentricity is the hyphenated name, especially beloved of Britons. Though they show up as often now on welfare rolls as in social registers, such names were originally the result of a man's taking a wife whose name was too distinguished to be submerged in his own. And once the two surnames were hyphenated and handed down that way, there was nothing to prevent a hyphenated scion from marrying into another hyphenated family—with occasional elephantine consequences. There have existed such names as Haldane-Duncan-Mercer-Henderson and Borlase-Warren-Venables-Vernon.

Even when a man's name was correctly and consistently spelled, there was no guarantee that everyone who saw it would pronounce it the same way he did. And a sufficient repetition of a certain pronunciation—even an egregious mispronunciation—could result in a change of spelling to suit. The immigrants who joined the early American melting-pot often found their names fused into strange new forms. The French Pibaudière became Peabody, Bon Pas became Bumpus, Beauvoir became Beaver. The Dutch Wittenacht became Whiteneck, the German Gebhardt became Capehart. H. L. Mencken lists page after page of such contortions in *The American Language*, most of them having occurred on the frontier, where literacy and precise language ran a poor second to a sense of humor; hence Archambault into Shampoo, Blancpied into Blumpy and Muqabba'ah into McKaba.

Other immigrants have rearranged their names with more deliberation and less exuberance, to give them an "American look" or to make them easier for the new neighbors to spell and articulate—e.g., the Finnish Määrälä into Marlowe, the Romany MiXail into Mitchell, the German Eisenhauer into Eisenhower and Krankheit into Cronkite, the Dutch Roggenfelder into Rockefeller. One of the most "American" of all corporate names was that of Ringling Brothers' Circus, but the father of those brothers was named Rüngeling until his hometown newspaper spelled it phonetically. When William

Falkner got the galley proofs of his first book and found that the compositor had set his byline as "William Faulkner," he didn't bother to mark a correction; he simply spelled his name that way from then on. There is no counting how many times a Schmitt has become a Smith, a Johansson a Johnson, a Rabinowitz a Robinson.

Similar acclimatization has occurred in other countries. A German Klein moving to France might take the French name of the same meaning: Petit. A Levy might Gallicize his name into LeVie. The Spanish name Zaragoza is an elided descendant of Caesar Augustus. The Norwegian composer Edvard Grieg's ancestors were Scottish, and named Craig. The Italian name Tagliaferro was so constantly pronounced "Tolliver" in England that many Britain-based branches of the family have long spelled it that way. Contrarily, numerous English names have maintained a spelling considerably different from the pronunciation that has come to be accepted. The name pronounced "Chumley" is still spelled Cholmondeley, "Pomfret" is spelled Pontefract, "Crunchell" Crowninshield, "Fanshaw" Featherstonehaugh, etc.

From time to time, government edicts have caused the creation, alteration or abolition of personal names. In the sixteenth century, Philip II commanded that all the Moors still resident in Spain must drop their Arabic names and take Spanish ones. This was rather myopic of him, since by that time many Spanish names in use, both of people and of places, had long before derived from the Arabic—e.g., Alcalde (al-qa'id, "the leader"). In the seventeenth century, the Scottish Privy Council for some reason developed a grudge against the Gregor clan, and for sixty years the death penalty threatened any Gregor or MacGregor who refused to change his name.

Toward the end of the eighteenth century, Austria, Prussia and Bavaria found themselves unable to cope with the Hebraic name-system of their Jewish citizens. The Jews identified themselves only by patronymics (e.g., Joel, son of Aaron), and a multiplicity of identically named Ben Aarons, Ben Judahs, etc., was gumming up the administrative machinery. It was decreed that all the Jews take permanent surnames, and commissioners were appointed to see that they did.

A Jew willing to bribe the commissioners could choose his own new surname. A Jew too poor or too proud to bargain would have one assigned to him. The official name-givers seem to have got as much fun out of the one as profit out of the other, because they gleefully devised and dispensed the most fiendish and outlandish of names. A sampling includes

Eselkopf, Fresser, Süssmilch, Wanzenknicker, Drachenblut, Schwanz, Saumagen and Schmutz—which mean, in order, Ass-head, Glutton, Sweet-milk, Louse-cracker, Dragon-blood, Tail, Sow-belly and Filth. Almost equally pitiful in their way were the names the more fortunate Jews chose and paid for: Grünberg, Rosenfeld, Blumenthal, etc., names evocative of vistas—Green-mountain, Rose-field, Blooming-valley—that they in their narrow ghettos could never hope to see.

Very few traditionally "Jewish" names are really Jewish, i.e., Hebraic in origin. The Jews have too often found it necessary, wherever they have settled, to assume indigenous names as a matter of protective coloration. Thus the majority of Jews in the world today bear names of German, Polish, Russian, Spanish, Romanian and other European derivations. When they emigrated from those countries to America, some of them took the further step to Anglo-Saxon-sounding names. Since the opening up of Israel in 1948, European and American Jews moving to that ancestral homeland have usually discarded their "foreign" names, however old and distinguished, and have taken Hebrew ones.

In the 1880s the United States government insisted that its civilized Indians adopt surnames and make them permanent. When an Indian child enrolled in school sans surname, he was given one; if he already had an Indian name it was usually translated into English. Since not all the school officials were capable linguists, some mistakes were made. Mencken cites one case where an Indian whose name meant Young-Man-Whose-Very-Horses-Are-Feared suffered a comedown in translation to Young-Man-Afraid-of-His-Horse. Many other names were deliberately mistranslated because they scandalized the schoolmarms. In their natural state the Indians hadn't learned to abhor nature; some of their native names were forthrightly "obscene." Name-translating *into* Indian languages is no easy thing, either. A few years ago, when a New York man was honorarily adopted into a Pawnee tribe, he was given the name Rah-wis-tah-rika, which means "Smoke Signal Son" and was as close as the Pawnees could come to rendering his occupational title. He was an advertising man.

Most name-changes have been instituted by the individuals concerned, and almost always have changed in the direction of euphemism. An early euphemist was Cardinal Grugno, who is said to have begun the custom of popes' taking a new name upon accession. Grugno had good reason to; his own name meant "swine-snout." So when he became pope in 1009 he took the name of three predecessors and became Sergius IV.

During the thirteenth and fourteenth centuries, when hereditary family names were first becoming fashionable throughout Europe, most of the outspokenly descriptive ones, the clownish and derogatory ones, were dropped by their bearers. Occasionally a less-than-nice name survived because a family had become so inextricably identified with it that it wasn't easily abandoned. But even some of these lost their infelicity after a while, through words changing their meaning. Parnell, for one, is now a respectable and unremarkable name, but originally—and God only knows the reason for its first bestowal—the word meant "a loose woman."

Conversely, through other changes in language and folkways, names originally innocuous became indelicate, or at least they came to seem so to the later, more fastidious generations wearing them. The English name Shittler, for example, had first meant simply a weaver, "shittle" being the earlier word for "shuttle." But in 1884 we find a J. R. Shittler changing his name to J. R. Rowden. By the early nineteenth century, even the lowest classes had achieved a state of literacy and social awareness that made a man squirm under an unflattering name and yearn to get rid of it. About that time began a wave of name-changes, both informal and court-arranged, that continued to crest for better than a century. Among the many thousands of legal changes recorded in Europe and America during that period, these few excerpted from English court calendars are typical:

In 1798 T. H. Cock became T. H. Lamb. In 1808 Mr. J. Freakes became J. Parson. In 1825 C. J. Crook became C. J. Noble. Mr. S. A. Yapp metamorphosed by stages; in 1838 he became Chapman-Yapp, and four years later asked the court's permission to make it just plain Chapman. In 1844 Mr. and Mrs. Gossip became Mr. and Mrs. Hatfield. In 1868 John McOstrich became John Carmichael. In 1871 Mr. W. Ffooks, a lawyer, became W. Woodforde. In 1877 the Ick family became the Broderick family, and Mr. J. E. Hogsflesh became J. E. Herbert. In 1880 Mr. J. Rump, a butler, became J. Ward. In 1882 J. Crapper became J. Foster. In 1887 Mr. Arthur Chucker-Butty became Arthur Goodeve. In 1892 Mary Ann Gotobed, a spinster, became Mary Ann Loft. In 1897 Mr. G. G. Uren became G. G. Wren.

Since we can't know the compelling circumstances, some of these changes seem no improvement at all, or even seem a turn for the worse. In 1797 Mr. J. Pine became J. Pine-Coffin. In 1807 Mr. F. French became F. Flutter-Steevens. In 1815 Mr. E. Cheese became E. Cheese-Carpenter. In 1871 Mr. T. M. Heaps became T. M. Heaps-Moore. In 1879 Mr. J. Balls became J. Balls-Woolby.

Smiths abound in these annals, forever changing or hyphenating the name to something else. Only a handful of petitioners changed their names *to* Smith. One who did was W. Jones in 1798, and his descendants must wonder what benefit he saw in the switch.

Name-changing still goes on, and doubtless will as long as word meanings are inconstant and fashions are fickle. Most such changes nowadays are, as ever, euphemistic: an Italo-American pianist uses the surname Carmen professionally because his real name, Guastafeste, means "wet blanket." But some changes are in the opposite direction: when Viscount Hailsham renounced his title in order to qualify for the House of Commons, it meant resuming his pre-peerage name of Quintin Hogg. And some name-changes are of indescribable nature: in 1964 the members of a rock quintet legally changed their names to Hub Kapp, Terry Kloth, Ty Klip, Rye Krisp and Rip Kord. And there is a black stripteaser who works under the name of Sybil Rights.

But throughout history there have been admirably unregenerate souls who've stuck stanchly to the surnames pinned on them by fate and forefathers. One of the first purchasers of land in William Penn's Pennsylvania was Richard Glutton. In 1849 the superintendent of the Cincinnati Lunatic Asylum was Absalom Death. An 1873 compilation of odd names in America ranged from Allchindus Allchin of Philadelphia to Pius Zwisley of Baltimore, and included such other wonders as Clapsaddle, Halfhead, Kickem, Liquorish, Sneezum, Quattlebum, Toadvine and Witherup. An otherwise undistinguished murder trial in San Francisco in 1897 aroused nationwide interest solely because of the defendant's name: Albert Frederick George Vereneseneckockockhoff. In 1940, when Antoni Przybysz of Detroit legally changed his name, he changed it to Clinton Przybysz. Almost any city directory or newspaper can supply similar examples: Opal Bonecutter, Lenore Hogaboom, Lean Belch, Emma Goof, Maxim Bugzester, Albert Shanker, Novella Cluts, Breece D'J Pancake, Hooshana Yowza. These are all real names.

Many thinkers have speculated on the part an individual's name plays in influencing the course of his life. Would Sir Francis Drake have been quite so dashing as Frank Duck? Would Pansy O'Hara have achieved fame and fortune if an editor hadn't changed her name to Scarlett? Would moviegoers accept Cary Grant as a debonair lover under his real name of Archibald Leach? No modern writer would dream of handicapping his intended hero with a name like Natty Bumppo. But then again, such movie stars as Meryl Streep and Sissy Spacek haven't suffered from using their real names. And the currently regnant prelate of the Roman Catholic Church in the Philippines is Cardinal Sin.

Parents have tried all sorts of theories when it came to picking auspicious names for their offspring. The ancient Greeks believed that the longer the name, the better. The early Christians left the decision to lot; they would select a number of likely names, mark each one on a separate candle and then name the baby according to which candle burned longest. Some Tatar tribesmen, evidently feeling unable to cope with the decision themselves, would name their child after the first person they encountered exactly six months after its birth. The name of every folk-hero, from messiah to matinee idol, has been perpetuated by the children born after him. Jesus is a common given name among the Spanish, and Moses among Jews. Caesar still has his European legions, George Washington is seemingly still fathering his country, and in the southern United States it's hard to find a citizen who *doesn't* have a Lee somewhere in his (or her) name.

In the 1860s, a Michigan couple christened their sons One, Two and Three, their daughters First, Second and Third. That was at least a more practical devisal than that of a Vermont couple of about the same time. *They* named their assumed-last child Finis. When, afterward, a girl and two boys came along, those had to be named Addenda, Supplement and Last Appendix.

It's a moot point whether a child named, say, Winston has a better chance of success in life than one named, say, Fauntleroy—except that a Fauntleroy is likely to suffer such a gruesome childhood that he'll grow up to be either a hermit or a Hitler. But if ever a child had a Christian cross to bear, it was the unfortunate son or daughter of the Puritans. Those perfervidly pious people were wont to make their children walking advertisements for the moral virtues, giving them names like Faith, Constance, Conscience and Fortitude. But some of their inventions surpassed even fanaticism and verged on the sadistic. A 1658 Sussex jury panel included these Puritan specimens: Faint-Not Hewett, Stand-Fast-on-High Stringer, Search-the-Scriptures Moreton, Fly-Debate Roberts and Be-of-Good-Comfort Small.

One poor girl was baptized Through-Much-Tribulation-We-Enter-into-the-Kingdom-of-Heaven Crabb. Her friends called her Tribby. Another youngster somehow survived to manhood with the given name of Kill-Sin; that was bad enough, but his surname happened to be Pimple. What his friends called him is unrecorded.

The most unimaginative sort of name-giving ,and, one would suspect, the most enfeebling to the child involved, is that of naming a boy after his father and making him go through life dogged by the dangling *Jr*. The actor son of actor Douglas Fairbanks, whose buskin tenure has by now more than doubled that of his famous father, is at this writing and at the age of seventy-four still being billed as Douglas Fairbanks, Jr. In many families obsessed with dynasty, this sort of blight extends even unto the IIIrd and IVth generations. And some American parents, notably lower-class southerners and blacks, now don't bother to give the son the father's name at all; they simply christen him Junior.

The Mormons had the custom of giving the name Doctor to a seventh son of a seventh son. Another favorite first name among them was Moroni, after one of the high-ranking angels in their pantheon. That is, it was a favorite name until about 1910, when psychologists adopted and popularized the word "moron" to describe a particular category of mental retardation; after that, Moronis began to be scarce.

American parents have become increasingly loath to depend on the long-time "established" names, and more and more children are being blessed with names of extravagant invention. Mr. and Mrs. Trees of Columbus, Ohio, named their sons Douglas Fir and Jack Pine, and their daughter Merry Christmas. Some others registered on birth rolls in recent years include (for boys) Arson, Dimple, Zurr, Comma, Lover, Voyd, Author, Faro, Onus and Alpha Omega; (for girls) Marionette, Emirbsa, Licelot, Hygiene, Ova, Nookie, Sireen, Xiomara, Uretha and Coita.

But of all sad names that have ever been, surely one of the saddest is that cited by Charles L. Wallis in his book *Stories on Stone*, and found on a gravemarker in Idlewild Cemetery, Hood River, Oregon. According to Wallis, the man who bore it was named by his unwed mother to lament her own misadventure. The tombstone is inscribed:

ASAD EXPERIENCE WILSON

1895   1946

So geographers, in Afric maps,
With savage pictures fill their gaps,
And o'er unhabitable downs
Place elephants for want of towns.
—JONATHAN SWIFT

From Å to Zsilyvajdejvulkan

T H E R E is just one spot on earth from which, in an
hour's driving time or less, a motoring tourist can
reach either Athens, Belfast, Belgrade, Bremen, China,
Denmark, Dresden, Frankfort, Limerick, Lisbon, Madrid,
Mexico, Naples, Norway, Oxford, Palermo, Paris, Peru, Poland or Vienna.

The spot is situated at about 44° 9′ north latitude, 69° 51′
west longitude, in the county of Sagadahoc, state of Maine,
U.S.A., and it is surrounded by towns bearing these names,
no one of them more than fifty-five miles away. This cosmo-
ramic aggregation, besides supplying fodder for innumerable
newspaper fillers, illustrates one way in which places get
their names—by frank imitation of other names which, in
their turn, were originally either descriptive, commemorative
or purely notional.

Why this southwest corner of Maine should have chosen to
become a map of the world in miniature can only be guessed.
The name of Maine itself comes from an ancient French
province, so it may have seemed fitting to honor the name-
sake country by founding another Paris. Athens and Oxford
may have hoped eventually to rival the originals as cultural
centers. Limerick and Lisbon may have been settled respectively by Irish and Portuguese immigrants who named them
out of homesickness. But there are not now, nor have there
ever been, enough Viennese and Chinese in Maine to account
for the Vienna and China. And why anyone should see any resemblance between the Maine Palermo and the Sicilian one—
or should want to—is beyond imagining.

This New World tendency to imitation, particularly in the

United States, has long been deplored and derided by visiting Europeans. The English tourist W. H. Russell wrote in 1863, "All that can be seen of the city of Troy is a timber house, three log huts, a saw mill and twenty Negroes."

As recently as 1911, in his *Words and Places*, another Englishman, Isaac Taylor, was likewise complaining:

We find the map of the United States thickly bespattered with an incongruous medley of names—for the most part utterly inappropriate, and fulfilling very insufficiently the chief purpose which names are intended to fulfill. In every state of the Union we find repeated, again and again, such unmeaning names as Thebes, Cairo, Memphis, Troy, Rome. . . . What a poverty of the inventive faculty is evinced by these endless repetitions, not to speak of the intolerable impertinence displayed by those who thus ruthlessly wrench the grand historic names from the map of the Old World, and apply them, by the score, without the least shadow of congruity, to collections of log huts in some Western forest.

Granted that the American place-namers were often dismally unoriginal, they had precedent. Surely, of the multitude of Caesareas that sprang up throughout the Roman Empire— in Palestine, Cappadocia, Mauritania, etc.—many must have been no more than "collections of log huts." And what of the numerous Devons later planted by nostalgic Englishmen from Baffin Bay and Jamaica to South Africa and Tasmania?

Of all the methods of naming topographical features and their man-made increments, imitation has been the easiest and oftenest employed. But there had to be something to imitate; where did the original names come from?

In a good many instances, no one knows. The origin and meaning of the oldest existing place-names are often hidden from us by eons of linguistic change or physical change in the places themselves. To illustrate, take a couple whose origin we *do* know: England's Isle of Ely hasn't been an island since the Venerable Bede's day, and the eels that gave it its name were extinct even then. The Picketwire River in Colorado, never trammeled by pickets or wires, got its American name through corruption of an earlier French one, the Purgatoire. As for one that's still a mystery: Berlin features a bear in its coat of arms, perpetuating the belief that the city was named for a legendary twelfth-century founder, Albert the Bear (*Bär*). But the city wasn't born until the thirteenth century, and there is every possibility that its name came from the Slavs' slighting epithet for the region: *berle*, meaning "wasteland."

Every pimple and pock on the face of the earth has been

given a name—if not several of them through the ages—
from Chomolungma to the Challenger Deep, from Å to Zsilyvajdejvulkan. Chomolungma is the original Tibetan name of
Mount Everest. The Challenger Deep, in the Pacific between
Guam and Yap, is the deepest known part of any ocean. Å is
a fishing village in northern Norway, and it has suffered: it
used to be Aag. Zsilyvajdejvulkan is a coal-mining town in
Romania.

The world's atlases are as full as its telephone directories
of unbelievable names: the English village of Happersnapper
Hanger, the Pis Pis River in Nicaragua, Great and Little Misery islands off Massachusetts, the town of Jenkinjones in
West Virginia, Poland's Puck Bay, the Tit oasis in Algeria,
the town of Tweed Heads in New South Wales, Pshish Mountain in the Caucasus, the village of El Boom in Nicaragua,
Cuckold's Cove in Canada, the Jenny Jump Mountains in
New Jersey, and thousands more.

But even where an odd place-name's origin and meaning
are obscure, we can usually assume that it had some simple
and self-evident meaning to its original namers. For instance,
the somewhat awful-sounding Twat, a hill in the Sahara, apparently is cognate with Tuareg (*Tawariq* in Arabic) and
must have been named for some association with the Tuareg
tribesmen. Conversely, a place-name which merely looks "foreign" to outsiders can sometimes prove to be a surprise when
translated—e.g., the Gniloye More in the Crimea is the Pu-
trid Sea.

The first place-names bestowed by early man would have
been descriptive ones, and it is likely that he invented individual names before he did generic ones. That is, he would
have named separate mountains in his area according to
their differences—High-Place, Flat-Top-Place, Place-Where-
the Eagles-Nest, etc.—long before he got around to recog-
nizing their general similarity and cataloguing them all together as "mountains."

In any locality or language, the majority of topographical
place-names are descriptive, calling attention to either a distinguishing peculiarity (Bald Mountain) or a recognizable resemblance to something commonplace (Table Mountain).
The pragmatic intent to give a place the most succinct and
fitting description has occasioned considerable independent
duplication of names; for example, there is a "bald" mountain in eleven states of the United States; in New Brunswick
and Manitoba, Canada; and in Queensland, Australia. In the
single state of Minnesota there are 99 Long lakes, 39 Round
ones, 91 Mud lakes and 32 Sandy ones. But some of the co-

incidentally identical place-names are not quite so obvious. America's Mississippi, Spain's Guadalquivir, Mexico's Río Grande and Russia's Volga all actually have the same name: Big River. England's Oxford was, of course, a convenient place for getting oxen across the Thames River. Turkey's Bosphorus means exactly the same thing—a cattle-crossing— but from a mythical rather than a real use of the strait. The Bosphorus is supposedly the place where Zeus, in his guise of a bull, swam away with the kidnaped princess Europa.

Many geographic names of resemblance, both individual and generic, have been derived from the human anatomy: headland, brow (of a hill), river mouth, ness (from the Old Norse for "nose," hence a promontory), foothill, the Finger Lakes of New York State, Elbow Cay in the Bahamas, etc. When William Byrd was laying out the boundary between Virginia and North Carolina, he dubbed two mountains in that area The Wart and The Pimple. But some anatomical descriptives are more delightfully evocative. The "big breasts" of Wyoming, the Grand Tetons, are famed in story and history. Less well known are the Paps of Jura, mammary mountains on a Scottish island near Islay; and the real curiosity here is that there are *three* of them. Also in Scotland is Perthshire's Schiehallion Mountain, its name derived from the Gaelic *ti-chaillinn*, "the maiden's teat." Two little hummocks in the Strait of Belle Isle, between Newfoundland and Quebec, are rather irreverently known as Our Lady's Bubbies.

Some place-names are descriptive of the original inhabitants, or are meant to be. Ethiopia got its name from a Greek word meaning "sun-burnt faces"—which is apt enough—and Patagonia, which means "land of the big feet," was so dubbed by early Spanish explorers who were evidently impressed by the clumsy clodhopper footwear affected by the natives. Oklahoma means "red man." But Indiana is just one of many places in the Western hemisphere which were ultimately misnamed because of Columbus' belief that he'd landed among the Indians of India.

Often the discoverer of a new place has given it a name befitting some inconsiderable part of it and that name has later been extended to the whole, in some cases incongruously. Iceland and Greenland, for example, evidently got their names from someone's first glimpse of them, though actually Iceland is mostly green and Greenland is seven-eighths ice.

To the annoyance and discommodity of European explorers, some North American Indians had the practice of giving a separate name to every bend, fork, shallow, rapid and stretch of a river. A white settler newly arrived on the bank of a certain Maryland stream, where it empties into Chesapeake Bay, might inquire of a local Indian the name of the river, and the Indian would answer, "Pocqueumoke," an honest and truthful description of this one piece of the water. Whereupon the greenhorn white man would append the name (since elided to Pocomoke) to the entire length of the river. Generations later, his descendant in a Delaware town somewhere on the upland reaches of the Pocomoke would have cause to wonder why a freshwater stream should bear a name that means The-Place-Where-Oysters-Are-Found.

A mountain in Korea, officially designated Kumo on the map, has five other popular names depending on what direction it's approached from. The mountain is the cornerpost of five counties, and the natives of each see in it a different shape, name it accordingly and invest it with fitting folklore. One district discerns in its shape a Korean "writing brush," and so that area, according to local legend, produces a high proportion of scholars. Another county makes out the shape of an old-time Korean "crown"; many ministers and officials supposedly are born thereabouts. From another part of the country, the mountain is a "skulking robber"; that county is allegedly full of thieves. To a fourth county the mountain looks like a "sheaf of grain"; many in that neighborhood become successful farmers and merchants. From the fifth county, the long ridge is supposed to resemble a "wanton woman" stretched out in a provocative pose; the women of that region are, in consequence, regarded rather askance.

The Spanish explorers who first landed on the western coast of South America found a Valley of Paradise (Valparaiso, in what is now Chile), while the Portuguese navigators who made landfall on the eastern coast found the Mouth of Hell (Pernambuco, in Brazil).

Sometimes a place can willfully switch back and forth from one name to another. In China there are two cities that do this regularly twice a year. The district of Lungchwan has a winter capital, the city of Shanmulung, and a summer capital, the city of Changfengkai. Each of these, during its season as seat of the government, changes its name to Lungchwan. One of Russia's most famous cities first honored the imperial establishment with the name Tsaritsyn, then the dictator as Stalingrad, and is now less showily the simple Volgograd.

Sometimes a name has existed independently and has roamed in yearning search of a place to light and stay. Ancient geographers gave the name Ultima Thule to the presumed northernmost edge of the world. According to the maps of Eratosthenes (*ca.* 220 B.C.), Ultima Thule lay somewhere in the northern part of Baltia, that is, the Norway-Sweden peninsula. By Ptolemy's day (*ca.* A.D. 150), the "farthest north" had been relocated north of Britain, in the Shetland or Faroe Islands. After touching down in numerous other places during the centuries, Thule has currently come to rest on the northwest coast of Greenland, where the U. S. Air Force maintains a radar station, an outpost that—at least the troops will aver—is indeed the farthest, Godforsakenest brink of the world.

A place may be aptly named until subsequent political boundaries are laid around it and frame it rather ridiculously. The Northwest River in Virginia was named that because it flows from the northwest to the sea. But its riverside town, also named Northwest, looks foolishly out of place, tucked as it is in the farthest southeast corner of Virginia. It is not unique, though; the town of North East, Pennsylvania, is in the extreme northwest corner of that state.

And there are some places that have been named by sheer mistake. When Spanish explorers first landed on a peninsula in the Gulf of Mexico, and asked the local Indians the name of the country, the natives replied, "*Yectetan.*" This meant approximately "What say?" or "How's that?"—but Yucatan it became and Yucatan it still is. Massachusetts owes its Marblehead to some marbleheaded name-giver who couldn't recognize the cape's rock as granite. Yreka, California, has an amusing if nonsensical yarn to explain its name. It was reportedly so dubbed by mistake, back in the days when it was a brand-new mining community jerry-built of laths and canvas. A passing traveler glimpsed a painted cloth banner being tacked onto a shopfront, assumed it to be the town's name, and spread the word that California's newest community was called Yreka. But he'd seen only part of the banner, and that from the rear; what the whole sign said, from the front, was "Bakery."

Many places have borne more than one name, and often conflicting ones, depending on how they appeared to different name-givers. That part of Canada now bleakly called the North Country was to the early French voyageurs Le Beau Pays, "the beautiful land." An island off Greece, long called Calliste ("the most beautiful") suddenly belched forth such a horrific volcanic eruption that the inhabitants changed their opinion of the island and the name of it, too. Ever since, it has been called Thera, "the beast." The Danube

River has a different name in every country it flows through: Donau in Germany, Duna in Hungary, Dunaj in Czechoslovakia, Dunav in Yugoslavia and Dunărea in Romania.

Books about the Civil War, written immediately after the event by veterans of the opposing sides, would superficially appear to be about two different wars. The reason is that the Union armies generally designated their battle sites according to the local topography, while the Confederates labeled them according to the nearest settlements. Thus the Yankees' Battle of Antietam (the creek) was the Rebels' Battle of Sharpsburg (the village); the Yankees' Bull Run (another creek) was the Rebels' Manassas (a railroad depot).

Some place-names require digging to get at their real meaning—*real* digging in the case of Sharktooth Hill, California. The map shows this to be more than a hundred miles from any sea and any shark, but diggers there have unearthed enough fossil shark teeth to prove that once it was at the bottom of the ocean. New York City's Gramercy Park is presumed by many of its residents to derive from the French *grande merci*, but old maps of Nieuw Amsterdam show the site occupied by a dog-legged pond called the Kromme Zee, "crooked lake." A little linguistic delving reveals that the English village of Bovy-in-Beer was not named for beer at all; evidently the community grew up around a cowshed—that is to say, a "bovine byre." In Iowa there is a little ghost of a mining town which appears on today's maps as Mystic. This is no sentimental reference to its ghostliness; it is allegedly a tidied-up rendition of the remark made by the first migrants who came there to work the coal mines: "This is a mistake."

The wee island of Calf of Man in the Irish Sea was named for neither kine nor mankind. It happens to nestle close to the Isle of Man, and "calf" is an old expression for a small island near a larger one. But the Isle of Man got *its* name from the Welsh *mān*, meaning simply "small"—thus the Calf of Man is literally "the smaller of the small." There is more than one offshore rock marked on British marine charts as the Old Man, but the descriptive was originally the Celtic *alt maen*, simply "high rock." And the Cornish headland now fearsomely known as the Dead Man was *dod maen*, the innocent "yellow rock."

Numerous other place-names are obviously descriptive but maddeningly ambiguous about *what* they were meant to describe. The name of Nagpoor, India, may mean "city of snakes" if it derives from the Sanskrit *naga* ("serpent"), or it may mean simply and rather sillily "city-city" if it comes from the Hindustani *nagura* and *pura* (both meaning "city").

The various English names like Blackmore and Blakeley would appear to be derived from "black" (or from the Middle English version, *blak*) but they could just as well come from the Old Norse *blakka*, which meant quite the opposite: "pale." A numerical label on a place may be an attempt at description, as in Canada's Thousand Islands. Or it may signify location: North Dakota's Thirty Mile Creek does not measure thirty miles in any dimension, it was thirty miles' journey from some prior landmark on some long-forgotten trail westward.

The descriptive name given to a topographical feature will often suffice for a human settlement in the neighborhood. Niagara Falls is the name of towns on both the New York and the Ontario sides of the river. Savannah, Georgia, gets its name from the Spanish-Carib term for the sort of flatland in which it is situated. Lizard Town in Cornwall is named after a nearby headland, called Lizard for its shape. Sometimes this method of naming-by-propinquity can work the other way around. Beside the English river Granta grew up a town, once called Grantebrycge and gradually softening its name through Cantebrigge to the eventual Cambridge. At this point, evidently, someone decided that if the town was Cambridge than the river must be the Cam. And so it has been ever since. Such derivative name-giving can sometimes make for gross misnomers. A mountain may aptly be named Granite Mountain, and a marsh at its foot will become, merely through nearness, an incongruous Granite Swamp.

Frequently a community will wear a name descriptive of its prime product, industry or claim to fame, e.g., Michigan's Cement City, Pennsylvania's Factoryville and Steelton. England's Bath is called that for its salubrious mineral springs. In Saxon times it was called the same thing, only more explicitly: Akemannesceaster, "aching people's camp." Before that, the Romans called it Aquae Sulis, "waters of Sul" (after a local deity). A street in a remote corner of Paris is called the rue de Carrières d'Amérique ("quarries of America") because, in the early nineteenth century, Paris exported to the States vast quantities of gypsum mined in that area (hence also the term "plaster of Paris"). The United States has numerous "company towns" like the acronymic Alcoa, Tennessee, seigniory of the Aluminum Company of America.

After descriptives, the next largest category of place-names consists of commemoratives—of a god, devil, saint or ordinary being, of an exploit or incident. There are numerous Jesuses, Marys and Trinities on the map, and Saints of all sorts. There is Gods Lake in Canada, the Dios Cays off Cuba, l'Ile du Diable off French Guiana, Mars Hill in Maine, Athenai in Greece, Diana Bank in the Bahamas, Mount Erebus in Antarctica, Hecate Strait in Canada, the Brahmaputra River in India. The province of Manitoba is named for the Algonquian Indians' Manitou, or Great Spirit.

The kind of mortal considered worthy of memorial in a place-name may be a Caesar or a small-town manufacturer of patent medicines. The former is immortalized in England's Isle of Jersey (a corruption of Caesarea) and the state of New Jersey (officially Nova Caesarea). Groton Junction, Massachusetts, changed its name to Ayer in honor of Dr. James C. Ayer, a local boy who made good (and made millions) by peddling Ayer's Cathartic Pills.

Some seemingly commemorative names are not. There may have been a man named Tom Kedgwick somewhere at some time, but the New Brunswick river by that name wasn't named for him. It got its appellation by elision—one might say creative elision—from the original Micmac Indian jawbreaker, Quahtahwahamquahduavic. And some commemorative names don't seem to be. Gibraltar derives from Jebel Tarik, "mountain of Tarik," the Moor who led the conquest of Spain. The name of Butterlip How, a hamlet in Cumberland, England, looks like anything but a memorial, until one reconstructs the original out of the latter-day corruption. It seems there was once a Viking named Buthar Lipr, and the village is the presumed site of his *haugr,* or "burial place."

Not long ago the inhabitants of a housing development in Stamford, Connecticut, demanded the change of their street's name to Club Circle. They were tired of living on Bubsey Lane. (Reportedly, it commemorated the nickname of the tract developer's little boy.) "We're always being held up to ridicule," complained one dweller there. Scranton, Pennsylvania, named for one of its leading families, had earlier tried Scrantonia and, before that, Harrison, Slocum Hollow and Unionville. None of these is particularly rhapsodic, but any one of them is better than the very first name that neighborhood bore: Skunk's Misery.

Not all commemorative place-names are bestowed in honor of hometowners. Athens memorializes a South African statesman in Jan Smuts Street. Paris is particularly partial to naming streets after other people's heroes. The first American immortalized there was Benjamin Franklin, with the rue Franklin, so dubbed in 1791. There is also a rue Edgar Poe, and in 1964 the quai de Passy became the avenue de President Kennedy. The early Virginia colonists, knowing which side of the ocean their bread was buttered on, laid out eleven counties named for various English kings, queens and princelings. Then, as if to take no chances on slighting any future monarch, they established a catch-all King & Queen County.

The state of Wyoming got its name second-hand, so to speak, as a commemoration of a description. The descriptive name Wyoming, from a Lenape Indian term meaning "hills and valleys," was first bestowed on a Susquehanna River valley in Pennsylvania. After an Indian massacre of white settlers there in 1778, the Scottish poet Thomas Campbell made the place world-famous with his poem "Gertrude of Wyoming." And so in 1868, when a new territory was organized in the Far West, it took the same name to honor the original Wyoming martyrs.

Early seafarers were wont to label a landfall in memory of something that happened to them there, and to judge from the resulting place-names—Point Anxiety, Fury Beach, Cape Wrath, Repulse Bay, Cape Hold with Hope, Wreck Reef— they encountered distress far oftener than they did delight. A whopping good adventure novel could be written from the outline provided by just the New Zealand coastline, with its Cape Foulwind, Poverty Bay, Doubtful Sound, Cape Kidnappers, Cape Runaway, Separation Point, Cape Turnagain and Cape Farewell.

The American frontiersmen would name a place to commemorate anything from a battle with bloodthirsty Indians to a rousing bout with delirium tremens—Hungry Horse, Killdeer, Death Valley, Massacre Rocks, Gouge Eye, Rum River, Powderhorn, Rifle, Gunsight Hills. But all their names weren't riproarers. Some have the ring of discovery, or the reminiscence of a life-saving oasis, or the serenity of the whispering wilderness—Bonanza, Sweetwater, Sweetgrass, Sleepy Eye, Dreaming Creek.

Hungry Mother Mountain in Virginia allegedly got its name when travelers came upon a cabin where a pioneer family had been wiped out by marauding Shawnees. The only survivor was an infant who, when found, was whimpering over and over, "Hungry, mother . . ." But the event memorialized in a place-name need not always have been a melodramatic one. Stingray Point got its name when Captain John Smith picked up a live sting-ray, and regretted it. New York's Spuyten Duyvil Creek is supposed to be where a headstrong Hollander vowed to swim the dangerous crossing "in spite of the devil." The North Dakota village of Seroco invented that name for itself because the first piece of mail delivered to its brand-new post office was a Sears Roebuck catalogue.

Individuals and events are not the only phenomena that

have been eternized in place-names. While the early founders of American towns often looked to the Good Book for inspiration—Bethlehem, Shiloh, Bethesda, etc.—succeeding generations have sometimes turned to less good books, e.g., for a name like Tarzana, California. According to the latest census figures available, there were (maybe still are) 226 prisoners of Zenda, Kansas. In 1950 Hot Springs, New Mexico, convulsed itself into Truth-or-Consequences in honor of a once popular radio quiz program.

Then there are the place-names of acronymic invention, most of them sounding like delicatessens run by a coalition of in-laws. Delmarva is the name inflicted on the peninsula shared by Delaware, Maryland and Virginia. Texarkana sits at the conjuncture of Texas, Arkansas and Louisiana. Calexico, California, and Mexicali, Mexico, confront each other across the border there. But even these have historical precedent of a sort. Tripoli means just "three cities," and the Tripoli in Lebanon was named in honor of the older cities of Sidon, Tyre and Aradus, which had joined in financing the settlement.

The colonists of every new country have borrowed many of their place-names from the original inhabitants, sometimes taking them intact, sometimes translating them into the new language, sometimes phonetically easing or distorting them. Folk-etymology is evident everywhere from the state of Washington's Humptulips River to Humpy Bang in Queensland, Australia; in each case a now forgotten native expression having been transformed into a pronounceable and recognizable (if nonsensical) English locution.

The various North American Indian tongues were alike in featuring thorny hedges of consonants separated by gutters of grunts—for example, one Occaneechee word for Virginia was Attanoughkomouck. So many settlers who used Indian words at all elided them into more manageable noises, and wrote them down in even simpler form. The "Indian" names on the current American map, then, would baffle the original name-givers. This state of affairs is an embarrassment to local historical societies, who yearn to translate the Indian names into license-plate poetry like "Land of the Sky-Blue Waters." Such translation demands a lively imagination, because the Indian words mean practically nothing in their present dilution, and seldom meant anything poetic to begin with.

Niagara was originally Oni-aw-garah, and, according to the more rapturous breed of historian, means "hark to the thunder." Why "hark," why not "listen to" or "hear"? Because "hark" sounds more Hiawatha-ish, that's why. As noted ear-

lier, Mississippi means only "Big River," not anything so lofty
as "Father of Waters." Missouri, popularly "People of the Big
Canoes," really means "Big and Muddy." Both Ohio and Allegheny mean simply "Good Waters." Chesapeake Bay, according to the meaning of its name, is under the misapprehension
that it too is just a Big River. If the Indian place-names had
any noteworthy virtue, it was their occasional portmanteau
capacity. For instance, Stjukson (now Tucson) somehow
managed to mean "Village of the Shaded Spring at the Foot
of the Mountains." And the Indian names have been put to
at least one extraordinary use, when in 1945 composer Ernst
Krenek used the place-names between Albuquerque and Los
Angeles as lyrics for his *a cappella* chorus, "The Santa Fe
Time Table."

Nowadays an "Indian" place-name is something traditional,
sacrosanct and dear to the hearts of the people who live with
it. As George R. Stewart remarks in his *Names on the Land*,
"People who cherish a name chiefly for such reasons do not
usually like to have it explained or translated." The citizens
of Chicago, especially, do not care to examine too closely into
the origins of the name. The first migrants who settled there
were never quite sure whether the Ojibwa word *She-ka-gong*
meant "Onion River" or "Skunk River" or something really
feculent; but it indubitably meant "Stinking River."

The very vastness of North America, its rapid exploration
and settlement, the multiplicity of new places discovered and
new communities founded—all demanding names—inevitably meant a lot of duplication. Why so many duplicates should
have been kept all this time, though, is not so understandable.
To consider just the town names in just one state: Virginia
today has two New Hopes, two Bethels, two Greendales, two
Midways, two Sandy Points, two Burgesses and a Burgess
Store, one each Mechanicsburg and Mechanicsville, two Dixies,
two Glasgows, two Summits and three Centervilles. Not one
would be worth treasuring, even if it were unique; two or
more of the same are unforgivable. And, as if deliberately
devised to drive postmen insane, the next-door state of West
Virginia also has a Dixie, a Glasgow, a Summit Point and a
Centreville.

Speaking of West Virginia, when the pro-Union mountain
counties of Virginia screwed up the courage to secede from
that state during the Civil War, they couldn't quite screw up
the additional courage to assume a new name at the same
time. They mulled over New Virginia, Kanawha and Alle-
ghany—all too radical!—before settling for the present West
Virginia, a name which is technically inaccurate, as Virginia

extends ninety-five miles farther west than West Virginia does.

The Americans, far from taking steps to weed out the duplicate names and improve the drab ones, have from the earliest days been more inclined to prune and pluck the few really distinctive ones. In Manhattan, the Street that Leads by the Pye Woman long ago became Nassau Street, Smell Street Lane became Broad Street, Tinpot Alley became Edgar Street. Portsmouth, New Hampshire, before it genuflected to the original in England, was Strawbery Banke. Virginia's enchanting Cape Tragbigzanda—named by Captain Smith for his Turkish paramour—became the sycophantic Cape Anne.

Stephen Vincent Benét was one of several poets who have written paeans like, "I have fallen in love with American names, / The sharp names that never get fat. . . ." But he had to delve far inland, to the stomping grounds of the uninhibited frontiersmen, to find sharp names like Medicine Hat and Deadwood and Lost Mule Flat. And trailing the frontiersmen came the euphemizers and the boosters—none of whom seems to have possessed any more wit or imagination than a real-estate promoter.

They brought their Havens and Dales and Glens and Views, all those names that sound like privately incorporated cemeteries. The sharp names that would never get fat got jettisoned instead, for the sake of the "community image." Skunk Grove, Iowa, became Rose Grove. Sodom, Utah, became Goshen. Canada's Pile o'Bones Creek became Regina Creek, and Maggotty Cove became Hoylestown. Even when a developer tried for novelty he often achieved ignorant incongruity. A housing development outside Clifton, New Jersey, for years bore a sign proclaiming itself to be "Sherwood Forest, a Community of Modern Ranch-Style Homes." Jackson Hole, the beautiful and historic rendezvous valley of the rugged Wyoming mountain men, has been deemed by their descendants to sound somewhat indelicate, and so has recently been pruned to just Jackson, WY.

In these flat acres of conformity, the few exotic names shine like good deeds. The French and Spanish place-names particularly, though they may be obvious or even crude descriptives, have acquired a glamour that is lacking in their Anglo-Saxonized counterparts. Prairie du Chien, Wisconsin, is a much more stylish address than Dog Field would be. The Malheur River is more inviting to a fisherman than it would be as the Bad Luck River. Boca Raton, however it got the name, is easier for the Florida Chamber of Commerce to promote than Mouse Mouth would be. Sans Souci sounds far more carefree than its translation, Without Worry (though it is quite often mispelled San Souci, as if to say "Sainted Solicitude").

Of course, the high regard for foreign-language place-names is no guarantee that their inhabitants can pronounce them. I have to confess that my own hometown of Buena Vista is called by everybody there Bew-na Vista. In some places around America a foreign name has actually stuck unrecognized. Ozark is simply a phonetic spelling of the French Aux Arks— a clipped expression meaning "at the place of the Arkansa tribe." And the Lemon Fair River was named by a Vermonter trying to pronounce Les Monts Verts.

But the nice-naming process still goes on. In 1959 an American millionaire bought the 700-acre Hog Island in the Bahamas, intending to set up a luxurious vacation resort there. The first luxury he installed was a new name: Paradise Island. In 1960 the crossroads hamlet of Tightsqueeze, Virginia, got itself into the newspapers by changing its name to Fairview. The citizens were so thrilled at having attained public print for probably the first time in history that they immediately switched the name back to Tightsqueeze, and thereby got into public print for probably the last time in history. The euphemistic name-change is not confined to America. In Russia, for a couple of centuries, four small hamlets bore names which translated as Dog Town, Fool, Flea Nest and Spit. But one day in February 1966, their inhabitants awoke to find themselves living in Spacious, Sunny, Happy Town and Little Cherry, respectively.

Sometimes, though, the process of renaming can actually sharpen up an originally suety name. Marthasville, Georgia, didn't lose anything when the Western & Atlantic Railroad picked it for a terminus and insisted it adopt the coined name of Atlanta. New York's Storm King Mountain certainly sounds much more rugged and craggy than it did as Butter Hill. And some places, originally named with wistful augury, might do well to change to a more realistic label. The mining towns of Happy Hollow and Beauty, in Kentucky, are two of the most dismal, impoverished and ugly specimens of America's "depressed areas."

There are few white blanks left on the world's maps, those tantalizing patches once marked "unexplored." But new names are still frequently required, and the most recent bestowals range all the way from uninspired Levittowns, sprouting like toadstools (housing developments all across the United States, planted by the Levitt corporation), to more imaginative creations like the Valley of Ten Thousand Smokes. This name, though it sounds like one of the Indians' better bequests, was actually coined in 1915 for a valley in Alaska's Katmai region, where a volcanic eruption in that year left the earth pocked and fissured with steaming geysers and jets of smoke.

Although the white gaps in earthly maps are fast giving way to plats as precise and unexciting as croquet lawns, there are still new places waiting to be named elsewhere. In 1959 the Russians sprinkled place-names all over an entire new hemisphere, after one of their space probes photographed the never-before-seen dark side of the moon. Still awaiting the first footfall of man are places like the Soviet Mountains, Mare Moscovianum, Mare Somnil ("Sea of Dreams") and the craters Tsiolkovski, Lomonosov and Joliot-Curie. The rival Westerners got their first chance to bestow a place-name on the moon in 1964, when astronomers convened after the United States' Ranger 7 probe took the earliest close-up photographs of the lunar surface. The area its cameras scrutinized was dubbed Mare Cognitum, "the Known Sea"—and one more blank was no longer.

> I knew then that "w-a-t-e-r" meant the wonderful cool
> something that was flowing over my hand. That living
> word awakened my soul, gave it light, hope, joy, set
> it free! . . . Everything had a name, and each name
> gave birth to a new thought.
>
> —HELEN KELLER

All Things both Great and Small

How did things get their names?

Well, to begin right there, a *thing* in Old Norse was an assemblage of people met to discuss matters of public concern.* The word gradually shifted from the get-together to the discussion itself, thence to the affairs discussed, and so on down to essentials. Now it can be applied to any "thing" from infinite to infinitesimal, from the trivial "thingumajig" to the ungraspable "thing-in-itself" (*Ding an sich,* the Kantian term for a noumenal Something so far beyond human ken that it can never be known).

The name given to a thing sometimes tells us as much about the namer as it does about the thing. The Polynesians call the frigate-bird the *iwa,* meaning "thief." The word may adequately describe the birds' unlovely habits (they steal each other's food, nesting material and even eggs), but the *iwa* birds have no conception of "theft"—the name is more pertinently indicative of the Polynesians' notions of right and wrong. The Shoshonean Indians called the giant condor the "thunderbird," on the assumption that some super-one of its species made the thunder by flapping its wings—thus the name is a revelation of one primitive people's attempt to assign a plausible cause to a seemingly causeless effect.

Not every thing-name, of course, admits of snap analysis. Most such words would require a whole volume apiece to explain the cultural and psychological gestalt of the people who coined them. But even at a glance some thing-names can

* A Scandinavian parliament is still a *Thing* or *Ting*—in Denmark, for instance, it is the *Folketing.*

[163]

give us insights into the personalities of language, and at least a few of them can show us the name-giver at the same time.

For an example, take the scientific thing-name *Vampyrotouthis infernalis*. Taxonomy (the naming of animals and plants to classify them according to phylum, genus, species, etc.) is a determinedly humdrum and unemotional science. But the name *Vampyrotouthis infernalis* translates as "vampire from hell," and reading it we can almost see the shocked and loathing recoil of the first scientist who looked upon this creature. It is a denizen of the ocean deeps, and it deserves the awful appellation. Its black body is covered with flickering green phosphorescence, and on either side of its neck it wears a flashing searchlight. Its head is almost as big as its body; it has multiple rows of white teeth, and its red eyes stare out from a tangle of ten continuously writhing tentacles. The "vampire from hell" would truly be a terrible monster—except that it is rather less than four inches long.

The glossary of thing-names is as vast as the universe. But, for the purpose of using them to sample the personalities of language, a wieldy enough selection can be culled just from the names man has given to his animate co-inheritors of the earth. Man has always been a nature-watcher; among the first things he named must have been the fauna and flora that surrounded him—"and whatsoever Adam called every living creature, that was the name thereof."

Even the flora-fauna category of thing-names would fill several libraries. In the East, there are philosophico-religious cults which have a different term for each separate concentric layer of an onion. But modern science can do even better than that, breaking the onion down into smaller and smaller entities: tissue, carbohydrate, water molecule, hydrogen atom, nucleus, proton. And an onion can be viewed from any number of semantic tangents; to the botanist it is a bulb of the lily family, to the gourmet it's an ambrosial delicacy, to the timid it's a social menace, to the flatulent it's a time bomb, etc.

But one need not explore esoteric byways in order to realize the astronomical varieties of thing-names; they are evident even in everyday usages. A particular family pet, for example, may be simultaneously a dog, a hound, a bitch, a puppy, a Weimaraner (a breed nicknamed by its fanciers the Gray Ghost); it may be registered as something like Lili Marlene von Kristalbach, and answer to something like Poochie. Eight names altogether. Add to these the various epithets a dog can get called from time to time: Man's Best Friend, Nasty Nuisance, Good Dog, Mummy's Ickle Peachums, etc. Then multiply all these by the world's two or three thousand different tongues—the current ones—plus maybe another couple of thousand languages that are now extinct.

And the voluminous roster of any single thing's many names can be complicated even further by changes of word-meaning within each separate language. In Saxon days *hund* was the generic name for all dogs of all breeds everywhere, while *dogga* designated a specific native breed (predecessor of the mastiff). Gradually the two words changed places; today "dog" is the generic term and "hound" refers to a rather limited category of hunting dogs. "Dog" has also come to be applied to other animals as well, to indicate the male of the species, as in dog-fox and dog-wolf.

This is no unique instance; the same sort of change has occurred in many thing-names. "Deer" once meant any kind of wild animal, from a moose to a mouse, and "venison" was any kind of edible game flesh. As "deer" narrowed down to mean what it does today, so did "venison" to mean specifically deer meat.

Nor are things always called by the same name, even at the same time, even in the same language. In different parts of the United States, the same bird is variously a woodpecker or a peckerwood, the same insect is a firefly or a lightning-bug, the mountain lion is variously cougar, puma and catamount. What is a guitarfish in America is a banjo shark in Australia, while the American cat shark is the English dog-fish. What Americans call the English walnut the English call the Welsh nut.

Oscar Wilde's observation that language is the only thing America and Britain don't have in common was inadvertently but amusingly illustrated by the English authors Joan and John Levitt in their otherwise unfaultable book *The Spell of Words.* In their chapter on "The American Language" they pointed out that "new compound words were made by the Americans," and went on to cite instances: "Two names for birds—*katydid* and *whippoorwill*—are made up in imitation of their songs."

I am tempted to reciprocate with a report that the European mangelwurzel gets its name from the slavering noise it makes while rending its prey; but I am reminded of a naïveté of my own, very similar to the Levitts' confusion about the katydid. I worked for a while, in my teens, as a fieldhand on a nursery farm. Once, when the proprietor was away, a woman drove up and asked to buy "some hens and chicks." I told her that we were a plant farm, not a poultry farm. But she persisted in the request, while I kept trying to impress on her that all we sold were flowers and shrubs. We were both exasperated, and convinced of each other's lunacy, when fortunately the boss arrived in time to prevent my losing the sale. "Hens and chicks," I learned to my mortification, is a quite common name for a quite common ground-cover plant.

An animal or plant common to a number of the world's inhabited regions will have many different names, and these will usually vary in meaning or significance according to how that plant or animal is regarded in each separate neighborhood. The English word "grasshopper" is sufficiently and amiably descriptive of that familiar insect. The Italians regard it slightly differently, but still affectionately, as a "little mare" (*cavalletta*), and the Spanish hyperbolize it into a "jump-mountains" (*saltamontes*). But the wee creature seems to have intimidated the stalwart Germans; their name for it, *die Heuschrecke*, means roughly "the terrible-hay-thing."

A single thing can also be variously regarded, and named, by different sections of the same society. The American flower known to florists and dandies as the "bachelor's button," a jaunty blue boutonniere, is known to farmers as the "bluebottle," a pestiferous weed that strangles their cornfields. Even when a thing is called by the same name by all speakers of a language, it can have differing connotations for different groups of them. For an oft-repeated example, take Dr. Johnson's definition of oats: "a grain which in England is generally given to horses, but in Scotland supports the people."

About the only thing-names which have a readily recognizable similarity in several different languages are those which imitate the sound a creature makes. The cuckoo's call is echoed in the Greek *kokkux*, the Italian *cuculo*, French *coucou*, Spanish *cuclillo*, German *Kuckuck*, Swedish *gök*, Danish *gøg* and Dutch *koekoek*. The owl's hoot is heard, with somewhat more variation, in the Greek *glaux*, the Italian *gufo*, French *hibou*, Spanish *buho*, German *Eule*, Swedish *uggla*, Danish *ugle* and Dutch *uil*. (The Finns were more impressed by the bird's unblinking solemnity; they call the owl *pöllö*, "the starer.") Another bird's distinctive cry earned it an echoic name in one language and a rather derisive descriptive in another. The Australian aborigines called the bird the *kookaburra;* later English settlers called it the "laughing jackass."

Animals and plants have been named for just about every imaginable reason, from their physical appearance to their hermitlike nonappearance. An instance of the latter is the "seventeen-year locust," which spends that long underground before making its unwelcome debut. The dandelion is one of many plants named for its appearance, that is, for its jagged-edged "lion's-tooth" leaves. In German the plant is *Löwen-zahn*, which means the same thing. Although we English-speakers call it by a Frenchified name (from *dent-de-lion*, courtesy of the Normans), the French themselves call it rather less cutely *pissenlit*—"wet-the-bed"—a presumed nocturnal result of eating it at dinner time.

The ostrich was once known descriptively as the "sparrow-camel." The giraffe's modern name is a corruption of the Arabic, but its popular descriptive name in earlier times was "camelopard," meaning that it was as big as a camel and spotted like a leopard. At the same time, the leopard's name was something of an indictment of its parents' supposed promiscuity; the animal was believed to have been born from the miscegenation of a lion (*leo*) and a panther (*pardalus*).

Things named for their real or imagined personality include the pansy, dodo and pug. The French thought the pansy looked pensive (*pensée*, "meditation"). The Portuguese who first visited Mauritius found the island's unique indigenous bird mainly unique for its clumsy helplessness, and named it "stupid" (*doudo*). The frisky little dog's name, pug, is cognate with Puck, the pooka, the bugaboo and numerous other goblins who derived their titles from the Greek *kobalos* ("sprite"). The "kissing bug" sounds like a cuddlesome creature, but a South American insect (the triatomid, an inch-long variety of bedbug) actually got that name because it prefers to bite people in the soft tissue around the lips or eyes—and its "kiss" imparts a most unlovable disease.

Some things were stuck, deservedly or not, with names that are rather less than polite. The shitepoke is so called because the bird allegedly empties its bowels when it is startled. The name of the partridge comes ultimately from a Greek word meaning "fart"—presumably because of the loud boom its wings make when it suddenly breaks from cover. The wild arum lily which Americans call jack-in-the-pulpit is known in parts of Britain as priest's-pintle, the latter word an Anglo-Saxonism for "penis."

The terrier was named for its usefulness. The word comes from the French for "hillock," because the dog's hunting role was to burrow for game that had gone to earth. Another creature named for its use is the "oil bird" of northern South America. It feeds on the oleaginous seeds of palm trees, and gets so greasily fat itself that the natives render it into oil to be used for fuel.

Two things named for the aftereffect of their use are the

"dead man's vine" and the "dummy's plant." The first grows in Colombia, where it is called *ayahuasco* by the Indians who use it in their magico-religious rituals. A sip of its brew sends the drinker into a maniacal fury and then into death-like coma. The *planta del mudo,* a Venezuelan herb, is supposed to have the faculty, when chewed, of rendering its user totally dumb for two days.

Many things are named for their resemblance to something else. The name orangoutang comes from the Malayan *oran utan,* "man of the woods." The word "lobster" is a derivative melding of two other words, one Latin (*locusta*) meaning "locust," the other Anglo-Saxon (*loppe*) meaning "spider." New England lobstermen still call that shellfish familiarly a "bug." The orchid is so named because its root resembles the human male gonads (from the Greek *orchis,* "testicle"). The "elephant shrew" is only three inches long, but it has a flexible proboscis; the "elephant's ear" is an ornamental plant with immense leaves; the "elephant's foot" is a vine with a massive rootstock.

The pineapple would appear to have no connection whatever with either a pine or an apple; why then the appellation? In olden times an "apple" was any kind of fruit or fruitlike growth, so the pine tree's cones were the original "pineapples." When the tropical fruit was discovered it was given the name because its shape and stiff scales resembled the pine cone's. But the resemblance inspiring a thing-name need not be physical. For other but quite cogent reasons the shark is called in several languages the "tiger of the sea." Surprisingly, some American Indian tribes which frequented inland areas and could hardly have been very well acquainted with the sea, were at least familiar enough with the temperament of its sharks that they named the rattlesnake the "little shark of the woods."

The resemblance between two similarly named things is sometimes so slight (or slighting to one of them) as to cast suspicion on the namers' eyesight or intelligence. The early English explorers in America came across a brand-new bird, big and handsome, magnificent in flight, in plumage and in the roasting pan. It deserved an equally magnificent name and, had it got one, it would probably be the "national bird" of the United States today. But the Englishmen, woefully unoriginal, named this new wonder after a scrawny sort of guinea fowl they had known in Europe. They called it a turkey.

Of all the things named for their coloration—blue jay, redwood, brown trout, coal-black flower-piercer, etc.—the penguin got its name (meaning "white head") from a people who never laid eyes on it. Breton fishermen trawling the Newfoundland banks gave the name (*pen gouin*) to a large, white-headed diving bird they found there. Much later, explorers in the Southern Hemisphere borrowed the name "penguin" for the fairly similar diving birds of those seas. Eventually the northern bird surrendered the name entirely and itself became an auk (from the Old Norse, meaning "fisher").

Things named for their aroma include stinking smut (a wheat fungus) and several varieties of stinkbug, stinkweed and stinkwood, plus some pleasanter things like sweet alyssum, spicewood, lemon verbena and babies'-breath. But the skunk, nonpareil of the odoriferous, got its name not so much from its scent as from its method of dispensing it. The various original Algonquian names (it was *asakunkuo* in Occaneechee, *segonku* in Abnaki, etc.) all appear to have derived from a root word meaning "urinator." This is also the meaning of "pismire," Anglo-Saxon name for one sort of ant.

Some animals are named for their favorite food. (So are a few plants, e.g., the "Venus's fly-trap.") In Italy there is the *beccafico,* or "peck-a-fig" bird. The "drugstore beetle" could ostensibly eat right through an entire apothecary shelf; it has been known to eat liniments, narcotics and lethal poisons with every appearance of enjoyment. The European polecat has no connection with poles; the name comes from the same source as "poultry," that being its favored prey.

Other things are named for their favorite habitats. The hippopotamus' name means literally "river horse." There is the moor hen and the chimney swift. There is watercress and land cress. The name salamander is the oddest of this category, in the way it came to be bestowed on a small, lizardlike amphibian. In the sixteenth century, the alchemist Paracelsus borrowed the name of a mythological Greek monster, the *salamandra,* to denote the "vital spirit" of fire (the *Ding an sich* of it, so to speak). Each of the other elements, according to him, had a similar life-spirit; the "undine" of water, the "gnome" of earth and the "sylph" of air. Paracelsus never succeeded in isolating the salamander or any other of these invisible entities. But his theory was widely known, and somewhere, sometime, an outdoorsman must have laid a stick on his campfire without noticing that it bore a stick-colored little creature frozen into camouflaging immobility. Then, presumably, the heat stirred the animal, and the man first descried it when it began to run desperately back and forth on its burning stick. Behold, here was a fire-born animal, or at least a fire-dwelling one—here was a salamander.

(For a long time, asbestos was thought to be the wool or the feathers of the salamander.)

Several specimens of fauna and flora have been named out of sheer admiration: the bird of paradise, the beam of the sun (one Indian name for the hummingbird), the angelfish, the iris (Greek for "rainbow"). And others have been named out of pure revulsion: the sloth, the devilfish, the black widow, viper's bugloss, the glutinous hag, the jackal (from the Turkish for "scavenger"). But some of the thing-names in this class describe characteristics that are hard to see in the things themselves. The horrid-sounding "mad-dog skullcap" is nothing but a mild, meek variety of mint. And the *Calliphora erythrocephala*, which means "red-headed bringer of beauty," is the hairy, nasty, carrion-loving, big blue blowfly.

One approach to thing-naming is the old one of timid euphemism: giving a dangerous animal a sweet and, it is to be hoped, soothing name. Since Saxon times, the English have known the bear only as a zoo or carnival exhibit, so it wears a merely descriptive name ("bear," like "beaver," comes from an older word meaning "brown"). But in early times in Britain the animal roamed wild, so the Celts' name for it was an inoffensive palliative on the order of "honey-eater." In northern lands the bear has remained until recent times a predator to be reckoned with, and so the Finnish euphemism is still in use there today: "honey-paw."

A great many things have been named by mistake or misapprehension. The dog called Great Dane is innocently wearing an alias; the breed was actually developed in Germany. The German shepherd is properly an Alsatian. And the canary bird wears a dog's name; it was so called for its native Canary Islands, and they got their name (from *canis*) because of the packs of wild dogs found there. The Spanish shark was so named because it made an unprecedented appearance in northern American waters in 1898—its usual habitat being the Caribbean—and the belief was that it had been driven northward by the concussion of artillery fire from the Spanish-American War then going on in Cuba.

To a Virginia Indian *powcohickora* was a gooey paste made of mashed nuts, any sort of nuts. But the white settlers mistook the name to mean the nut itself, one specific variety of nut, and applied the name—first as "pokickery," then "pohickery," finally "hickory"—to the whole of a certain tree.

Other things have been named for their places of origin— the Scotch terrier, the Japanese beetle, the pekingese, the spaniel (Spain). The cantaloupe came from Cantalupo, Italy; currants came from Corinth; tangerines came from Tangier.

The jimson weed was originally the Jamestown weed, named by the starving colonists there who desperately tried eating it, and discovered that it provided more hallucinations than calories.

The tarantula spider got its name from Taranto, Italy, and proceeded to write that name large in history. In the sixteenth and seventeenth centuries, Italy was the source of dancing manias that sporadically swept all Europe. Individuals or the populations of whole towns would suddenly start dancing and continue until they dropped. Contemporary observers, unable to account for the phenomenon, put the blame on the tarantula's bite and called the hysteria "tarantism." The word is still medical terminology for a fit of uncontrollable dancing, and a fast, whirling Italian dance of modern times is reminiscently called the *tarantella*.

Mispronunciation, mistranslation and folk-etymology can account for some offbeat thing-names, bestowed when people of one language discovered a foreign novelty and attempted to naturalize its foreign name. The Norse word for a certain domesticated deer was *hreinn,* meaning that specific kind of deer. The English amplified the name into "reindeer," which would thus literally mean "reindeer-deer." The African animal called by the Khoi-Khoin the *ngu* was not much improved in its English rendition, "gnu." (The Boers did rather better; in Afrikaans the animal is a *wildebeest*.)

Consider the tomato. Spanish explorers discovered it in Mexico, where it was called *tomatl,* and took it home as the *tomate.* When the Italians imported the plant from Spain they called it *pommo dei Mori,* "apple of the Moors." The French got it next, and folk-etymologized the Italian name into *pomme d'amour*—"love apple"—which one might regard as typical of the Gallic turn of mind. This mistranslation engendered a whole aphrodisiac legend about the tomato which persisted into the nineteenth century. Meanwhile, the Germans in turn translated the French tomato into *Paradiesapfel,* evidently deeming it the fruit that had tempted Eve. Since those days, the Italian word has shrunk into today's *pomodoro,* which could quite legitimately translate as "golden apple," and seemingly involve the tomato in the Helen of Troy legend as well.

As we have seen in earlier chapters, folk-etymology often substitutes a familiar word or sound for a homophonic foreign one, whether or not the sense is anywhere near the same. For example, the plant called in English "wormwood" is neither wormy nor woody; its original Teutonic name was *wermut,* from *wer,* "man," and *mut,* "courage," indicating its stimulating qualities in beverage form. The Abnaki Indians called a certain river rodent the *muskwessu,* "it is red." The white man elided this into "musquash" and then folk-etymologized that into "muskrat," on the evidence of the animal's musky odor and ratlike appearance. In early France, a certain freshwater crustacean was called a *crevice.* This was itself a misnomer, as the word already meant "crab," which this thing wasn't. But when the English took over the word, they heard a "fish" in the second syllable and so the creature became a "crayfish." Later, American folk-etymology changed the first syllable, on the analogy of "crawl," and made the thing a "crawfish."

One such word-change converted a real animal into a fabulous monster. The animal was the crocodile, and its original name was the Greek *krokodilos,* rather an understatement, meaning "gravel-worm." This became *crocodilus* in Latin, but was often miswritten by medieval bestiarists as *cocodryllus,* and was translated into the popular languages as *cocodrilo, cocadrile* and eventually *cockatrice.* Now, not many people had ever seen a cockatrice—that is, a crocodile—but they had heard it was a sort of monster reptile. And popular mythology already included a monster reptile, the basilisk, which according to tradition was hatched from a cock's egg (*oeuf coquatri*). The common man could see a cock (or *coq*) in the name of the cockatrice; the natural assumption was that this creature must be the basilisk under a sobriquet. Thus the cockatrice (now equipped with the basilisk's supposed power of killing with a glance) got into mythology, and stayed there even long after the real crocodile had got into natural history under its own name.

The Western world's mythology is full of imaginary creatures, and some of their names are as well known as those of any real beings—the sphinx, dragon, phoenix, unicorn, werewolf, etc. Theologians have been trying for centuries to validate two biblical beasts, the behemoth and the leviathan. The former is generally presumed to have been the hippopotamus (Egyptian *p-ehe-meu,* "water ox"), and the latter a whale. But there have been multitudes of other fantastics which enjoyed less renown.

There was the manticore (from a Persian word meaning "man-eater"), which had a lion's body, a scorpion's tail and a human head. There was the yale, a sort of antelope with movable horns, like directional antennae. There was the bishop-fish, which wore a miter, cowl and gown all made of scales and fins. Even less familiar to us now are the legendary creatures of other cultures—e.g., the *makara* of India, which could be part-elephant, part-fish, or almost any other amalgam of animal components; the *cigouave* of Haiti, a voodoo beast similar to the manticore; the Melanesians' *thu,* a three-legged, fork-tailed human female with one green and one red eye; and the Cree Indians' *wendigo,* an indescribable night-prowling thing whose skin oozed blood.

Some of these nonexistent beings have actually come into reality, or at least have bequeathed their names to reality. The amphisbaena, a mythical serpent with a head at both ends, gave its name to a real tropical lizard whose stumpy tail looks very much like its head end. The Norwegians invented a sea monster called the *kraken;* the name has become a synonym for the giant squid. There is a European wild goose still called the barnacle goose. Tit for tat, there is a gooseneck barnacle. This crustacean, when its neck is extended, does vaguely resemble a goose; for this reason (and because the geese were migratory and never seen to breed in Europe), the belief was that the birds were merely grownup barnacles. One medieval naturalist wrote that the barnacles "hang by their beaks, like seaweeds attached to timber. Being in process of time well covered with feathers, they either fall into the water or take their flight in the free air."

A scrivener who wanted to describe a mythical animal, or a limner who wanted to draw one, often had to depend on its name for clues to its appearance. A unicorn, for example, was undeniably a creature with "one horn," but that left a lot of leeway. Medieval naturalists presented it in every guise from a "very small animal like a kid" and a "one-horned ass" to a "monster with a horrible howl, with a horse-like body, with feet like an elephant." So folk-etymology came to be as imaginative as folklore. According to T. H. White's translation of a twelfth-century bestiary, bees were called *apes* in Latin "either because they cling to things with their feet (*a pedibus*) or else because they are born without feet, for they only grow their feet and wings later on."

Indeed, folk-etymology has not always been just an attempt to explain some oddment of folklore. It has often been the operative *cause* of that folklore—as in the queer case of the beaver, or *castor,* as it is called in Latin.

In early times this animal's testicles were more valuable than its fur; they yielded an oil, castoreum, used in making medicines and perfumes. Overzealous etymologists confused the words *castor* and *castrare,* and therefrom got the notion that a castor was so called because it would readily castrate itself. According to bestiarists who followed this theory, the beaver was intelligent enough to know that any pursuing hunter was mainly interested in its testicles, and so would nip them off itself, drop them in the hunter's path and thus save itself from capture or death. One fabulist even averred that if a beaver, having already pulled this trick once, was again cornered by a hunter, it would hoist its tail and *point* to its missing privates so the man would let it go in peace. These rather poignant little tales did have some small plausibility; a beaver's testicles being internal, it really doesn't appear to have any.

Some of the creatures of legend, though never more than names, have left odd implantations in mankind's memory. The mermaid was remarkable for three things: her beauty, her tail and her fey propensity for seducing human males (a hobby which she shared with those other sea-beings, sirens and undines). Seafarers really believed they had seen mermaids; nowadays we know that what they must have seen were dugongs, or sea-cows. These creatures do have two breasts, they do sometimes rear upright at the ocean surface, and from a distance they could have looked human. A close-up glimpse of a dugong is enough to evaporate the mermaid legend—the sea-cow is as ugly as the sea-maiden was beautiful—but a vestige of the old belief persisted in at least one area. Until very recent times, any fisherman of the Indian Ocean who caught a dugong and hauled it to market had to take oath, before he was allowed to sell it, that he and the beast had not indulged in sexual intercourse.

Probably the oddest of all the creatures in the mythological menagerie was the Jenny Haniver. That was the generic name for a corpse, or mummy, of an animal that had been in life quite real and ordinary, but masqueraded after death as any one of the whole zoo of unreal and extraordinary monsters.

Jenny Haniver was a sailor's prank. Seamen on long voyages, bored with carving scrimshaw or tattooing themselves, were ever eager for a diversion and ever on the lookout for some prize that promised profit. In almost any waters a man could drop a line and land himself a skate or ray or manta. With a sharp knife and a bit of imagination, a man could perform interesting plastic surgery on these big pancake-shaped creatures: carve and nick and twist it just so, and leave it in the sun. With the proper manipulation as it dried, the heavy leathery skin would harden into some fantastic shape. Thus the sailors brought home and sold to credulous collectors the guaranteed mummies of honest-to-god basilisks, bishop-fish, monkey-fish, mermaids and even dragons.

The tomfoolery went on for some three hundred years between the thirteenth and sixteenth centuries. There is no

All Things both Great and Small

knowing exactly when the homefolks began to suspect the fakes, or exactly why they took to calling them Jenny Hanivers. It has been suggested that the "Haniver" is a corruption of "Antwerp," that being probably the busiest seaport of the time.

But even the Jenny Hanivers had their sentimental value. The town of Bregenz, Austria, acquired one—the "mummy of a mermaid"—in the thirteenth century, and hung it in a street archway. When, after six hundred years or so, the thing began to succumb to decay, the town fathers had an exact stone replica made to take its place. At last report the statue was still there.

But the legendary animals were finally so thoroughly debunked that natural scientists were unprepared to recognize some of the real oddities that did and do exist in our world. When the first cadaver of a duck-billed platypus was sent from Australia to England, the zoologists there flatly declared it a fake.

The practice of making up names for made-up animals, and vice versa, does not belong entirely to the Dark Ages. The early American outdoorsmen did it too. There were enough unfamiliar animals in the country anyway; people were generally ready to believe in any new one, however weird. Texas had the galliwampus, described by O. Henry as a mammal with fins on its back and eighteen toes to its feet. Vermont had the guyascutus, a breed of cow with shorter legs on one side, developed so it could circumambulate the steep New England hills. (In this it was similar to a western beast, the sidehill-dodger.) The guyascutus, according to Charles E. Brown, "is never seen except after a case of snake-bite." There was the beazel, a fur-bearing trout; the canteen-fish, which carried its own water; and the sugerino, a corkscrew-shaped worm whose life work was letting the water out of irrigation ditches.

Then there was the sooner. Mencken described this as a breed of dog "so bellicose that it would sooner fight than eat." But here, for once, the Sage of Baltimore may have been deceived by a politely euphemistic sham. I always heard of the sooner as a hound too lazy to be housebroken; that is, he'd sooner do it indoors than go out in the yard.

Some of the mythical beings man has invented were superstitious delusions, others were merely humorous diversions. But whether they mark man as ignorant or imaginative, they also proclaim the power that sheer language holds over him. Once a notional name has been invented, or an idea verbalized—no matter how nonsensical it might be—he has been

[175]

as reluctant to let go of the word as of any other treasure he has ever found or made. And holding on to the word has too often meant holding to the rationale built around it. For a simplistic example, one name for the dragonfly is "devil's darning needle"; ergo, rustics tell their children it will sew their eyelids closed if they don't watch out.

This tendency to explication has been a harmless quirk in the case of pretty legends like the mermaid. It has been something else in the case of baneful bugaboos like the wendigo and werewolf. And, while man has outgrown many of his infantile fears, he has not yet outgrown that primitive regard for the word as an entity in itself. We have seen, in the chapters on euphemism and obscenity, how readily man will delude or frighten himself by perceiving mirages in inert sounds and symbols. We will go further into that trait of human personality in the closing chapter of this book.

But first let's look at a few other, more lightsome, gladsome and utilitarian uses to which language has been put.

Papa belong me-fella, you stop long heaven. All 'e
sanctu 'im name belong you. Kingdom belong you 'e
come. All 'e hear 'im talk belong you long ground
all-same long heaven. Today givem kaikai belong day
long me-fella. Forgive 'im wrong belong me-fella, all
same me-fella forgive 'im wrong all 'e makem long
me-fella. You no bringem me-fella long try 'im. Take
'way somet'ing no-good long me-fella. Amen.

—THE LORD'S PRAYER

Pidgin English and Pig Latin

IF a professional linguist were to be set down suddenly in
a strange country, he'd probably have enough training in
linguistic fundamentals to grasp the new language fairly
quickly. But a layman in similar circumstances would either
have to find some short cut to communication or suffer all the
handicaps of a deaf-mute. And many times laymen *have* found
themselves in just that helplessly speechless predicament.
Necessity being the mother of invention, they have created
whole new languages—on the spot and on the spur of the
moment, one might say, considering the centuries of gesta-
tion a language usually requires. An informal, short-cut communication like this is variously called *lingua franca*, compromise language, contact vernacular or trade language, but
is best known as "pidgin."

The earliest compromise language of which we have record
was that compounded by Mediterranean traders in about the
ninth century. Common to seamen from all the countries
ringing the sea—Spanish, French, Greek, Italian, Arab—this
was the original *lingua franca* (because the Arabs called all
non-Muslims "Franks"). That tongue, known to its speakers
as Sabir, was still in use until the seventeenth century, and
the Maltese language still retains traces of it. A similar makeshift was the polyglot jargon with which the Crusaders made
themselves understood in the various countries they crossed
during their eleventh-century expeditions to the Holy Land.

But the pidgin that is most in use today, and most familiar to the rest of the world, is the variety born on the China coast three hundred years ago, when the Western nations first began to trade there.

Most laymen call it "pidgin-English" and all they know of it is the Chinese laundryman's traditional "no tickee, no shirtee." But it is not just a quaint or comic relic of the old opium-and-warlord days. This particular pidgin is a language both viable and valuable and although it is variously ignored, derided and marked for extinction, it quietly continues to gather converts throughout a good part of the world, and could even become a new weapon of the Cold War.

This variety of pidgin came into being because the crewmen of merchant vessels visiting China, and the staffs of trading posts set up there, were disinclined to bother learning Chinese, and the Chinese saw little sense in the involved grammatical locutions of the traders' languages. The representatives of the two cultures compromised by adopting the Westerners' words and adapting them to Chinese syntax. The resultant amalgam became known to both parties as "business" language or—because the closest a Chinese could come to pronouncing "business" was "bishin" or "bijin"—eventually "pidgin." Other varieties of the language are known in some parts of the Pacific as *bêche-de-mer* and beach-la-mar, both of these names folk-etymologized from the Portuguese *bicho-de-mar* ("sea worm," a marine slug prized as a table delicacy in China, and a staple of trade there). Elsewhere, the language is sometimes scornfully called Beachcomber's English or Sandalwood English.

The pidgin of the coast trade gradually became an admixture of English and Portuguese words (these two nationalities having been the earliest traders), of Chinese words, and a sprinkling from other languages—German, Bengali, Malayan, French—all of them subtly transmuted by the vagaries of pronunciation.

Thus we have the word "cumshaw," ubiquitous in the Orient, meaning gratuity or bribe or rake-off. The expression was originally "come ashore money," a sailor's tip to the launch boatman. "Savvy," meaning to comprehend, is a corruption of the Portuguese or Spanish *sabe*. The word "chow" comes from the Chinese *ch'ao*, meaning to fry or broil. "Joss," indicating something holy, was originally either the Portuguese *deus* or Spanish *dios*. "Pickaninny" was the Portuguese *pequeninho*, meaning small, and is used in pidgin languages from the South Pacific to South Africa to mean also child or offshoot. Other pidginisms that now spice the English language include "look-see," "Stateside," "can do," "no can do," "make do" and "long time no see."

Another form of pidgin developed along the same lines in Australia, where exiled British convicts were among the first settlers to consort with the aborigines. Still another variety of pidgin was spread among the island chains of Polynesia and Melanesia by sealing and whaling fleets and the "blackbirding" slave hunters.

One edition of the *Encyclopaedia Britannica* dismisses pidgin as "a weed-grown jargon . . . filled with nursery imbecilities, vulgarisms and corruptions," but has to concede that it is "above all, utilitarian." L. and M. S. Herman, in their book *Foreign Dialects*, more charitably characterize it as "a sort of shorthand language." Pidgin's prime virtue is its extreme simplicity. Each variety has a vocabulary borrowed from foreign languages (predominantly English, by now) consisting of anywhere from 400 to 1,000 nouns, 40 to 50 verbs, 100 or so adjectives, pronouns and adverbs—the whole given its distinctive flavor by the inclusion of some 40 to 50 common native words.

To be sure, pidgin's limited vocabulary can engender some laughable quotations, such as the oft-reprinted and probably apocryphal description of a piano by a New Guinea native: "Him big-fella box, you fight 'im, 'e cry." Or the classic announcement by a Chinese servant that his master's prize sow had given birth to a litter: "Him cow pig have kittens." And in some situations the language is admittedly unwieldy, not to say dangerous. A special handbook issued to American and Australian troops in the Pacific during World War II instructed guards to phrase their "Halt or I'll fire!" in this manner: "You-fella you stand fast. You no can walkabout. Suppose you-fella walkabout me kill 'im you long musket." If the trespasser *did* turn out to be an enemy, chances are the guard wouldn't get to finish that oration.

But pidgin's seemingly imprecise vocabulary can be almost poetic at times. There could hardly be, in any language, a friendlier definition of a friend than the Australian aborigine's "him brother belong me." Or consider his description of the sun: "lamp belong Jesus." Pidgin can be forthright, too. An Aussie policeman is "gubmint catchum-fella." An elbow is "screw belong arm." Whiskers are "grass belong face." When a man gets old, he is "no more too much strong." When he's thirsty, "him belly allatime burn." When he's angry, "him proper hot inside head." An onion is "apple belong stink" and perfume is "water belong stink."

Those who deride pidgin as "baby talk" have the erroneous

idea that they can speak it merely by tossing off an occasional "catchee" and "allasamee." But despite its simplicity and its lack of familiar textbook grammar, each pidgin tongue does have a set vocabulary and rules of construction which do take a little while to learn. The ignorant tourist who bellows his conception of pidgin-English at a bewildered Noumean stall-keeper might just as well be fulminating in Swahili.

There do not yet exist any definitive textbooks or comprehensive dictionaries of any variety of pidgin—and the otherwise omnifarious Berlitz does not teach any of them. So about the only way to learn pidgin is to go and live among the people who use it daily. American GIs of World War II spoke it to the natives of the South Pacific. Others encountered it, and made use of it, during the Japanese Occupation, the Korean and Vietnam Wars.

One incident from my own stay in Korea illustrates several salient features of the language form. A young lady of Taegu once had occasion to ask me, "Hey, you PX go mo s'kosh', catch me Grennecks?"

"Grennecks?" I said, puzzled. I had understood most of her request, but I'd never heard of that last; it sounded like a breakfast cereal. "What means Grennecks?"

"*Grennecks!*" she repeated, exasperated at my thickness. She spent some time making descriptive gestures and repeating the word. Finally she had to go next door and borrow a box of it from a neighbor, to enlighten me. It was a box of Kleenex.

Her request translates as "Hey, if you're going to the Post Exchange anytime soon, how about bringing me a box of Kleenex?" This demonstrates how pidgin adopts only the most basic verbs ("go"), and utilizes only one tense (the present); how one verb ("catch") can serve for infinite different meanings—get, fetch, buy, bring (it can also mean "sleep with"), etc. The little speech also demonstrates how pidgin borrows and transmutes foreign words. "Mo s'kosh'" is a slight elision of the Japanese *mo sukoshi*, literally "soon a little," and is used here to mean shortly, soon or a little while. "Grennecks" is of course a mere mispronunciation, partly because of the Korean inability to enunciate the *l* sound.

While the several varieties of pidgin are superficially alike in that they lack case, gender, tense and number, they differ in such areas as intonation patterns and use of "function words." More important, each such language must rely on word order to make sense, and that word order is determined by the syntax of the native language which serves as its foundation. Thus it would not be possible for, say, a Taiwan Chinese and a Melanesian Kanaka to chat together in their different pidgins, any more than they could in their separate native tongues. But even so, pidgin has on occasion been the sole means of contact among widely disparate cultures. There is the story of an English consul in China who was once asked to officiate at the wedding of a young Danish sailor and a Chinese girl—no one of the three knowing the others' languages. Accordingly, the English official said to the bride:

"This man wantchee take you home-side makee wife-pidgin. Can do, no can do?"

Said she demurely, "Can do," and the consul pronounced them man and wife.

Considering the sort of tramps who were the original progenitors of pidgin—illiterate seamen, uncouth convicts and piratical slavers—and considering the sort of locutions the American troops have contributed since then, it is hardly surprising that pidgin is lacking in high-toned elegance and is replete with impolite vulgarisms. For example, here's how to ask the way to the men's room in one pidgin dialect: "House peck peck, 'e stop where?" A Solomon Islands chieftain, watching U.S. Navy ships offload vast mountains of supplies onto a beach during World War II, was moved to mutter, "Mission fella, 'im 'e say God make everyt'ing. Bullshit. Amer'ca make everyt'ing."

However, most such vulgarisms are used innocently, either as simple intensives or with meanings far different from their originals. (A building's foundation is "arse belong house.") It's not too easy to cuss in pidgin, but it's easy to pray. The Roman Catholic Mission in New Guinea has published since 1935 the monthly magazine *Frend Belong Me* ("My Friend"), written entirely in a phonetic pidgin. It contains religious articles, jokes, fairy tales, even crossword puzzles. The mission also publishes pidgin Bibles, songbooks, prayer books, etc. Far from losing any beauty or sanctity in translation, these Gospel tracts often exhibit a childlike purity and refreshing viewpoint. For example, the book of biblical stories *Jesus Is Our Leader* is titled in pidgin *Yesus em i forman belong yumi*, or "Jesus, him the foreman belong you-me."

Pidgin, in one form or another, is still the *lingua franca* of a goodly portion of the Pacific lands. Its usefulness cannot be slighted—the natives of the Papua-New Guinea area alone speak more than seven hundred tongues, but are enabled to converse and trade by means of one pidgin common to them all. Young men from New Guinea's most backward backcountry tribes often set out to seek their fortune by first deliberately committing some crime serious enough to merit a few years' sentence in a white man's jail. The imprisonment affords an ambitious man the chance to learn the ways of civilization and, most important, to become fluent in pidgin. Thus highly educated, his future success is assumed a certainty.

Pidgin is omitted from most lists of the world's principal languages. But various researchers have estimated that from 30 to 50 million people now speak some variety of the language, either solely or as an adjunct to their native tongue. Even if we accept the smallest estimate, the collective pidgin language should rank about twentieth among humanity's tongues, sharing the place with such others as Polish and Korean. Or, to put it another way, more earthlings speak pidgin than speak Norwegian, Greek, Armenian, Hebrew, Albanian, Estonian, Latvian and Lithuanian *combined.*

And yet many linguists and ethnologists have long refused to acknowledge pidgin *as* a language. Tourists abroad have regarded it merely as "cute." Colonial administrators have long sought to supplant it with their Old World tongues. It has traditionally been the language one used to lackeys, not to equals. Just a generation ago, a British Army officer remarked, with a pomposity worthy of a Colonel Blimp, that the pidgin tongue "usually takes a form in which the language of the ruling or more powerful race is adapted to that of the ruled or weaker race."

But at least one variety of pidgin has quite recently achieved dignity and status for itself, with the emergence of Indonesia as an independent republic after World War II. What is now the official language there, "Bahasa Indonesian," was originally a kind of pidgin, and perhaps the oldest of them all. Centuries before the Europeans arrived in that part of the world, Arabian and Malay traders were using a very simplified, pidginized form of Malayan as a trade language among Indonesia's many islands, cultures and tongues.

When the Dutch colonized Indonesia in the seventeenth and eighteenth centuries, they found this so-called Bazaar Malay to be the only tongue common to all their holdings, and so formalized it as the official administrative language (only changing its written form from Arabic to Roman script). Now independent and fiercely nationalistic, the islands are proud of their Bahasa Indonesian. But the fact that it *was* legislated onto them by their former governors is certainly one factor in the Indonesians' anti-Dutch (even anti-Western) feeling, and in their 1969 success in ousting the Dutch from New Guinea, the Netherlands' last foothold in that area.

Pidgin has long been in use, unhonored and unsung, in some of the United States' far-flung Pacific protectorates. But since 1959 pidgin has rightfully been entitled to call itself a part of the American language. That is to say, pidgin is right now a working and workaday tongue in Hawaii, the newest of the fifty states.

A correspondent writes me, "The island pidgin draws its rich and varied vocabulary from many sources—Hawaiian, Samoan, Japanese, Chinese, Korean, several Philippine dialects, Portuguese, and God knows what else, strung on a frame of more-or-less English. Much of the business of the islands is conducted in it. My wife, who nursed in a plantation hospital on Oahu at one time, still recalls her shock at hearing the doctor address the workers in pidgin. The 'innocent vulgarisms' made quite an impression on ears fresh from Philadelphia."

Lately, in their rampant concern about equality for all mankind, the Western world's policy-makers have become ashamed of pidgin, as a reminder of the ugly old caste system, and now seek to uproot it. In this latter-day compulsion to "civilize" every backward nation in sight, pidgin is invariably considered one of the first backwardnesses to be jettisoned. This could prove to be a mistake.

In 1953 a United Nations Trusteeship Council investigated conditions in the Australian Mandate of New Guinea, and proceeded to recommend—among other suggested improvements—that the pidgin language in use there be abolished and gradually supplanted by English. Among the immediate and vociferous dissenters was Cornell professor Robert A. Hall, Jr., who championed the existing order in a book entitled *Hands Off Pidgin English!* In summing up all the arguments for (and the trivial few against) the use of Melanesian pidgin, he pointed out that the normal New Guinea native can learn pidgin well enough in six months to begin instruction as a medical assistant. To achieve a command of English sufficient to undertake the same instruction would require five or six years.

Professor Hall contends that a hortatory use of pidgin could be a factor in the Cold War struggle for supremacy in the Far East. Pidgin is as fluent a language for preaching doctrine as it is for preaching religion or hygiene. During the many years it would take the Westerners to teach English to any or all of the Pacific peoples, Communist infiltrators speaking the familiar old pidgin would have plenty of time to propagandize, indoctrinate and convert those same peoples. If it would make the UN feel better about retaining pidgin as the language of Melanesia, suggests Professor Hall, some of the taint of caste-symbol might be removed by renaming the language Modern Melanesian or Neo-Melanesian.

Still, by any name it has ever known—pidgin, beach-la-mar, Beachcomber's English, weed-grown jargon, baby talk, or whatever—the Pacific pidgin appears to be here to stay for a while, beyond the powers of prohibition of any paper edict. English is now, by UN proclamation, the official language of New Guinea's trust territory. But in 1962, when the UN invited one of the native members of its Trusteeship Council— a prosperous copra planter named Somu Sigob—to address a meeting at the New York headquarters, he nonplused the delegates by addressing them in pidgin.

There have been many other pidgins besides the Pacific varieties, and some of those, too, are still in use. French colonials developed an African pidgin (Petit-Nègre) on that continent and disseminated it, via the slave trade, to the West Indies and Louisiana, where it became known as Creole. Only traces survive in the Louisiana dialects, but in Haiti it is the everyday language of the lower classes. What might be called Dutch Creole is still spoken in the Dutch West Indies, and a Portuguese Creole in the Cape Verde Islands. The blacks of South Carolina's offshore islands still speak Gullah, a pidgin dialect compounded of English and several African tongues. Around the turn of the twentieth century, Russian and Norwegian trappers in the Arctic communicated by a pidgin-mixture of their two languages, called Russonorsk.

Afrikaans, the language of the Republic of South Africa, began as the Dutch of the seventeenth-century settlers in the Cape Colony. But in the course of time it got considerably pidginized, simplifying its grammar and absorbing many native African words. The white South Africans also speak an even more certifiable pidgin, "Kitchen Kaffir," to their native servants.

The English colonials in India developed a jargon called "Hobson-Jobson." The name is supposedly a corruption of the Muslim processional chant, "Ya Hassan! Ya Hussein!" The English used the jargon more as a snobbish "in-group" slang than as a language of Anglo-Indian communication, but many of its borrowed words (bungalow, shampoo, dungarees, etc.) have stuck to the mother tongue, and so have some of its idioms. The "big cheese" is a Hobson-Jobsonism from the Hindi *chīz*, meaning "thing," and a "grass widow" was originally an English wife who vacationed in the cool green hills each summer while her husband sweated for the Raj in the suffocating city.

The first settlers in America conversed with the East Coast Indians in a sort of pidgin ("Great White Father send you much wampum"). Later, and farther west, the frontiersmen learned to use a means of trade communication that was already common among the Indians: the sign language. They had to. Sometimes a single and insignificant tribe would have its own individual spoken language, incomprehensible to any other Indian as well as to the whites; but the one standard sign language was understood by all of them, from the midwestern plains to the far western mountains. In the Northwest the Indians, American farmers, French trappers and even visiting Russian seal-fishermen all shared a pidgin called Chinook (but more familiarly known just as "the jargon" to the speakers).

The various immigrant nationalities that came to America developed contact vernaculars very like pidgin, but these seldom lasted beyond the first generation. The Italians' use of *sanemagogna* has already been mentioned; another such construction was *ghenga di loffari* ("gang of loafers"), English words transmogrified by Italian grammar and spelling. The Irish kept few of their native locutions, except for exclamations like "cushlamachree" (properly *cuisle mo chroidhe*, "vein of my heart") and the seigneurial "himself" to refer to the man of the house or any other autocrat.

The American language is still a patchwork of regional dialects, and the speakers of one are inclined to be as patronizing about another as they would be about a Fiji Islander's quaint gaucheries. The Jerseyite who says "youse" feels superior to the Alabamian who says "y'all," and vice versa. How many of the American ways of speech might be said to qualify as pidgins is a matter of some dispute among linguists. Some claim that the Spanish-English of the Mexican border country is as much a pidgin as is Gullah. Dr. Beryl Bailey has suggested that the contemporary American black speech (e.g., "He say he glad he go' get married") is not an ignorant mishandling of "good English" but is structurally a pidgin-type contact vernacular. Anyway, there are two other dialects spoken in the United States which most linguists will concede as pidgin-types: Pennsylvania Dutch and Yiddish-American.

Most people are aware that Pennsylvania Dutch was never Dutch at all, the name being merely a corruption of *Deutsch,* the Rhenish German spoken by the early settlers there. The reason for the dialect's survival is partly the clannishness and Old World traditions perpetuated by the strict Mennonite sects to which most of the speakers belong. But another reason is that tourists find the language so enthrallingly quaint. Nowa-

[185]

days the Mennonites are taking a more liberal attitude toward modernism, and are taking on the trappings of civilization. They themselves probably regard the dialect as being as obsolescent as the "hex signs" on their barns, but if there's one other thing these people are notable for, it's hard-headed pragmatism. Chances are they'll go on speaking Pennsylvania Dutch as long as it attracts the free-spending outlanders.

The peculiarities of this dialect consist mainly in its extraordinary ways of tormenting ordinary English words into German syntactical constructions. This leads to ambiguities of subject and object, like "Throw the baby out the window his blanket" and "Throw Mama from the train a kiss goodbye." Or this invitation to dinner: "Come in and eat yourself." Or "Look the window out and see if it makes down anything."

To "make down" means to rain or snow, but "make" has other meanings, too. Pennsylvania Dutch most resembles pidgin in that one word can often substitute for a good many others. "Make the door open" is obvious enough, but to "make up the hill" means to climb it, and "make the fire finish" means to put it out. "All" likewise has numerous ways of signifying a negative conclusion: "The dinner is all" (the meal is finished). "The train is all" (we've missed the train). "Grosspapa is all" (Grampaw just died).

Sometimes the grammar is English enough, but applied in a blithely freehand way: "Outen the light and so to bed." Or consider the housewife's lament: "The hurrier I go, the behinder I get." And sometimes a recognizable English word has been given a new, unrecognizable and even portmanteau meaning: "My off is on" translates as "My vacation has begun." The English "ain't" is used in its familiar meaning, but also as an oral question mark ("is it not so?") like the German *nicht wahr* and the French *n'est-ce pas*. For example: "You're coming with me, ain't?"

Many Yiddish-American constructions are similar to those of Pennsylvania Dutch—for instance, the inverted sentence structure: "Married I can always get"—because Yiddish too was originally a German dialect. Some German words are common to them both, and both unhesitatingly Americanize them, as in putting English endings on German verbs: "grexing" (whining), "schlepping" (carrying, moving, hustling), etc. Both have borrowed the element *ge-*, common to German past participles, and have made it a passive prefix to English verbs: "The flat tire is ge-fixed." *Bei mir* has been literally translated for uses like "By me it's O.K."

Pennsylvania Dutch is not quite so prone to vocal tics like

"so," "already" and "yet," but they are ubiquitous in Yiddish-American speech: "Hurry up already!" "So it matters I'm late?" "An argument he gives me yet!" Yiddish-American slang adds the German *schm-* sound to English words in various ways, to express disapproval, derision or sarcasm, as in the doubling "bargain-schmargain." Yiddish also includes words from Hebrew and from Baltic, Balkan and Slavic languages, so these too have emigrated into Yiddish-American. For example, the Slavic diminutive suffix *-nik* was in use (e.g., "nogoodnik") long before *sputnik* made it world-famous.

Yiddish remains the second language of many American Jews, but the compromise language of Yiddish-American would probably have dwindled and died long ago except that it, like Hobson-Jobson, became a sort of ethnic "in-group" fad. And in big cities like New York—where the population is 20 per cent Jewish—even the non-Jews have deemed it fashionable or fun or "hip" (or simply good business) to sprinkle a few Yiddish tags into their conversation.

These quasi-pidgin languages, like the true pidgins, were all concocted out of sober expediency, to bridge a gap in communications. But a man also has occasional practical need to restrict his communications to a select coterie. For this, conventional language just won't do. Thus there are made-up languages like the Cockney rhyming slang, the underworld's jargon and the "carny talk" of circus and carnival people.

There also exist made-up languages which are not all work and no play. Although the urge to communicate is rooted deep in man's being, he has an urge sometimes to cut himself off from communication entirely. Every once in a while a man seems to need just to babble, to sing hey-nonny-nonny, to throw off his linguistic inhibitions and utter (or listen to) noises that mean nothing, suggest nothing and commit him to nothing. This holds true from diaper-age to dotage; children will babble-soliloquize for hours, and senior executives will pay good money for entertainers to lecture their convention meetings in double-talk. A number of ex-generals and after-dinner speakers do this unintentionally, but I mean professionals like the late vaudevillian Al Kelly, who had more speaking engagements than he could fill. "The bladgets, you see, are attached to the portisframe . . ." but his outrageous monologues were better heard than seen in print.

This whimsical trait of human personality might well explain the intermittent popularity of such linguistic phenomena as scat singing, religious glossolalia, rock lyrics and certain elder statesmen's unghosted speeches. Double-talk has got into literature, too—and again I mean the deliberate instances, like Lewis Carroll's "Jabberwocky." James Joyce made quite a good thing of rattling off passages of nonsense-language, often with tongue in cheek but sometimes seriously intending subliminal communication.

The languages made up by children of school age fall somewhere between secret clique languages and nonsense double-talk. They are more often spouted just for fun than for any purpose of concealment, because they're too easily deciphered. But evidently the use of them gives youngsters some illusion of privacy, and at the same time affords an opportunity for showing off. Sometimes these play-languages are carried on as far as college, but by that stage they are only fads of the same order as weird hair styles.

The play-language fad seems particularly endemic to girls' boarding schools. At one such junior college some years ago the language spoken was Alfalfa. (Maybe it still is; anyhow, at reunions, some middle-aged alumna will generally resurrect it, with giggles.) Alfalfa is typical of the simpler play-languages; it consists only of interpolating the syllables of "alfalfa," in that sequence, between successive syllables of whatever is to be said. For example, "Better late than never" would come out "Betalterfal late-fa thanal nefalverfa." A newcomer to Alfalfa is bound to stumble, even reading a prepared translation like this one. But some of the girls at that college could jabber the jargon so glibly as to confound their schoolmasters and housemothers.

The granddaddy of play-languages must have been Pig Latin, as it is referred to in English literature as far back as the 1600s. (It is not to be confused with Dog Latin, Sham Latin, Kitchen Latin, Apothecary's Latin, etc. These appeared even earlier, in several European countries, and were macaronic medleys of the national tongue plus Latin words and word-endings, the intention being to simulate erudition—or deride it.) Pig Latin can claim no infusion of real Latin, but it is slightly more complex than Alfalfa in that it uses sound-transposition. Pig Latin starts each word with its first vowel, switching any preceding consonants to the end of the word and suffixing an -ay sound. Thus "Better late than never" becomes "Etterbay ate-lay anthay evernay." Even with the transposition it's easier to unscramble than Alfalfa.

Another American play-language is Double Dutch, unique in that it utilizes a syllabary (b is bub, c is cash, d is dud, f is fuf, etc.). In translating from conventional English, vowels remain intact, but most consonants change to these syllables. Our specimen phrase would translate "Bubbetutter lullate thannun nunnevuvver."

[188]

The American "carny talk"—anything but playful—comes in several versions. Most are as simple as Alfalfa, and presumably are just as flabbergasting to the rubes and hirams marked for euchring. One variety inserts the sound *eez* after each syllable: "Betteeztereez lateez thaneez neveezereez." The Paris underworld used to communicate in the *argot de boucher* ("butcher's slang"), where every word began with *l* and ended with any nonsense-sound that came to mind. Our phrase "Better late than never" (and to avoid any additional confusion, let's keep it in English) might come out something like "Letteroo latitch lannik leverwow."

Probably every language has had its play-languages. In Balzac's *Père Goriot,* some of his characters are so impressed by their visit to the cyclorama that thereafter they converse in a jargon that tacks *-rama* onto almost every word. Also in the nineteenth century, France had the language called *javanais* ("Javanese"), which tucked an *av* somewhere in every word: "Bavetter lavate thavan naveer."

Belgium had the *Pekestaal* or "language of the little *p*'s," in which each syllable was repeated, beginning it with a *p* sound: "Betpet-erper late-pate thanpan nevpev-erper." Germany's *Be-Sprache* worked the same way, using a *b* sound. The Danes had the *Kragesprog* ("crow language"), so called because that's what they thought it sounded like. It merely inserted a *ber* after every syllable: "Betberterber late-ber thanber neberverber."

The Dutch play-language substituted *edi* for every vowel. The Japanese *nosa-nosa kotoba* inserted *nosa* after the first vowel sound in each word. A Ukrainian play-language threw a *k*, plus any vowel, in between syllables: "Betkaterky late-ko than-koo nekaverky" (which makes even the English phrase sound Ukrainian enough). Finland's play-language may have been the most complex and undecipherable of them all. In the Finnish *konnti* ("knapsack") language, *k* took the place of a word's first consonant, which moved to the rear of the word, and *-onnti* was added onto that: "Ketterbonnti katelonnti kanthonnti kevernonnti."

Pidgin and play-languages may seem to some philologists to be just candidates for a museum of linguistic oddities. But even the simplest and silliest of made-up languages may intimate much about the ways "real" languages came into being, and may possibly point ways to improving them. Dr. Ludwig Zamenhof pored over play-languages for a full year before he began work on the creation of Esperanto, to date the most useful and most used of "universal" languages. Pidgin is supposed to have given Charles K. Ogden the idea of compiling his 850-word Basic English, a system whereby non-English-speakers can learn to express themselves in that language clearly, correctly and in a wonderfully short time.

The *raison d'être* of play-languages may be a trifling one, but so long as they have some use—even if only of amusement—they are not to be despised. As for pidgin, it has amply proved its worth and, even if it is eventually superseded by conventional language, there are indispensable bits of it that are sure to survive.

In some far distant day, an earthling spaceman may land on the first-discovered inhabited planet outside our solar system. And when he announces himself to the natives—speak though he may in electronic beeps or laser blips—it's a safe bet that he'll use some equivalent of the time-honored pidgin greeting: "Me friend."

U O a O but I O U,
O O no O but O O me;
O let not my O a O go,
But give O O I O U so.*
    —WILLIAM WHEWELL

Cloak, Dagger and Bacon

I T has often been said that men are only grown-up little
boys, and a good argument to that effect is their eager
preoccupation with what one might call "grown-up play-
languages." The secret grips and signs and cryptic communications of fraternities, Freemasonry and international cloak-
and-daggery are only a short step removed from the passwords
and countersigns of boyhood's backyard clubhouse. The clubhouse itself likewise tends to mature. In one instance it has
grown up to be the multi-million-dollar office complex of the
U.S. National Security Agency, whose "secret membership"
totals some twenty thousand employees and whose "club
treasury" spends hundreds of millions of dollars a year just
on the making and breaking of codes and ciphers.

Codes and ciphers are certainly not language per se, but
they have long been involved with it, as both help and hindrance to communication. And like every other aspect of language they have influenced the course of human history.
Mary, Queen of Scots, lost her chance at the crown of England—and the head on which to wear it—when one of
Elizabeth's astute courtiers intercepted and deciphered the
secret messages Mary was sending to her co-conspirator Bab-
ington. Napoleon lost two of his most crucial battles (at
Leipzig in 1813 and Waterloo in 1815) partly because his
military cipher was so wonderfully complicated that on both
occasions his field instructions got garbled and misinterpreted.

* You sigh for a cipher, but I sigh for you,
  Oh sigh for no cipher, but Oh sigh for me;
  Oh let not my sigh for a cipher go,
  But give sigh for sigh, for I sigh for you so.

The Zimmermann Incident, which helped provoke the United States into entering World War I, is not yet ancient history. Early in 1917 Arthur Zimmermann, Germany's foreign minister, sent a code message to the German envoy in Mexico City, empowering him to offer Mexico a chance to regain its former territory in Texas, Arizona and New Mexico—if that nation would declare war at the back door of the United States. When English agents intercepted the message, decoded it and revealed its contents, an infuriated America saw the German proposal as the ultimate insult, and President Wilson had no choice but to declare war.

Cryptic messages fascinate many an ordinary man as much as they do counterintelligence cryptanalysts, historians and paleographers. There are almost as many fans of newspaper cryptograms as there are of crossword and acrostic puzzles, and they'll devote hours, if necessary, to deciphering an item like:

L UHMRLFHG WR ILQG VRPH RLQWPHQW
LQ PB OLWWOH SRW RI IOLHV.

Secret writing owes its existence and its popularity respectively to two parallel human traits: the desire to keep one's own business private, and the urge to snoop into other people's. The first accounts for our busy devisal of multitudinous ciphers and codes, and the second explains our unflagging passion to decipher them—even when, as in the case of the newspaper cryptogram, a mountain of labor brings forth a pretty puny mouse.

The biographers who translated Caesar Augustus' enciphered epistles were rewarded with such pasty gems as: "*Ave* Tiberius—We observed the Festival of Minerva most enjoyably by gambling for five days straight. Your brother Drusus grumbled mightily about his luck, but actually he just about broke even. . . ."

The scholars who deciphered the private shorthand in which Samuel Pepys wrote his diaries may have felt a bit better repaid with tidbits like this entry of January 28, 1661: "To the Theatre . . . and here, I sitting behind in a dark place, a lady spit backward upon me by mistake, not seeing me; but after seeing her to be a very pretty lady, I was not troubled at it at all."

Of course, secret writings have been oftenest employed by people in prominent or precarious positions: heads of state arranging secret alliances, conspirators contriving revolutions, warlords plotting conquests, popes conniving with all three—

and commoners secretly scribbling bitter commentaries on all four. For a long time, ordinary writing alone sufficed for secrecy. Those who could do it and read it were such rarities that the reticent among them didn't have to worry much about their private business becoming public gossip. But as literacy became more widespread, people with secrets to keep became increasingly wary about committing them to a medium that any busybody could comprehend.

Hence the longtime verdure of cipher and code, and right here it might be pointed out that there is a technical difference between the two, though the terms are often mistakenly used interchangeably. A code converts whole words or even whole passages of the "plain text" (the message to be encoded) into other words or symbols. A cipher changes individual letters of the plain text into something else.

A code depends upon the sender's and receiver's agreement on a glossary of what is to be substituted for what (e.g., AABAA = secret, BABAA = plans, CABAA = stolen, etc.). Even a red light is a code message, in that everybody has long agreed that it means "stop" or "danger." The early Christians used a code sign to refer to the Christ. In Greek the initial letters of "Jesus Christ, Son of God, Savior," taken acrostically, compose *ikhthys*, "fish," and so a stylized drawing of a fish became the Christians' secret symbol.

Seldom is a code simple enough to be carried in the head: "one if by land, two if by sea." Since it must provide a substitute for every word that may foreseeably be required, it generally means that both sender and receiver carry identical codebooks. But in a pinch, practically any bound volume of words can serve as a codebook—an ordinary dictionary, cookbook, Silhouette Romance novel, *Casket & Sunnyside* magazine—so long as both sender and receiver possess identical copies. In such a case the code message would consist entirely of numbers, specifying the page of that volume, the line and the place on that line where each word of the plain text is to be found.

We tend to think of codes as being the special property of the military and diplomatic services, but they are also in everyday use in everyday life. Shorthand is a code. So are such handy abbreviations as R.S.V.P. and c/o and I.O.U. So are glyphs like $ and © and ♂. There is the postal system's "zip code" and the telephone "area code." A newly fashionable sort of code-plus-cipher has become so common as to be almost an irritant: those ads and commercials where a salesman urges you to dial or peck on the telephone a word instead of an old-fashioned number. The device is of course

[193]

not meant for hiding anything, but for ease, convenience and cutesiness. A putative customer or patron, instead of having to memorize a string of numbers, has only to remember a catchy word. *"Uptight? Dial DEPRESS!"* Do, and you discover that that number consists of only two digits.

Space probes report back to earth in code. We utilize a quite complex code when we order a piece of merchandise by catalogue number; a single designation like 24To6-3N3 may include the article's description, size, color and price. So do those ribbons of black bars now printed on almost all product labels; they're a code readable by supermarket check-out computers. Cable companies maintain copious codes for the use of their customers; a lengthy phrase like "in accordance with the instructions in your letter" can be compressed into a single code word and thus cost only the one-word rate for transmission.

Ciphers are not so universally useful, their single function being that of concealment. Outside of the military and the various intelligence agencies, there is probably no person more familiar with ciphers—and more pestered by them— than a schoolteacher of the fifth or sixth grade. She has doubtless had to confiscate hundreds of enciphered notes being smuggled back and forth (at least among the boys) in her classroom. Several of my own best cryptographic efforts at P.S. 15 were thus thwarted by a long-suffering Mrs. Atkins.

A schoolboy's cipher is usually of the simplest substitution sort—perhaps writing 1 for *a*, 2 for *b*, etc., or reversing the alphabet with Z for *a*, Y for *b*, etc.—and this type of cipher was among the first employed by the ancients. Julius Caesar used one in which the cipher substituted was merely the third letter following in the alphabet; that is, he wrote D for *a*, E for *b*, and so on (in today's alphabet, "Caesar" would be FDHVDU). His successors used similar ciphers; according to Suetonius, Augustus just wrote down the letter following the one he meant (B for *a*, etc.) and could write it as rapidly as straight text. This childish sort of substitution is still known to cryptologists as the "Caesar cipher," though it had doubtless been in use for centuries before Julius' time.

Substitution is one of three basic sorts of cipher; another is transposition, in which the letters of the plain text message keep their identity but get shuffled around according to some predetermined system. It might be as artless as mere reversal—"Caesar" becoming RASEAC—or it might be a more complicated system (though still laughably simple to the experienced cryptanalyst) like this columnar transposition based on a four-by-three square:

"This is cipher" is written T H I S
                              I S C I
                              P H E R, and then is transcribed
from the vertical columns into the message TIPHSHICESIR.
Or one could use a diagonal transposition, say, from lower
left to upper right: PIHTSEHCRIIS. Or a route transposition,
perhaps a spiral starting from the top left, down and around
and in: TIPHERISIHSC. In any case, the recipient of such a
message deciphers it by reversing the agreed-upon transposition process.

The third basic type of cipher is the concealment variety,
akin to the music student's familiar old acrostic, "every good
boy does fine," in which the first letters of the words give the
G-clef staff-notes in proper order. Where a message in substitution or transposition cipher unavoidably proclaims itself a
secret message and boldly risks decipherment, a concealment
cipher is intended to get past any censor or interceptor without arousing suspicion as to its nature and content. In a concealment cipher, the letters of the plain text keep their identity and their relative positions as well, but are hidden by
being scattered throughout a "cover text" according to some
prearranged pattern. This puts quite a strain on the one doing the enciphering, as he has to concoct a sensible-sounding
message to surround the scattered secret text, and this is not
always practicable. A spy in some hot, tight spot is not about
to set down a verbose essay.

But deciphering such a message is considerably easier.
Sometimes this is done by laying a perforated card over the
page of cover text and reading off the letters that show
through the holes. Cardinal Richelieu used this system. More
often, the secret message is found by some letter-counting
method. For example, in the last sentence of the preceding
paragraph there's a three-word message, or moan, discernible
by reading off every sixth letter.

A very easy variant of this system is to send a page or
more of ordinary printed material, with the message letters
(or even whole words) indicated by pin-pricks in the paper,
nearly invisible until they're held up to the light. In the nineteenth century, when mail rates in England were prohibitively
high but newspapers could be sent free, a great many people
used the pin-prick system for sending personal messages.
During World War II numbers of servicemen overseas managed to circumvent the censors and notify their families of
their whereabouts by similarly pin-pricking superficially innocent letters.

Both ciphers and codes have their advantages and disadvantages as modes of secret writing. A code, being a completely arbitrary and random substitution of symbols for words, is extremely hard for an "enemy" cryptanalyst to crack unless he somehow gets hold of the secret codebook. His next best hope is to intercept a whole stack of the coded messages so that he can try to spot frequently repeated symbols. Knowing the general subject matter, he can reasonably expect certain words to keep reappearing. Also he can match the code symbols against the known frequency of word repetition in the encoder's language. (For example, the five oftenest-repeated English words are, in order, *the, of, and, to* and *a.* The most frequently recurring French words are *de, il, le, et* and *que.*) The main disadvantage of using code is that it does require both headquarters and the agent in the field to depend on a codebook. If an urgent message finds the spy without his codebook handy, he's in trouble, and if the enemy finds him *with* it, he's in even worse.

Cipher has no need of the clumsy and incriminating codebook. A tremendously complex cipher can be based on a system, pattern or key that can be memorized—or at worst will require only some easily concealable or quickly disposable apparatus. The drawback to cipher is that any system or pattern which one man can contrive, some other man can manage to duplicate. Given a sufficient sample of a cipher message—and sometimes one word may be enough—an experienced cryptanalyst can read it as easily as a *chef de cuisine* can tell the ingredients of a sauce from a single sip. It may seem incredible, but an expert can frequently decipher a message written in a language of which he doesn't know a word.

The examples of cipher given in this chapter are, of course, the simplest sorts devisable, and would be small potatoes to even a newspaper cryptogram fan. The ones actually in use, whether by a U. S. Central Intelligence agent prowling inside Nicaragua or a General Motors spy reporting on Ford's test runs of next year's models, are of a complexity to stun anybody but a professional cryptographer. Just the technical names of a few standard systems are enough to discourage an amateur from tackling them. There's the "Vigenère polyalphabetic substitution," the "true Beaufort reciprocal," and so forth.

The ciphers in use today are usually combinations of both substitution and transposition types (concealment ciphers are now considered old-fashioned). And often, to achieve maximum message security, they're used in conjunction with code. For an extremely oversimplified illustration, say an American ambassador has an urgent, top-secret message to transmit to Washington, and say one word in it is "H-bomb." From his codebook he gets the code substitute for "H-bomb"— maybe ALOHA. This he will then encipher (assume a Julius Caesar substitution: D for *a*, etc.), getting DORKD. Now he may re-encipher this by a transposition method—say simple reversal, getting DKROD. Even this garble can be superenciphered by running it through other, different ciphers again and again. Should an enemy agent intercept the message and manage to backtrack through all these steps, he would fetch up only at ALOHA again, and, assuming he didn't have a copy of the codebook, he'd hit dead end there.

The realist is aware, however, that even the most tangled cipher and jealously kept code will eventually be cracked. The best that can be hoped for any secret message is that it will baffle the enemy just long enough for its contents to be valueless to him by the time he does read it. And, ideally, the codes and ciphers will be changed frequently, so that when an enemy does decipher one message, his knowledge of its key can't help him unravel subsequent ones.

The efficacy of a code or cipher is considerably heightened if it can be transmitted by some means that defies detection or interception. So spies have learned to "write" messages in such unexpected ciphers as the placement of stones in a garden wall, the position of pieces on a chessboard, different sorts of candy in a Valentine box, the notes in a bar of music, stitches sewn in a seam, beads of a necklace, even the twinings of a hair about the teeth of a comb. There is also voice transmission by telephone or radio with an electronic "scrambler" at the sending end and an "unscrambler" at the receiver; any eavesdropper in between would pick up only an idiot babble. One method of concealment that hasn't yet outlived its usefulness is the hackneyed old idea of "invisible ink." Inventors have come up with all manner of complicated formulas for this stuff, but a not-too-fastidious spy will find his urine as practical as any, and handier than most. (Heating the paper brings out the writing.)

Secret communications are being used today more than ever before; the climate of the times encourages their proliferation. New electronic machines concoct codes and ciphers more hellishly complex than any human ever could. For example, the U. S. Army's suitcase-sized machine, the KW-9 (used during the Korean War; it is surely obsolete and has been replaced by now) enciphered and deciphered messages by a wink-quick system of multiple substitution, in which each separate letter was encrypted according to a whole new cipher, this being automatically keyed by the combination of all the letters preceding it. Machines like the KW-9, while making ciphers and codes harder to crack, have also made them easier to utilize and transmit, so now they abound in every field from international diplomacy to commercial competition. But their occasional embarrassing breakdowns aren't talked about, and their triumphs can't be.

However, there have been codes and ciphers aplenty in literature, from classic to hack. Indeed, their flamboyant performances as plot gimmicks, rather than their comparatively prosaic uses in real life, are what is mainly responsible for their familiarity and popularity among laymen.

Edgar Allan Poe sparked a hot interest in cryptograms during the 1840s, first with his essay *Cryptography* and then with his story of *The Gold Bug*. Poe rode the crest of the craze for a while, challenging readers of his magazine columns to send him a cryptogram he *couldn't* solve. Evidently he was never stumped at this, but then he defied readers to crack an "unsolvable" cryptogram of his own (one of the "polyalphabetic substitution" variety), and was dumbfounded when a Mississippi subscriber promptly did. Poe maintained to his dying day that the man must have somehow peeked at an advance copy of the issue containing the solution, but anyway his own passion for cryptology rather cooled after that.

Balzac included in his *La Physiologie du Mariage* a long and cryptic passage that baffled would-be decipherers for nearly half a century, until an officer of France's intelligence service demonstrated that it was nothing more than nonsense deliberately contrived to look like cipher. Dickens' *A Tale of Two Cities* begins with Mme. Defarge knitting, and her knitwork turns out to be a code or cipher list of prospective candidates for the guillotine. Jules Verne's story *Mathias Sandorf* turns upon the puzzle of a cipher message (of the "Cardan revolving grill" variety). Conan Doyle had Sherlock Holmes tackle a simple substitution cipher (really rather beneath his talents) in *The Adventure of the Dancing Men*. More recently, Andrew Garve's mystery novel, *The House of Soldiers*, depended for its climax on a message enciphered in Ireland's ancient ogham alphabet.

But the literary codes and ciphers which have generated the most febrile excitement have been those which existed only in the minds of their discoverers. At least they have never been proved to exist anywhere else.

In the ninth century, a number of rabbis founded the mystical philosophy of Kabala on the belief that the Hebrew Scriptures contained secret ciphers, and that anyone who correctly interpreted them would have a head start on understanding all of nature, science and the secrets of the universe. The Kabalists assigned numerical values to each Hebrew character, then played anagrams with the words of the Scriptures, added up their numerical equivalents, and found vast esoteric "truths" in the coincidental recurrence of various numbers.

Inevitably the books of the Kabala became the textbooks for magicians, alchemists and divines of later centuries, who believed or pretended that they contained formulas to work any kind of sorcery, and prognostications of everything forthcoming in the future.

Among the most beguiling and controversial ciphers ever unearthed are those which "prove" that Shakespeare's plays were not written by Shakespeare. The fact that no such ciphers have been irrefutably demonstrated does not deter a goodly body of people from believing in them and disbelieving in Shakespeare.

The doubts about Shakespeare's authorship became vocal within a century after his death. The earliest argument, and the only plausible one yet put forward, was that that "upstart crow" simply did not have the breeding, background, education, culture, broadening travel and entrée at court to account for the scope and quality of his writing. Really rigid anti-Stratfordians insist that Shakespeare's only contribution to the plays was his byline; that the name was assumed by some personage of more gentlemanly and scholarly credentials. That person has been variously identified—Edward de Vere, Robert Cecil, Christopher Marlowe, *et al.*—but the most favored contender is Francis Bacon, Baron Verulam.

Other anti-Stratfordians believe the plays to have been composed by a whole committee of collaborators. One theory is that such a committee—including Shakespeare, Bacon, Marlowe, Fletcher, Beaumont, *et al.*—was organized by Elizabeth and supervised by de Vere or Raleigh, as a sort of wartime Propaganda Department, not so much to entertain audiences as to feed them candy-coated chauvinism.

Anyway—according to the anti-Stratfordians—either for personal reasons or out of consideration for national security, the true author (or authors) of the plays took no credit at the time, and recognition has been refused ever since. But might not the author(s) have slipped some hint of the truth into the very playscripts themselves? The sly concealment of messages in literature was by no means uncommon. The Elizabethans were almost tiresomely fond of constructing acrostic poems. And in the very year of Shakespeare's death appeared an otherwise anonymous work in which one Bishop Francis

Godwin asserted his authorship by spelling out his name with the chapters' initial letters.

The first suggestion that Shakespeare's works might hold similar hints came from a Mrs. C. F. Windle in 1882, when she published a pamphlet entitled *Discovery and opening of THE CIPHER of Francis Bacon, Lord Verulam, alike in his prose writings and in the "Shakespeare Dramas," proving him the author of the dramas.* Actually, she had found no cipher at all, in the technical sense of the term; her conclusions were based on a farrago of far-fetched puns and anagrams, laboriously pieced together from fragments of the play texts. But her mere suggestion seems to have been an eye-opener for other anti-Stratfordians. Since then, innumerable ciphers have been "discovered," assigning the plays to every one of the aforementioned claimants and others besides.*

But Francis Bacon remains the front-running contender among the cipher cultists. And here his boosters have the makings of a very persuasive argument, because Bacon was himself no mean cryptographer. He wrote on the subject, and even invented a biliteral cipher of his own—the "Biliterarie Alphabet" he called it—so practical and ingenious that it is still used. Unfortunately for the Baconians, professional cryptologist have been unable to find his cipher or any other in the plays, and have, to date, demolished the delusions of all the eager amateurs who believed or hoped or pretended that they had done so.

It would be both unfair and untrue to lump all the anti-Stratfordians in an intellectual class with flying-saucer faddists and that crowd. But it can't help but be noticed that one of the more vociferous supporters of the Baconian cipher theory, Dr. Orville Owen, took time out from cryptography to try to sell the U.S. government his invention of "a machine to defy gravity." And that another dedicated cipherist, Ignatius Donnelly, dabbled in spiritualism and was the author of a book intended to validate the legendary Atlantis.

Several cipher-hunters have seized on the famous "long word" in *Love's Labour's Lost*—honorificabilitudinitatibus—because the same word appears as a doodle in Bacon's papers. Although this appears to have been a fairly common

* On the other hand, a pro-Shakespeare cryptologist once waggishly asserted that the Bard was the author of the Book of Psalms. For "proof," look to the 46th Psalm (King James Version). Check the 46th word from the beginning of that psalm, and then the 46th word from the end (excluding "Selah").

nonsense expression of the time (and had appeared in a Latin work a century earlier), the Baconians have made much of it. Dr. Isaac Platt anagrammatized it into *"Hi ludi, tuiti sibi, Fr. Bacono nati"*—even more dreadful Sham Latin than the original—meaning, according to him, "These plays, produced by Francis Bacon, guarded for themselves."

By arbitrarily repeating some of the letters, Edwin Bormann got *"O subitat in id utili: Baconus ironicus,"* or "Oh, he conceals in it something of use: the ironic Bacon." Still another version hauled a new and rather anachronistic challenger into the fray: *"Ubi Italicus ibi Danti honor fit,"* or "Where there is an Italian, there Dante is honored." One English anagram of the long word came out "But thus I told Franiiiiii Bacon." Its deviser explained that the *i*'s were the Roman numeral six, and that "six" should be pronounced in the French manner. Hence "Francis."

Some of the cipher-fanciers' conclusions have been no more weird than the ways they went about reaching them. Dr. Owen, he of the antigravity machine, wrote a book, *Sir Francis Bacon's Cipher Story,* based in part on his decipherment of passages from an English translation of Bacon's *Feliciam Memoriam Elizabethae.* But the translation had not been made until more than twenty years after Bacon's death, and any cryptograms that he might have concealed in his original Latin text could hardly have survived the translation.

In the 1930s the researches of Mrs. Maria Bauer somehow convinced her that the original manuscripts of the plays (presumably in Bacon's handwriting) had been smuggled out of England by one of Bacon's seventeenth-century immigrant descendants, and had been buried at Williamsburg, Virginia. At the time she conceived this notion, the Rockefeller Foundation was in the process of restoring Williamsburg as a national showplace, so Mrs. Bauer hurried there to poke among the excavations. She found nothing but more tantalizing hints. For example, she espied the names "Anne" and "Graham" on a tombstone and immediately inferred "anagram"— to her, unmistakable evidence that she was on the right trail. Unhappily, the Rockefeller people didn't agree; they found Mrs. Bauer a nuisance, and sent her packing.

Some of the cipher-hunters have found deep significance in the plays' italicized words, typographical errors, misspellings, brackets, hyphens and other punctuation. Others have found meaningful patterns in the placement of words, letters, even printers' signature marks on a page—and these not only in the First Folio but even in nineteenth-century editions. The imagination boggles at the conspiracy this would have required amongst author, publisher, typesetters, printers, apprentices, binders—and all their descendants. But those who cherish such theories brush away objections with the explanation that all the conspirators were, like Bacon, Freemasons or Rosicrucians, and so entered readily into his intrigue.

Maybe. But some of the discovered ciphers are so complex that the plays exist only as vehicles for them, and not a word of the plays could be changed without addling the ciphers. It is fatuous to suppose that Bacon, or anyone else in his right mind, wrote the plays merely to conceal proof that he wrote the plays. Even if this were remotely possible, it requires a transcendent faith on the part of the Baconians to believe that his "cover text" just happened to turn out to be the most sublime writings in all of English literature.

There have been anti-Stratfordians who buttressed their arguments with testimony from spirit seances and Ouija boards. But even rational ones have sought a message from beyond the grave, by attempting to decipher Shakespeare's epitaph; that is, the version of it which was supposed to have been inscribed in an "uncouth mixture of large and small letters," thus:

> Good Frend for Iesus SAKE forbeare
> To diGG TE Dust Enclo-Ased HE.Re.
> Blese be TE Man T̯ spares TEs Stones
> And curst be He T̯ moves my Bones.

Admittedly, this mishmash invites speculation. But the speculators have only the word of one Shakespearean scholar that the epitaph was ever so written. The present stone on the playwright's grave is a nineteenth-century replacement of the eroded original, and is inscribed in quite ordinary English orthography. So may have been the original; at least none of those who saw it placed commented on any oddity about it. But an editor of an 1801 collection of the works mentioned the "uncouth mixture," and so would-be decipherers have been chipping away at it as long as they have at the playscripts.

By juggling words and letters, omitting some, repeating others, inverting still others, and then applying all manner of imprecise cipher systems, and still again contorting these systems at their convenience, various decipherers have produced such provocative messages as "Shaxpere Ate Francis Bacon. Why Roarer!" and:

Cloak, Dagger and Bacon

Dig Honest Man dost THEE forbeare
I SHAKE-SPEARE England's Tvdor Heire
Graved belovv these mystic Stones
The mystery codes yet gab of bones.
                                                    F. B.

The Shakespearean Ciphers Examined is the title of an entertaining and erudite book by professional cryptographers William and Elizebeth Friedman. This husband-and-wife team came to the subject after many years of U.S. government service, including long tenure as chief cryptanalysts of the War Department and the Secret Service, and they brought scientific detachment and disinterest to the Shakespearean controversy. Indeed, they were almost saintly in resisting the temptation to chortle at frequent instances of crackpottery and skulduggery among the cipher-cultists. They took up each of the likelier ciphers and let it demonstrate its own failure.

Some of the cipher systems are so ramshackle that they permit decipherment of a multitude of messages from the same piece of plain text. Other ciphers are logical enough in their construction but are faultily (or trickily) applied in order to coerce a message. In some cases, a seeker has pieced together some hoped-for message and then contrived a vastly involved "cipher" to fit—but it produces nothing but hodgepodge when tried on some other part of the text.

The Friedmans took one of the popular systems, an anagrammatic transposition cipher, and showed that it can be applied to derive a message proving that the true author of the plays was Samuel Clemens. They took another system, the pride and joy of a Dr. Wallace Cunningham, and had it prove the true author to be Theodore Roosevelt. With B. M. Ward's acrostic system, they came up with Lewis Carroll. And with the "Kay cipher," a numerological system rather like the Kabalists', they revealed the true authors of the plays to be "Wm. & E. Friedman."

The Friedmans asked only two things of any system. It had to be applicable without ambiguity, cheating, stretching-to-fit or other jiggery-pokery. And it had to produce a message which made sense. But they found that the Shakespearean messages achieved by the most nearly valid means were the ones most "semantically bizarre, grammatically weak, decrepit in spelling, or just odd altogether." And they concluded, rather sadly, "Of crypto-systems which pass our two-fold test—we have to announce a disappointment: none does."

Hardly necessary to add, this judgment is not likely to disillusion or deter new seekers. If the history of cryptology proves one thing about the human personality, it is this: man loves a mystery, and the satisfaction of occasionally manufacturing one of his own is only excelled by that of unmasking another's.

Why, if a fish came to *me*, and told me he
was going a journey, I should say "With what
porpoise?"

—LEWIS CARROLL

Without Tongue or Words

S O M E of the codes and ciphers man has devised are in
the nature of communications bridges rather than barriers. And his penchant for unscrambling "secret messages" has found employments rather more noble than mere
snooping.

In investigating these manipulations of language, we are
again dealing with techniques and systems that are not languages in themselves. But in their application we can see
how man has sought indefatigably to improve and adapt his
linguistic facilities. Sometimes his attempt has resulted in
making human intercourse easier, as with the invention of
shorthand. Sometimes he has succeeded in preserving things
that were formerly perishable, as with the introduction of
music notation. Sometimes he has managed to express a concept that was formerly incommunicable, or to provide a
tongue for the formerly voiceless. But whether the seeking
man has been a Congo witch doctor fumbling for a mumbo-
jumbo that his gods would heed, or an electronics wizard
compiling a mathematical vocabulary for his computer, every
such effort has had the aim of expanding man's horizons and
aggrandizing his dominion within them.

Of the various codes intended to clarify language instead
of conceal it, the most commonplace and most generally useful is shorthand. There are numerous systems of it in use today, and there have been countless others in the past. We
don't know when man first tried to write as fast as he could
talk, but there is every likelihood that there were "stenographers," in a sense, even before writing was invented. These
would have been professional memorizers, constantly at the

[205]

elbow of kings, priests and the like, and in attendance at
every important meeting—no doubt working in shifts—
committing to memory at least the gist of everything that
was said.

The first written shorthand system of which we have any
record was invented about 63 B.C. by a Roman freedman
named Tullius Tiro, who used it to take down verbatim some
of the orations of his good friend Cicero. To judge from the
angularity of its characters, Tiro scratched his shorthand on
a wax tablet with a pointed stylus, but it was equally suitable
for penning on papyrus, parchment or paper. The system,
known as "Tironian notes," was clumsy compared to later
shorthands, but it was practical enough to outlast the Roman
Empire, being used by European scribes for nearly a thousand years.

The Greeks had a shorthand system of their own in the
fourth century A.D., and the Vatican was using a private system in the eleventh. The first shorthand to be popularized in
modern times appeared in England in 1588 with the publication of Dr. Timothy Bright's *Characterie: an Arte of Shorte,
Swifte, and Secrete Writing by Character.* Bright was followed by numerous other innovators and improvers, and
shorthand writing became quite a seemly accomplishment
among the illuminati, many of them contriving their own
private systems. The decipherers of Pepys' diaries assumed
that his writing was a private code designed for secrecy; it
was not until fifty years after they had sweated over it that it
was identified as merely his personal adaptation of a not at
all mysterious shorthand of the day, a system devised by one
Thomas Shelton.

From Tiro's to Shelton's, all of these were orthographic
shorthands. That is, they aimed at rapidity by simplifying
the spelling or writing of a word, but were still based on the
ordinary alphabet. Two orthographic systems are still in use.
One is Speedwriting, which advertises to white-collar aspi-
rants that "u kn ri 120 wpm & gt a gd jb & mo pa." The other
is Stenotype, which uses a sort of simplified typewriter to do
the same thing.

The first entirely phonetic system, transcribing the sound
of words without regard to how they look, was conceived by
William Tiffin in 1750. He made up his own alphabet, which
bore little relation to the English one but, once learned, was
much easier to write down in a hurry. Isaac Pitman, in
1837, devised a still simpler phonetic alphabet, and his system was soon *the* shorthand in both Britain and America.

Pitman's method (he called it first "stenography," then "phonography") depends on the placement of characters in relation to a base line and includes angular characters that are distracting to draw. John Robert Gregg's "Light-Line Phonography," introduced fifty years later, has the advantage of being written in the same smooth, forward slant as ordinary handwriting, all in curves and loops, with no stop-start angles and no variations in placement. Easily adaptable to any spoken language, it is today the most widely used system in the world.

But there is still room for a shorthand system that can be learned in hours instead of months, and without the necessity of tedious practicing, so new systems are occasionally proffered by hopeful inventors. Among the more recent ones was Rae Greenburg's 1956 contribution, Shortrite, "a nu e-z shorthand" of the orthographic persuasion. But if its textbook's ponderous "memory guides" are any indication (sample: "Dot the letter for the long *i* sound, / Cross the letter if with a *t* it is bound"), Shortrite is hardly the desideratum.

Shorthand is a pretty dry subject, but some innovators in the field have juiced it up a bit. About 1882 an Englishman named Thomas Waghorn applied for a patent on what might be called a "committee system" of shorthand, or a throwback to the prehistoric professional memorizers. It involved fifteen stenographers all working at once, but none of them had to know a thing about shorthand. Seven of them sat side by side at desks in one row, another seven at a row of desks behind them, and the whole phalanx was supervised by a leader armed with a long pole.

When dictation began—at the very first word—the supervisor would tap the first man in the first row with his cuestick. That man would write down the first word, and as many more as he could scribble (in longhand, remember) before the speaker got too far ahead of him. Meanwhile, at perhaps the fourth or fifth word of the speaker's dictation, the supervisor would tap the second man in the front row, who would likewise start writing for dear life. So on down the front row, each man in turn getting a few words of the speech on paper—and after the seventh man, the leader would tap the first one again. As each front-row man finished as much writing as he could manage in one spasm, he'd fling that sheet of paper over his shoulder to the man behind him in the second row, and then wait to start scribbling again as soon as the cuestick poked him again. The seven men in the back row would be equally busy with the scraps they were tossed, feverishly collating the disjointed fragments and deleting their duplications, to make a coherent continuity.

Within moments after the speaker was finished—or so claimed inventor Waghorn—a complete and easily readable transcript of his speech would be ready for his inspection. Waghorn conceded that this fifteen-man system would be unwieldy for office use, but saw no reason why it wouldn't be perfectly practical in court. Not surprisingly, his "invention" was denied a patent. We can get some idea of the enthusiasm it kindled at the Patent Office by the fact that Waghorn went straight home and wrote a book entitled *The Bitter, Bitter Cry of Outcast Inventors.*

Long after both ordinary writing and shorthand were available to put man's words onto paper and into history, he still lacked a means of eternizing some other precious noises— songs, for example. The words of ballads or chants could be written down, but there was no way of indicating at what pitch they should be sung or how long each note should be held. The earliest music, like the earliest folk tales, had no hope of perpetuation but to be memorized and dinned into the ears of each new generation.

From about the year 900, the notes of the musical scale were designated by letters of the alphabet (at one time, the scale ran from A through P), but this provided no fixed pitch. That is, the scale could start anywhere; the low A might be any note that was convenient to the deeper male voices. So, even when attempts were made at a system of graphic notation, there was no real standardization. One tenth-century method was to write the lyrics in syllables jiggling up and down across the page, to indicate the approximate high and low notes. Alternatively, neumes (from *pneumae,* "breaths") were inserted above the words. These little dots, dashes and hooks worked passably well for indicating the duration of a note, but they were still incapable of telling exactly *what* note. One try at remedying this deficiency was to put the neumes on different colored lines, but this probably did more for the decor of the hymnals than for the quality of the chorale.

The modern system of musical notation dates from about 1040, when Guido d'Arezzo got the idea of multiplying those neume pitch-lines. He extended them into a staff of four; various later musicians tried other numbers, as many as fifteen lines. About 1500, by which time musicians had learned to make use of the spaces between the lines, too, the staff steadied on five lines, with the addition of ledger lines when needed. The neumes had become notes (known then by names like *maxima, brevis, semiminima,* etc., and drawn in the shape of squares and lozenges). The letters which once had been drawn on the colored pitch-lines, F, C and G, were gradually stylized into today's clef marks. Vertical bars were introduced into the staff to mark off measures. Key signatures and time signatures were clumped together at the head of the staff, and a host of other code signs came into use to indicate sharps, flats, trills, rests, slurs and all the other musical necessities.

When it was realized that a musician's eye can without difficulty read a number of staffs at once, it became the practice to write separate musical parts on separate staffs ranged one beneath the other and united in "accolade." A single voice accompanied by piano, for example, means two staffs, while a symphonic score will occupy as many concurrent staffs as there are instrumental parts.

By the seventeenth century, the musical notation system was essentially what it is now, and a *Miserere* composed by Lully in 1665 can be performed today, three hundred years later, exactly as he wrote it. The few changes in the system since that time have been only minor refinements, and for these three centuries musical notation has been one of the few undeniably universal languages. It seemed impossible to improve upon. Until now.

Now composers are writing into their scores parts for such instruments as garbage cans, cap pistols, doormen's whistles, balloons (for popping), tire chains and sandpaper-soled shoes. Though the codebook of musical notation is a hefty one, it has no provision for such outlandish newcomers as these. To score a part for flush toilet or sonic boom is just as impossible with staff and notes as it would have been with neumes and colored pitch-lines. So modern-day composers are inventing their own notation systems, with the result that many of their scores look to nonmusicians (and to conservative musicians) like a busted-open ant hill. What kind of music they make is best indicated by quoting from Earle Brown's preface to his own composition, 25 *Pages.* It may be played, says he, "in any sequence; each page may be performed either side up; the total time-duration of the piece is between 8 minutes 20 seconds and 25 minutes. . . ."

Along with music, another sort of cultural performance long lacked its own written language, or code, and that was the dance. The movements of folk dances and religious pageants were handed down from generation to generation, but no doubt they changed at least a little with each transfer, and there is no telling how many spontaneous performances worth recording were forgotten after one showing. All we know of such early frolics as maypole and morris dances is what can be reconstructed from static drawings and inexact folk memory.

Words were even less adequate for recording the dance than they were for music. A practical dance notation would have to take cognizance not only of the notes being played, and the duration of them, but also physical action. Even as simple a step as the waltz involves more than just scuffing the feet along a plane surface; the entire body is moving in three dimensions. One simplistic sort of dance notation, with which most laymen are familiar, is the plan of footprints and dotted lines common to texts on ballroom dancing. But its inadequacy is apparent in some modern discotheque dances, in which the feet are often the only parts of the body that *don't* move.

One early attempt at dance notation was Thoinot Arbeau's book *Orchesographie,* published in France in 1588. Arbeau gave each step a name and a detailed explanation, then wrote the step names alongside the corresponding notes of the music for each dance. But to make the system at all comprehensible he had to use simple steps and simple dances, and there was no way of adapting his system to notate a group performance.

In the 1700s Raoul Feuillet compiled a considerable body of choreography, describing the dances performed at the court of Louis XIV, but his scheme of notation was a predecessor of the footprint-plan and gave no idea of what was happening above floor level. Even so, his books were exceedingly popular at the time (a contemporary curmudgeon complained that the court ladies oftener had a Feuillet choreography on their night tables than a Bible), and they remain a valuable if incomplete record of dances that would otherwise have been forgotten.

Other aspiring choreographers used such devices as little stick figures dancing along the staffs of music scores. But these were limited in their depiction of three dimensions and, while they could show different positions, they couldn't show how the dancer got from one position to the next. The first really practical system of graphic dance notation, and to date the best, did not come along until 1928, when Rudolf Laban published a book on his "Kinetographie Laban" (more familiar to dancers now as Labanotation).

Laban's most significant break with preceding notations was to dispense entirely with music's five-line horizontal staff. His system uses a vertical staff of three lines. The center line divides right from left, and the spaces on either side of it contain code symbols to show the steps of each foot and attendant leg movements. Parallel columns outside the lines are used for the symbols pertaining to body, arm, hand and head movements.

Not to get into a too technical explanation, just let it be said that the Laban system is capable of recording or directting *everything* that occurs during a dance—steps, gestures, *entrechats*, even somersaults and cartwheels—right down to finger movements. Furthermore, it can show the direction, timing and force or delicacy of these movements, whether they occur consecutively or simultaneously. Each staff provides for the activities of a single dancer, but the staffs can be ganged together, like the orchestral staffs of a symphonic score, to show the different simultaneous movements of a whole ensemble.

Though Labanotation was conceived as a "shorthand of the dance," and that remains its prime function, it has other potential uses. Its capability of delineating every possible movement of the human body could be put to work, for example, in time-motion studies of industrial workers, the training of athletes and even in directing the null-gravity activities of astronauts.

While shorthand, music and dance notation and other such codes were being devised for the ease and enrichment of normal human communications, there existed great numbers of people who were denied even the bare bones of language. The deaf and mute were variously deprived of the spoken word, and the blind were deprived of the written. It was not until comparatively late in human history that any effort was made to help these unfortunates, linguistically, and the reason for this longtime neglect was a simple one: the equally longtime illiteracy of the greater portion of mankind. In an era when only a handful of people could read and write, the blind man was no worse off in that respect than anybody else. By the same token, it would have been useless to teach some kind of visual alphabet to the mute and deaf when the alphabet was unknown to everybody else they were likely to want to communicate with.

The Renaissance saw the first attempts to provide reading matter for the blind when, in Spain in the sixteenth century, simple texts—prayers, proverbs and the like—were carved in wood, sometimes embossed, sometimes intaglio. But these panels were too clumsy and elementary to serve as much more than tactile comforters to the afflicted, and a rosary served better for that. In the next century someone tried sticking roundheaded pins into cushions in the outline of letters. This system had the advantage of being rearrangeable, to allow for an occasional change of text, and could even be used by a literate blind man for writing. Other experiments included the use of cut-out cardboard letters and sets of wooden blocks with raised letters.

A real advance came in the early nineteenth century when Valentin Haüy, head of France's National Institute for Blind Children, demonstrated that letters could be embossed on sufficiently thick, soft paper. By this time, too, workers in the field had come to realize that a literature for the blind needn't slavishly copy traditional orthography. The keen touch of the blind could identify just a fragment of a letter (for example, ∧ instead of a complete A). A man named William Moon reduced the Roman letters to their merest rudiments and printed embossed books, some of which are still in use. Moon's books had one distinction: he set them up in the manner of the ancient Greek *boustrophedon*—in lines reading alternately left to right and right to left, "as the ox plows," so the reader never had to lift his finger from the page.

But others had already proved that the blind had no need whatsoever of the standard alphabet. They could memorize by touch any sort of symbolic substitutes, and the simpler these symbols, the easier they were to write, emboss and read. In 1821 a French Army officer, Charles Barbier, introduced the first pure cipher for the blind, a system based on various combinations of twelve raised dots. His invention was rather too cumbersome, but when Barbier demonstrated it at the Institute, it inspired one blind boy there to carry it to perfection. Louis Braille had lost his sight at the age of three, in an accident in his father's leather-working shop. He had come to the Institute at thirteen and Haüy had kept him on as a junior instructor. He was only fifteen when in 1824 he conceived the cipher system that bears his name.

Braille writing is based on a rectangle, or "cell," of six raised dots, three high and two wide, each cell easily spanned by even a child's fingertip. There are sixty-three possible combinations of the one to six dots in varying positions within that rectangle. Twenty-six patterns are used for the letters of the alphabet and the remainder for contractions, punctuation, diphthongs, etc. Second only to its reading simplicity is the fact that a blind writer can so easily emboss the dots into paper with a stylus and guide slate. It has made possible such tools for the blind as Braille-calibrated micrometers, thermometers, slide rules, clocks and watches, and even Braille typewriters. Braille himself devised a version of his system for musical notation, and others adapted it to mathematical notation.

Various refinements in the system have been made since its introduction, and today there are two systems taught to the blind. The beginning student learns "Braille A," which is a cipher like the original version, the dot cells substituting for individual letters. When the student has become proficient enough, he goes on to learn "Braille B," which is more of a code, or shorthand, in that more complex dot patterns stand for whole words or even lengthy locutions.

But, disappointingly, a survey in the United States once revealed that only 15 per cent of the blind population ever become sufficiently at home in Braille to find pleasure in reading it. The other 85 per cent much prefer "talking books" (phonograph recordings by professional readers). So the search for a more advantageous alternative still goes on, and recently some startling experiments have opened new vistas for speculation.

In 1962 Soviet researchers reported that they were studying a 22-year-old Russian girl who could read ordinary print with her fingers while blindfolded. Western scientists were inclined to skepticism until, in 1964, along came a Michigan housewife with the apparent ability to identify colors with her fingertips, while blindfolded or in total darkness, even when the color swatches are under glass. She pretended no explanation of how she did it, saying only that "the light colors are smoother or thinner or lighter in weight. The dark colors are thicker or rougher or heavier. Red, blue and green just feel like red, blue and green."

The American scientists have suspended disbelief, temporarily at least, and are conducting controlled studies into the phenomenon. A test of students at Barnard College indicates, according to the examiners, that perhaps five to fifteen people in every hundred have a similar sensibility without ever knowing it. And a science writer was moved to comment, "If the nature of the stimulus could be learned, then it might be possible to build equipment to produce and amplify the stimulus, and so help a large part of the blind population to read."

Nothing so dramatic seems to be in the offing as a linguistic boon to the deaf and mute. They are still making do with the same talents of gesture and lip-reading they had to cultivate back in the Dark Ages—though of course both these means of communication have been somewhat sophisticated over the years.

Schools for the deaf nowadays concentrate on teaching lip-reading as the best means for equipping the deaf to commune with ordinary folk. By the same techniques, the schools have managed to give speech to many former mutes, those who are dumb through no organic indisposition but because they were born deaf. Lip-reading is easiest accomplished, of course, when a speaker enunciates clearly, i.e., visibly. And so the family of a deaf child, to learn not to mumble in his presence, are encouraged to practice the same recitations which his teachers use in instruction. Sample: "If a plaid-clad caddy-laddie's daddy had a fad for adding, would the plaid-clad caddy-laddie's daddy be an adder?"

But among others like themselves, the deaf and mute find sign language a valuable accessory. For one instance, a lecture spoken to a deaf audience would reach only the first few rows of lip-readers, whereas sign language can communicate to the whole hall. The sign language most generally in use today is a combination of cipher and code. The cipher part is a one-hand alphabet involving a different gesture for each letter and numeral, first compiled by the Abbé de l'Epée three hundred years ago and little changed since. The code part is a system of gestures, using one or both hands, which stand for whole words and concepts. This is a now standardized outgrowth of the gestures that the deaf and mute of long ago contrived spontaneously—just as the normal person instinctively makes shooing gestures to mean "Go away."

The alphabet signs are necessary for spelling out uncommon words. But the code signs have quite a remarkable range of expression and, since they deal with ideas rather than spelled-out words, can even enable the deaf of different nationalities to converse with some degree of mutual comprehension.

To signify "hell," for example, one simply points downward. "Jesus" is indicated by tapping the middle finger of each hand into the palm of the other; this represents the nails of the cross. While the gestures for less concrete concepts are not always immediately obvious, they still transcend the limitations of spelling and pronunciation. The gesture of open, crooked hands moving several times from the waist up along the sides, as if clawing the ribs, might seem inscrutable but it's not hard to figure out. It represents someone tearing his clothes and, depending on the vigor with which it's acted out, stands for "anger" in any degree from "displeasure" to "fury."

"Love" is indicated by crossed hands pressed to the breast. "Attention" is signified by placing the open hands against both sides of the face, to stand for the blinders on a horse. "Hello," "goodbye," "thank you" and "you're welcome" are all conveyed by the gesture of throwing a kiss. "Idle" or "holiday" is indicated by placing thumbs in armpits and waggling the fingers, the very picture of a happy loafer. That the sign language has been in use for a good long time is evident in the signs for "female" and "gentleman." The former is done by stroking a closed hand down the right cheek toward the chin, indicating an old-fashioned bonnet's string—and the latter by placing the open hand against the chest, moving it slightly outward and downward, indicating the jabot or ruffle once worn by men of quality.

It must be acknowledged that the development of linguistic prosthetics for sensorially crippled individuals is sadly laggard, compared to other modern-day technologies that are helping the mass of mankind to communicate better and faster. One new communications technique which is proving increasingly helpful is that employed by the proliferating computers—though it's not *quite* the miracle some make it out to be.

The most complex computer is capable of comprehending just one expression, the question "Yes or no?" And it is capable of responding with just one of two answers, "Yes" or "No." It replies, not on the basis of logic, intelligence, opinion or guess, but only after making a cold, mechanical choice between alternatives. And its alternatives are limited to whatever bits of information are already stored in its memory banks. Merely to add 22 and 22, the computer must, in effect, flick through every possible total from 23 on up, asking of each one "yes or no?" When it serves up the answer "44," it is not because the computer "knows" this to be the "right" answer, but because it was the first one (and therefore mathematically the only possible one) that was not provably wrong.

However, if you think about it, the most complicated question—barring the metaphorical and metaphysical—can be broken down into components answerable with "yes" or "no." A computer cannot answer a question like "Is ice cold?" But, assuming that its memory banks include the information that ice, to be ice, must have a temperature of at most 0° centigrade, the computer can answer "yes" or "no" to a whole string of questions like "Is ice colder than molten lava?" and "Is ice colder than blood heat?" After a series of answers, the questioner should be able to decide for himself whether ice is cold.

The electronic computer is a valuable tool because its memory banks can hold an almost limitless amount of information, and because it makes its choice among alternatives at the speed of light. Thus, no matter how complicated the problem it is posed—that is, no matter how many intermediate "yes or no" components are involved—the computer can reply almost instantaneously. The only "computer language" is binary arithmetic, a system based on just two digits, as against the decimal system's unwieldy ten. The two digits, 1 and 0, essentially correspond to "yes" and "no." A mathematical equation is easily translatable into this system for "programing" into a computer, and nonmathematical questions can be put to an information-handling machine by using combinations of the digits as either a literal cipher or a verbal code.

The machines have been put to various linguistic uses, the most practical being that of translation from one language to another. A computer's memory banks can be stocked with all the words in, say, the Russian vocabulary, together with their equivalents in English, and perform a translation by the simple process of matching them. This works well enough for translating scientific and technical texts of cut-and-dried data couched in charts and lists. But no computer yet can cope with the amorphousness of syntax and grammar—not to mention idiom and slang—so attempts at translating more "literary" literature have so far fizzled. A computer can, however, recognize an author's syntactical idiosyncrasies and tabulate their frequency, a talent which should be useful, for example, in settling long-standing disputes over the authorship of certain New Testament epistles.

Every once in a while, computer technicians show off their machines by programming them to "compose" some literary work of their own. This, like the proliferation of night-school "creative writing" courses, has not caused any wholesale melancholia among flesh-and-blood professional writers. The International Business Machines Corporation some time ago displayed with paternal pride a sentence concocted by one of its computers, all on its own: "What does she put four whistles beside heated rugs for?" A newspaper reporter, pressed for a plaudit, said, "Its typing is immaculate." Not even IBM has yet thought to update that old law-of-averages proposition about sitting twelve monkeys down to twelve typewriters—by plunking them down at twelve computer terminals instead—to see how long it'll be before their random pecking results in a print-out of the complete works of Shakespeare. Human stenographers may have slightly more cause for anxiety, but not much. Another dream of the computer-builders is to make shorthand obsolete by inventing a type-writer that will operate direct from dictation. But so far they've been stumped, again, by the vagaries of human languages. The machine has to contend both with individual quirks of pronunciation and with the inconsistencies of orthography. It just can't write right. In 1961 the Radio Corporation of America allegedly had its experimental phonetic typewriter make out its own application for patent, like this: "the ultimit objekt is too develup a tipriter which tips in respons too wurds spoken intoo a mikrophon the outpoot being imediatli legibl and usabl. . . ."

The electronic computers might well turn their talents to the decryptment of the several ancient languages that still defy the best efforts of paleographers. It's too bad they weren't around to ease the punishing wear and tear on earlier decipherers. Even after the lucky discovery of the Rosetta Stone, and with its aid as a "codebook," it took Egyptologists more than twenty years to unlock the secrets of hieroglyphics. When, one day in 1822, the 32-year-old Jean Champollion finally translated the first of them, he shouted, "I've got it!" and fainted. He had spent his health in getting it; he died enfeebled ten years later. When George Smith, in 1872, deciphered a cuneiform tablet, he exclaimed in ecstasy, "I am the first to read this text after two thousand years of oblivion!" Then he began gibbering and trying to rip off his clothes. He never quite recovered, and died at the age of 36.

In 1964 Russian scientist Nikolai Andreev claimed to have perfected a "linguistic key" which, in company with a computer, can analyze mathematically and thus decipher any text in any writing, known or unknown—including Venusian and Martian, if such things be. But Western scientists have long been preparing for any eventual encounter with extra-terrestrial languages, by delving into nonhuman languages right here on earth.

Ever since man first learned to talk, he has been wondering whether animals could or can. Certainly some of the more intelligent species, both domesticated and wild, have been able to learn a few commands in human tongues. And pets learn both to obey their master's words and to express themselves in a sort of charade fashion—it is impossible to misunderstand the message of a dog fetching its leash in its mouth, and a cat's tail is as expressive as a maestro's baton. But, although it was eons ago that man established this minimal communication with his animals on his terms, it was not until very recently that he had any hope of ever learning any language of theirs.

Scientists long ago concluded that such languages must exist. While the more obvious animal noises—a dog's bark, a cat's miaow, a bird's twitter—might be mostly instinctive or emotive reactions, it was impossible to believe that the complex society of a beehive could function so smoothly without some form of quasi-intelligent intercourse. In 1950 apiologist Karl von Frisch announced that the bees do indeed have a language, and that he had deciphered parts of it.

According to von Frisch, when a worker bee finds an estimable source of nectar she reports it to the rest of the bee community by "dancing" on a vertical wall of the hive. Her repeated contortions trace a geometrical pattern, using the position of the sun as a reference point, and indicate both the direction and the distance of the new food supply. Von Frisch further discovered that, come swarming time, scouts would be sent out to seek likely sites for a new home. These would return, report on their findings in another geometrical dance, and the rest of the community would compare the "enthusiasm" of the various scouts before deciding where to relocate. Von Frisch's thesis was backed by enough evidence and observations to make it theoretically acceptable, but it was conclusively validated nine years later when another zoologist actually talked to the bees.

In 1959 Dr. Wolfgang Steche built an artificial bee, an electronically remote-controlled robot. He secreted a supply of sugar-water in a place his laboratory bees had never yet visited. Then he slipped his robot bee into the hive and put it through a dance, according to von Frisch's geometrical code, telling where the nectar was. The real worker bees watched, comprehended and flew directly to the spot.

Various other researchers are studying such putative animal languages as those of chickens, crows, meerkats and monkeys. Dr. Erich Baeumer claims to have found that all chickens, regardless of nationality, breed or color, speak an "international chicken language" made up of thirty basic sentences. Hubert and Mabel Frings have recorded the calls of crows from different localities and have discovered some anomalous national variances. For example, Maine crows pay no attention to the alarm cry of French crows, but Pennsylvania crows get agitated when they hear it. The Fringses decided that this is because Maine crows are stay-at-homes and therefore are limited in their comprehension. But Pennsylvania crows fly south every winter, where they hobnob with other crows, and so seem to acquire some cosmopolitanism and a smattering of "foreign" crow languages.

Dr. Malcolm Lyall-Watson, who claimed to be already "on speaking terms" with a number of monkeys and chimpanzees in the London Zoo, took off for South Africa in 1964 to study the "tail talk" of meerkats (a species of ground squirrel). About the same time, Professor Denzaburo Miyadi concluded that Japanese monkeys have a vocabulary of some thirty different words—ranging from *kwaa*, "let's go," to *howiaa*, "here's food." This would set the monkey rather higher on the linguistic ladder than the gorilla; George Schaller, after living among the African mountain gorillas for a solid year, could distinguish no more than twenty-two different utterances.

Someone has described flowers as "prayers that say themselves." But, beyond the sentimental messages that humans read in them, flowers do have a vague sort of communicational capability. For example, the petals of the yellow daisy absorb all ultraviolet light, except at their extreme tips. A bee, which is blind to the color yellow but can distinguish ultraviolet, thus sees the daisy as a ring of bright points surrounding the dark heart where the nectar lies, and can zero in on it as readily as an airplane pilot following a runway's landing lights. The daisy's signal is of course no "conscious" communication, but a mutation fortuitously developed over an eternity of generations. Still, it serves the purpose of language—here advertising payment in nectar for the opportunity of pollination—just as effectively as if the flower crooned a siren song.

It is not likely that men will ever sit down to confabulations or kaffeeklatsches with hens, bees or daisies. But there is one nonhuman whose linguistic ability—and the intelligence behind it—may be on a par with our own. The porpoise, or dolphin, has for centuries been known to seamen to have both sense and a sense of humor. In recent years, skindivers and the proprietors of marine museums have discovered that porpoises are unafraid of men and even affectionate toward them, that they are exceptionally quick to learn, that they are capable of a wide range of vocalizations, and can even mimic human talk.

Among themselves, porpoises bark, whistle, creak, quack, click and squawk, and evidently when they put their minds to it they can reproduce any human noise. Lorus and Margery Milne, in their book *The Senses of Animals and Men,* tell how one porpoise at Florida's Marine Studios "imitated a man's voice so well that his wife laughed heartily. Promptly the porpoise imitated her laughter."

Neurophysiologist John C. Lilly spent several years in a determined effort to learn the creatures' language. This project attracted the interest of some rather crass outsiders. The American fishing industry seems to have entertained high hopes that the animals may be trained to find and track schools of fish, or even herd them into fishermen's nets. The U. S. Navy seems to have gone so far as trying to train them to snitch on enemy submarines, or even to volunteer as suicide carriers of small torpedoes. If the porpoises have co-operated in that, they're not as smart as we'd like to think they are.

Considering the porpoises' talent for mimicry, it may be a toss-up between them and mankind as to who will learn whose language first. But if communication could be achieved, it would be far more epochal in its own right than in any brummagem military or commercial advantage it might bestow. It would be the first intellectual intercourse between two different species on this earth. As the Milnes point out, "By finding features in common between the operation of a porpoise's brain and a man's, we stand a good chance of discovering the essential basis for elusive qualities such as memory, learning and intelligence."

Besides the opportunity it would give man for knowing himself better, it would mean incalculably valuable insights into an alien intelligence—and that the product of environment in an alien element. There is the possibility, remote though it may seem, that man *will* eventually come in contact with extraterrestrial intelligences whose nature he cannot yet begin to guess. In converse with the porpoise he might get some idea of what his relations with nonearth nonhumans may be like. Just as porpoises have traditionally "piloted" man's ships into safe harbor, they might someday help to guide his course of conduct in the seas between the worlds.

> I dare say that this [a universal language] is the last
> effort of the human mind, and when the project shall
> have been carried out, all that men will have to do
> will be to be happy.
>
> —GOTTFRIED VON LEIBNITZ

Tuta per Unu & One for All

I T is perhaps paradoxical that men should be seeking to
converse with subhuman beings here on earth and possible superhuman beings out among the stars, when
they have such a deal of trouble talking to each other. Without an interpreter, Dr. Lilly couldn't tell Professor Andreev
about his research into the porpoise language, and Professor
Andreev couldn't explain to Dr. Lilly how his Martian-
translation system works. But men have been studying this
human-human problem, too, for some three centuries, and
the solution—if there is one—may be closer now than ever
before.

There is a light touch of the goad in Professor Andreev's
good-humored boast that his linguistic-key-and-computer system might someday translate Martian. He did not say "West
Martian" or "Hyperborean Martian" or "Australo-Martian."
Taking the pixie premise that Martians exist, he further pretended that the ones living on opposite sides of the planet's
"canals" would not be as linguistically various as, say, the
earthlings living on opposite sides of the River Dnestr. The
intimation is that a really intelligent and mature race—
(and all extraterrestrial civilizations are automatically supposed superior to ours)—would long ago have disencum-
bered itself of polyglot confusion.

Ever since Babel, humanity has been lamenting its linguistic fragmentation. For a long time, there seemed nothing to
be done about it, beyond a passive reliance on the fundamentalists' assurance that if we'd all just be good and do
right, God would someday rescind the edict of confusion. It
was not until the seventeenth century that a few thinking

men began to contemplate the possibility of taking the matter out of God's hands and somehow contriving an "Earthian" language themselves.

The idea was an outgrowth of an earlier speculation. As far back as the thirteenth century, Western philosophers had suggested compiling some code of symbols—based on concepts rather than words, and thus independent of spoken tongues—that would serve as a common writing for people of all languages. But the notion was only half-heartedly bandied until about 1600, when the Western world began to take notice of Chinese ideographic writing and its use as a common script among people speaking a multitude of mutually incomprehensible tongues. This evidence that a supralanguage writing *was* practical aroused a new enthusiasm for the idea and encouraged even bigger ambitions. René Descartes was the first known proponent of a universal language to be spoken as well as written, and he was also the first to propose that it be an artificial one, invented from scratch.

However, when Descartes and his contemporary confreres spoke of a "universal language," they didn't necessarily mean a common tongue for everybody everywhere, but one suitable for intercourse on the rarefied level of philosophy and scholarship. The seventeenth-century commoner had no use for any spoken language but his own, and he already had his symbolic code writing in the rebus pictures on tavern and shop signs. International commerce was still of such meager extent that the traders could make do with an improvised pidgin wherever they landed. Mass immigration and tourism were unknown.

Even the scholars and philosophers didn't really need an intercultural language; they already had one. Every learned European of the time spoke fluent Latin, and it was hard to find any work of science, technology or philosophy written in any other language. Cromwell asked that his biography be written in Latin to make sure that future generations of Englishmen would be able to read it. But for all its ubiquity and utility, Latin still had faults common to every other human language. Even the classical Roman writers had sometimes lapsed into ambiguity and uncertainty of expression, and a Latin word could still—like any English word or French word—have different meanings to different people.

What the seventeenth-century philosophers were seeking was what the twentieth-century semanticists still are seeking: a language free of fuzz, fog and mumblefug. They wanted a language capable of analyzing and systematizing ideas, of pinning down abstractions and shades of meaning, of clarifying confusion, of expressing thought in unmistakable terms. What they meant by "universality" was that each word in the new language should have the same concrete meaning to every user, whatever his race, nationality, cultural heritage or environment. They never came near achieving such an ideal. But the seventeenth-century experiments did blaze trails for later attempts at a more exoteric and democratic world language.

It was in 1629 that Descartes sketched the first outlines of a practical artificial language. He envisioned it as having a bare minimum of grammatical rules and, most important, a vocabulary based on some classification of ideas in a system as logical and precise as that of mathematics. Descartes was satisfied just to state the criteria, and left it to someone else to build a language to fit them. A generation later, and independently of Descartes, the Scottish educator George Dalgarno set about devising a language along those very lines. He published it in 1661 as *Ars Signorum.*

As the basis for his "Art of Signs," Dalgarno divided "all of human knowledge" into seventeen broad categories, each designated by a consonant whose function was to be the base for a word. For example, K stood for all "political matters," and this category was subdivided into more explicit classifications by the addition of a vowel; thus *Ku* covered all matters pertaining to war. With the addition of each succeeding letter—alternately consonant and vowel—the category was narrowed still further, and the final result would be a polysyllabic but pronounceable word meaning a specific thing, individual, action, quality or whatnot.

Seven years later an Anglican bishop, John Wilkins, published his *Essay towards a Real Character, and a Philosophical Language,* which was rather prematurely hailed by several members of the Royal Society as The Answer to the quest for a universal language. The bishop was a man of diverse interests: he had suggested building "an Ark for submarine Navigation"; he had written on the possibility of life on the moon, and on the feasibility of constructing "a chariot" to fly there. But the final years of his life were devoted to promoting and puttering with his "philosophical language." As gossipist John Aubrey wrote, "This last was his Darling, and nothing troubled him so much when he dyed, as that he had not compleated it."

Wilkins' language coined its vocabulary according to an incremental system, similar to Dalgarno's but even more densely pocked with categorical pigeonholes. The system worked rather like the Dewey decimal classification of library books. To concoct the Wilkinsian word for "diamond," for instance, one had first to be aware that the gem was catalogued in a sub-sub-sub-sub-sub-sub-classification under the rubric of "Substance Inanimate." To wit:

Substance Inanimate
  I. Sensitive
 II. Vegetative
    A. Perfect
       (Plants, etc.)
    B. Imperfect
       1. Metals
       2. Stones
          i. vulgar
         ii. middle-prized
        iii. precious
             a. less transparent
             b. more transparent
                (*a*) diamonds . . .

Wilkins had earlier invented a shorthand system, and had made a hobby of cryptography, so he was well qualified to undertake a new system of writing (the "Real Character") to go with his philosophical language. Each classification carried not a letter, but a geometrical symbol, and in writing a word these various components were strung together or overlaid. Though the "real character" word was intended to perform the Chinese-ideogram function of conveying a concept instead of a noise, Wilkins gave each component symbol a monosyllabic sound (*da, gi, de,* etc.) so the words *could* be spoken if desired.

Both Wilkins' and Dalgarno's systems seemed to follow the Cartesian precept of a quasi-mathematical system, but they had few other endearing qualities. Though their "progression of ideas" was superficially logical, a user of either language would have needed a superhuman patience to clamber up and down the referential staircase every time he wanted to piece a word together, and he'd also have needed a monumental memory to remember which consonant, vowel or symbol was arbitrarily assigned to each category.

Anyway, the systems *were* only superficially logical, because they were too rigidly based on the sum of human knowledge as it stood, and the seventeenth century was not overfreighted with knowledge. In order to accommodate any new discovery or invention that eventuated in any field, either of these languages would have had to be torn down and rebuilt. For example, the scientific revolution already under way in Wilkins' time would soon have demolished his conception of "Substance Inanimate."

Dalgarno and Wilkins were followed by a score or more of other would-be interlinguists during the remainder of the seventeenth century, including mathematician-philosopher Gottfried von Leibnitz. His grail was a language that would be "an algebra of thought." At one time he seriously espoused Chinese ideograms as a writing system compatible with any and every national language. At another time, he proposed a language written entirely in numerals.

During the ensuing hundred years of search for a new language, all those proposed were of the artificial, symbolic, esoteric variety. But a new approach was tried in 1765, in the *Langue Nouvelle* suggested by M. Faiguet, then Treasurer of France. He disputed his predecessors' assumption that a manufactured language must be completely artificial, and favored synthesizing one out of available materials, that is, borrowing the most advantageous and adaptable elements of languages currently in use. Faiguet didn't provide any suggested vocabulary for his *Langue Nouvelle*, but his outline of grammar was admirably peeled down to easy essentials, and some of his ideas were creditable enough to be incorporated in the later Esperanto.

All the hundreds of languages devised since that time have fallen somewhere between the two extremes of *a priori* inventions (like Dalgarno's and Wilkins') created from totally new elements and structurally unrelated to any known language, and *a posteriori* concoctions (of the sort Faiguet favored) based on familiar elements and commonplace constructions.

The advantages of an *a priori* language are manifold. Its vocabulary can be logically based on some relationship of word to thing, its grammar can be exiguous, it need have no dead wood like English spelling or German genders or French irregular verbs. But its very newness may be self-defeating. A student has to start learning from the ground up, with no familiar reference points or similarities to his native language. He must memorize an entirely new vocabulary, sometimes a formidably odd one. And with some systems he must learn to write all over again as well.

An *a posteriori* language is bound to be somewhat haphazard, illogical and unwieldy, because it is derived from a naturally grown language or languages, and that's the way they are. Its supposed advantage is that, because it is not so utterly alien, it is easier for people to learn. This is a moot generalization. A new language based, say, on Russian rudiments would be fairly easy for any Slavic student to pick up; to a Japanese or Italian it would be just as rocky as ordinary Russian. If the new language were an amalgam of Russian and Latin elements, it would be less difficult for the Italian, less easy for the Slav, and still an abomination to the Japanese. Add an infusion of Japanese to the mixture and it's not going to be very easy for any of them. And so on: the new language's appeal and potential universality will continue to diminish as its eclecticism increases. Most of the artificial languages have combined *a priori* and *a posteriori* systems in varying proportions, in hope of getting the virtues of both and canceling out each other's vices.

After the seventeenth century's initial spate of proposed new languages, the first fine flush of enthusiasm seems to have waned suddenly and considerably. During the next 150 years, only a handful of new ones were devised. Shortly after the French Revolution, a Citizen Delormel proposed to the National Convention the adoption of his *Langue Universelle*, a symbolic, philosophical system quite similar to Wilkins'. The republicans were busily erasing all traces of the old regime—contriving a new calendar, new place names on the map, even new personal names for themselves—but apparently an abandonment of the old language was too revolutionary even for revolutionaries.

A few years later, another Frenchman, Jean-François Sudre, came up with the most wondrously strange of all artificial languages yet conceived. His Solresol was based, as the name indicates, on the notes of the musical scale. Using only the syllables *do, re, mi, fa, sol, la* and *ti*, it was capable of compounding more than 11,700 words of up to five syllables. (Sample: *Dore milati domi*, "I love you.") Sudre pointed out that Solresol could be comprehensibly played on an instrument, sung, whistled or hummed, as well as spoken. It could be written in either standard Roman script or in the already international symbols of musical notation. Solresol had a necessarily cumbersome grammar, and its arbitrary vocabulary—like that of any *a priori* language—demanded the memory power of a computer. But it was well received on its appearance in 1827; such luminaries as Victor Hugo and Napoleon III approved of it. Solresol was widely popular for fifty years (though no practical use was ever made of it), and still had devotees in many countries in the early 1900s.

But the mid-nineteenth century experienced a new wave of interest in universal languages, and Solresol soon had a host of competitors. The new interest was engendered by great advances in literacy among the common people, by increased international trade, travel and immigration, speedier transportation and communications systems, and the opening up to the world of new countries and cultures. A universal language was no longer just an ivory-tower dream; it was coming to seem a virtual necessity. Admittedly, the kind of people who invented such languages were still mostly of the moony visionary breed, and most of their followers were of the little-old-ladies-in-tennis-shoes type, but now even hardheaded businessmen and politicians were beginning to see merit in the notion of "one world, one language."

Among the nineteenth-century candidates were Lingualumina, Kosmos, Communia, Universalsprache, Néo-Latine, Pasilingua, Chabe Abane, Luftlandana, Monoglottica, Blaia Zimondal, Alwato, Mundolingue, Lingua and Latinesce. As is evident from the names of many of these, the Latin language, or some derivation or simplification of Latin, has figured prominently in the history of invented languages. It stands to reason. Latin *was* at one time a nearly universal language, and it has maintained that status in the field of medicine and in the Roman Catholic Church. It was also the ancestor of all the Romance languages and has contributed heavily to other Western tongues. Almost any European, undertaking to learn a new, Latin-oriented language, would find enough recognizable elements to make the task easier.

Of the *a posteriori* languages which have not leaned on Latin, almost all have been based on some other Indo-European tongue. Lucien de Rudelle's 1858 proposal, Pantos-Dîmou-Glossa, though its name meant "All People's Language," combined elements only from Greek, Latin, English, German, Russian and the Romance languages—all of Indo-European origin. A. Budilovich's 1891 attempt at a Pan-Slavic language, Obshcheslavyansky Yazyk, though it hardly sounds like a hot prospect for universal use, was also a stepchild of the Indo-European family. Even the completely artificial *a priori* languages have to have some kind of syntax, and so they too have tended to depend on constructions that would be least alien to Western tongues.

The reason is, of course, that the world-language movement began in Europe and has been most active there. Comparatively few interlinguists have been fluent enough in Asian, Amerindian, African or Oceanic languages to find any of them preferable as a foundation for an artificial language.

The first manufactured language which actually won international usage and an appreciable body of speakers, readers and writers was Volapük. One would expect that just the name—with its umlauted *u*—would have repelled the millions of people who have no such thing in their native languages. Almost as many would have found even the *k* an alien letter. But Volapük was an overnight success and spread far beyond Europe. Within five years after its appearance, it had some two hundred thousand speakers, and Volapük clubs and societies had sprung up in the United States, Mexico, Australia, South Africa and China. There were hundreds of books and periodicals published in and about the language.

Volapük was the 1879 creation of a German cleric, Monsignor Johann Schleyer, and it was introduced to the world in 1885 in his book *Grammatik der Universalsprache für alle Erdbewohner* ("Grammar of the Universal Language for All Earthlings"). The book was destined to be translated into some two dozen other languages during the heyday of Volapük. And a heyday it had. Mario Pei, in his *One Language for the World,* reported that "at a Volapük congress held in Paris in 1889 not merely the delegates, but even the waiters and porters spoke Volapük."

In Volapük, *volapük* means "world-speak," but why the world took to it so warmly is a mystery. Its vocabulary was supposedly based on English words, but Volapük's distorted versions of them were almost as arcane as Solresol's earlier musical abstractions. Volapük was as capricious as any *a priori* system in its use of word roots and affixes—for example, *vat* meant "water" and *lu* was the prefix for "nastiness," so *luvat* meant "urine." Its grammar was no model of simplicity either; nouns had Germanic case-endings and verbs had a bewildering array of affixes to show tense and mood. One of the language's minor failings was rather ludicrous. In his earnest desire to cater to "all earthlings," Msgr. Schleyer took care to omit *r* from Volapük's alphabet, because the Chinese have such trouble articulating it. He consistently substituted *l*, and thereby unwittingly exiled some 120 million Japanese and Koreans.

Volapük's downfall was as meteoric as its rise had been. Its devotees were well aware of its deficiencies and, at that 1889 congress, suggested some eminently worthwhile improvements, including the deletion of the language's "German frills." Father Schleyer unaccountably bridled at this show of impertinence from the earthlings, and refused to let anyone tamper with "his" language. The result was schism.

The numerous separatists went ahead anyway with unauthorized variations and improvements on Volapük—systems with names like Dil, Balta, Veltparl and Langue Bleue (named for the universal sky). Other dissenters divorced themselves entirely from Volapük and dreamed up totally new languages—Idiom Neutral, Mundolingue, etc. What had been a concerted movement was suddenly a cluster of cliques, each dedicated to one offshoot language and inimical alike to Volapük and all the other variants. Within ten more years, Volapük was nearly as defunct as Sanskrit, and so were all the neo-Volapüks.

Now came Esperanto into the ascendancy. This had been introduced in 1887, when Volapük was in showiest flower, and consequently hadn't excited much stir. Esperanto was not then *its* name, but the pseudonym of its inventor, Dr. Ludwig Zamenhof; he had presented it as *Linguo Internacia de la Doktoro Esperanto* ("by Dr. Hopeful"). Esperanto's earliest popularity was, oddly enough, in Russia. From there it spread through Scandinavia, and so was waiting on the doorstep of the Continent when Volapük began to fall apart, at which time many leading ex-Volapükists transferred their loyalty to this newcomer. One man, Louis de Beaufront, even abandoned his own language project—though he'd already spent twelve years working on it—to spread the gospel of Esperanto in France.

What was odd about Russia's acceptance of Esperanto was that the language was and is based on Teutonic and Latin-Romance elements, making it as difficult for a Russian to learn as English or Spanish would be. To read it the Russian had to learn the Roman alphabet, and to speak it he had to contend with the *h* which doesn't exist in his own tongue. Esperanto's *h* is also a trial to speakers of Romance languages, while its Germanic *ch* sound (as in *Reich*) is alien to English-speakers. In addition, the Esperanto alphabet uses half a dozen diacritical superscripts (for example, *h̆* represents that *ch* sound) which pain printers in practically every country.

Esperantists claim that their language is easier to learn than any natural one. But it would be easier still if it hadn't clung to so many of the natural languages' impediments: noun cases, plural adjectives, verb conjugation endings, etc. Zamenhof's vocabulary is less than easy to memorize, partly because of his whimsicality in deciding which things should get their names from the Teutonic tongues and which from the Latinic. *Knabo* is "boy," from the German *Knabe*, but "brother" is *frato*, from the Latin *frater*. There are some eight thousand such root words in the Esperanto dictionary, and these can be infinitely multiplied by the use of affixes. For example, the infix *-in-* means "feminine" and the prefix *bo-* signifies "by marriage," so *frato* ("brother") can become *fratino* ("sister") and *bofratino* ("sister-in-law").

But many of the affixes are Zamenhof's own inventions, with no relation to either Teutonic or Latinic elements, and no other logical *raison d'être*. Furthermore, Esperanto often departs from the ideal of simplification to indulge in questionable and sometimes ridiculous hairsplitting. In a vocabulary of a mere eight thousand basic words, Esperanto yet deemed it desirable to distinguish between a "kiss" (*kiso*) and a "noisy kiss" (*śmaco*, pronounced "shmock-o"). The Esperanto lexicographers are to be congratulated, however, on two handy locutions they found worthy of inclusion—*damnu!* and *kondamnu je infero!*

Esperanto, like Volapük, early had its critics. Zamenhof, unlike Schleyer, encouraged criticisms, suggestions and improvements, and Esperanto incorporated many of them. Even so, some obstreperous reform groups insisted on setting up splinter languages. De Beaufront, who had sacrificed his own dream language for Esperanto's sake, recanted and swore allegiance to a variant called Ido. Others were Nov-Esperanto, Esperantido and Esperido.

Esperanto suffered rebuffs from outside the ranks, too. Russia, its earliest patron, turned against it and banished the movement's periodical *La Esperantisto* after it ran a translation of a Tolstoy article that peeved the Tsar. Thirty years later, Nazi Germany banned the language because it wasn't "Aryan" enough. The League of Nations refused, despite persistent pressure by Esperantists in high places, to lend its sponsorship to the movement's drive for international acceptance. And those non-Esperantists who cherish their own mother tongues have had unkind things to say about this would-be usurper; e.g., English writer John Moore's description of Esperanto as "this bloodless, backboneless, witless deformity."

It has been continually challenged by one competitor after another: Völkerverkehrssprache, Tutonish, Interlingua, Ro, Nepo, Adjuvilo, Perfekt, Nov Latin Logui, Timerio (written in numerals: 1-80-17, "I love you"), Uniala, Hom-Idyomo— these and scores of others made their appearance during the first quarter of the twentieth century, and most made their disappearance as well. In just one year, 1928, the world was dubiously enriched by five different new languages—Etem, Novam, Ido Reformita, Oiropapitschn (a modified German) and Novial.

This last was something unique, in that it was conceived by a professional linguist, the Danish savant Otto Jespersen. Linguists generally have inclined to treat artificial languages with a tolerant skepticism. But Jespersen had been hopefully enthusiastic about Volapük, Esperanto and Ido in turn, and in turn had found them wanting. His Novial, constructed along the lines of English, with an eclectically European vocabulary, showed many improvements over its predecssors, but failed to budge Esperanto's solid entrenchment.

The search for the perfect universal language has not yet slackened. In 1943 statistician-philologist Lancelot Hogben submitted Interglossa, a language very much akin to pidgin. Its vocabulary is wholly from Latin and Greek, but its syntax is Chinese. Another on the same order is Kenneth Littlewood's Mongling, which has the further Chinese-y distinction of consisting entirely of one-syllable words. In 1957 appeared both H. Heimer's Mondial, actually a simplified Spanish, and Dr. Barnett Russell's Suma. This is a purely *a priori* invention, with an arbitrary vocabulary of just one thousand words. There are no noun declensions or verb conjugations, no articles, no plurals, not even any capital letters.

In 1964 Hans Freudenthal presented the very first *truly* universal language, that is, one intended for use by the whole universe. His Lincos (Language for Cosmic Intercourse) is a mixture of linguistic, mathematical and biological symbols, translatable into the binary code, transmittable by radio or laser to any inhabited planets out yonder, and allegedly comprehensible by any intelligences who tune in on it.

The current standing of all these various languages, in comparison to Esperanto, can be gauged by the fact that practically nobody but a professional linguist has ever heard of them. Almost every man in the street, any street, knows at least the name of Esperanto.

It made its biggest gains right after World War I, during that fleeting moment when international amity seemed within reach. Its record of acceptance since then has continued to be a rosy one. Post-revolution Russia reinstated it as an optional second-language study in schools. Albania made it a compulsory high school subject. Universities in China (pre-Communism) offered courses in it. Today it can be found in more than six hundred schools around the world. The movement has published nearly eight thousand books, both Esperanto texts and Esperanto translations of standard literary works, and more than a hundred periodicals appear regularly. Esperanto is one of just two supranational languages which the world's telegraph union has authorized for cable communications; the other is Latin. Various European radio stations make regular broadcasts in Esperanto. Several countries have commemorated its anniversaries by issuing special postage stamps.

There are Esperanto speakers (who can be recognized by a little green star worn in the lapel) in just about every civilized country, and active Esperanto societies in such diverse places as New York, Tokyo, Rio de Janeiro and Oslo. It has had its greatest appeal to the people of smaller nations—Belgium, Holland, Denmark, etc.—whose own languages outsiders consider too parochial to be worth learning. The *World Almanac* lists Esperanto among the "principal languages" of mankind, and gives it one million speakers. The figure is extravagant; while the Esperanto movement may have as many as *eight* million supporters, probably only about half a million of them are actually capable of making practical use of it. But even so, it astronomically outranks any other artificial language now or ever in use.

Its only current competitor of note is Interlingua, and this in a fairly limited area. Interlingua was first conceived (as Latine sine Flexione) by the mathematician Giuseppe Peano in 1908, and early came to be a sort of *lingua franca* of science and technology. Its vocabulary is wholly Latin, but uses only those Latin words which survive in and are familiar to the European languages of today. Its grammar is next to no grammar at all. Interlingua has been continually improved and updated by its users, and is now the common language of many international scientific congresses.

But other universal language movements are afoot, besides those advocating manufactured systems, and have been since Descartes' day, when the Moravian bishop Johann Comenius pointed out that *any* language could be a universal one; it had only to become universal. Comenius suggested that the then leading languages extend their dominion until one of them (Russian) became the sole language of the Eastern world and the two others (French and English) shared the West. According to some present-day proponents of the "natural-language" theory, something of the sort may yet come about.

The natural-language theorists are not all of one accord. Some suggest that an international committee, or a United Nations commission, select one of today's living languages on the basis of utility and practicability. This would then be inflicted by fiat as a compulsory second-language study in schools everywhere. Others demur, with an eye on the gulfs of jealousy and suspicion that currently divide East and West, and suggest that a world language be selected on the basis of its "neutrality"—perhaps Hindi or Swedish. Some are even more wary of national pride and tetchiness, and aver that several million feelings are bound to be hurt if *any* national language wins out over others. They recommend a weaseling adoption of one of the dead languages. Latin is naturally the oftenest proposed, but there have been advocates of Greek, Hebrew and Sanskrit.

Still another group is sure that the only solution lies in a language combining two or more of those now in use. Perhaps the most extreme example of such an agglomeration has been suggested by the Rev. Theodore Leidenfrost, a Lutheran missionary. His notion of the happiest universal language is one that would blend ten "representative languages."

Other interlinguists favor a natural language naturally universalized. They believe that by the time a universal language is really imperative it will have evolved as a matter of course, and will automatically be the one that best serves the greatest number of people. There is no lack of candidates for this honor. The Chinese point out quite truthfully that Mandarin is spoken by more people than any other two languages put together. French was the international "language of diplomacy" a hundred years ago, and the French would like it to be again. Russian is, by decree, the second language of all the Soviet satellite countries. Spanish is the official language of all but four of the independent nations in the Americas (the exceptions: the United States, Canada, Brazil and Haiti).

Luigi Barzini, in *The Europeans*, makes the latest argument, and a most persuasive one, that Europe and the whole world would be much improved if all the nations of that continent were to meld into one supra-nation which would "forget its trivial disputes and rivalries, put its own house in order, set up authoritative common democratic institutions, arrange its financial affairs according to more or less uniform criteria," etc., etc., and "speak with one calm majestic voice." But *in which language?* Nowhere in a book full of erudition and wisdom, ideas and recommendations, does Signor Barzini dare to put forth any suggestion in that regard.

However, there is one language that was already beginning to suffuse the world well before Descartes first posed the desirability of a universal language. This is, of course, English. During the past century, and especially since World War II, it has been well on its way to becoming the whole planet's second language. That English has won so many speakers all over the world is due both to its intrinsic merits and to the fact that a person of any nationality and station in life is handicapped nowadays if he *doesn't* know English. Professor

William F. Marquardt, one of the stanchest proponents of English as a world auxiliary language, cites some of the reasons for its widespread and still-growing acceptance:

It is spoken as a native language by more than 270 million persons in such strategically dispersed countries as Great Britain, the United States, New Zealand, Australia, Ireland, the Republic of South Africa. It is used as an official language in some thirty other nations situated on every continent. It is the language most essential to military operations in most countries of the world. Knowledge of it is one of the surest ways to advancement in government, business or education in most non-English-speaking countries. There are more publications in English in the fields of science, technology, education, politics and literature than in any other language. It is the common language of aviation, and the one most used in international conferences, commerce, travel, the United Nations. It is currently being taught in more schools in non-English-speaking countries than any other language. Some 70 per cent of the world's mail is written in English. More people speak it as a second language than any other language, and more *literate* persons speak it than any other.

Perhaps what best betokens the virtues of English is the fact that it has succeeded so well in spite of its own most hideous vice: its archaic, irrational, execrable spelling. English orthography stumps even native, lifelong, fluent users of the language—some of its most accomplished literary stylists can't spell—and it is the very Trials of Job to a foreign student.

A total spelling reform is not inconceivable. Russia has several times revamped its orthography, and Turkey managed a wholesale switch to an alien alphabet. But neither of their languages was so rock-solidly supported, as is English, by a stupendous stockpile of literature. Any spelling reform drastic enough to do English any good would necessitate transliterating every page that has ever been printed in it, and that *is* inconceivable.

If English can't be simplified, then the educators' next best hope is to smooth the students' approach to it. Some heartening steps in this direction have lately been taken in England and the United States, where numerous elementary schools have been experimenting with a new "transitional alphabet." The idea is to teach children to read and write a vastly easier orthography which, once grasped, allows them to graduate to standard English without too much of a jolt. The Initial Teaching Alphabet (devised by Sir James Pitman, grandson of Isaac of the Pitman shorthand system) has 44 characters, 24 of them old standbys, 14 of them ligatures of standard characters, and 6 completely new letters (for example, ʒ stands for the sound of *s* in "vision").

Though the alphabet is longer, it is simpler in that each character stands for a single sound and one sound only. England's Minister of Education has called the ITA experiment "a remarkable success," and American educators seem to agree. Children taught by the new method are more than a year ahead of those taught in the normal way, and when, at a certain level of proficiency, they are confronted with the standard alphabet, it fazes them not at all. There seems no reason why this transitional alphabet, perhaps in conjunction with Ogden's Basic English vocabulary of just 850 words, could not similarly help foreign students ease their way into the English language.

But even though English is already a *de facto* auxiliary language throughout the world, there is little immediate likelihood of its being officially recognized as such. Monolithic opposition could be expected from the Soviet Union, on ideological grounds; from China, on sheerly numerical grounds; and even nook-and-cranny Third World nations would deem it a colonialist encroachment on their insect autonomies. But any "more acceptable" language proposed for universal use—whether a natural, artificial or resurrected one—would now find English an almost insuperable obstacle to acceptance.

What seems probable is that national languages will long retain their intranational hegemonies—though regional and tribal dialects and curiosities like Basque will begin to wither away. English will increasingly monopolize international communications, and will continue to advance its status as the second language of even the commonalty of every nation. In time—and granting it will take a long, long time, and assuming no sudden world-wide revulsion—English will prevail, and even the most stalwart national languages will themselves eventually become relics for antiquarians.

In the process English grammar is bound to undergo some mutation, and its vocabulary is sure to absorb countless new locutions and constructions from the tongues it overwhelms. The eventual English-for-everybody will itself be a very different language from the one we know today. But the world will have its universal language at last, and we can hope, as Leibnitz hoped, that then "all that men will have to do will be to be happy."

SOCRATES. When anyone speaks of iron and silver, is not the same thing present in the minds of all?
PHAEDRUS. Certainly.
SOCRATES. But when anyone speaks of justice and goodness we part company and are at odds with one another and with ourselves?
PHAEDRUS. Precisely.

What's the Good Word?

A one-world language may well turn out to be the best tool ever provided for building Utopia. But no tool is any more efficient than its wielder, and man has shown some discouraging ineptitude in handling the ones he already has in his kit. When the day comes that a Swede and a Swahili can understand what each other says, will they understand what each other *means*? The semanticists won't bet on it, and with good reason. Swede, Swahili, New Zealander or New Yorker—no man has ever yet attained more than limited communication with even his identical twin brother. The barriers erected by polyglot confusion, penning apart nations and ethnic groups, are frail things compared to those of semantic confusion, which lock every separate individual into solitary confinement.

Once upon a time, when mankind was young, language meant what it said. It said very little, of course, but that little was plain: the grunt for "rock" meant "that hard lump there." As man's sapience increased, so did his vocabulary— no bad thing—but so did the associations connected with each word. "Rock" came to mean alternatively "weapon for bashing" and then "tool for hammering," and so on up the ladder of semantic separation into "granite, gneiss, gypsum, *et al.*" and "nonmetallic mineral matter" and "a physical entity occupying space and time" and on and on. Say "rock" today: a geologist thinks of the earth's building blocks, a jewel thief thinks of a diamond, a priest thinks of St. Peter.

At the same time language was fogging its focus of defini-

[236]

tion and delimitation, man was encountering concepts that couldn't be defined anyway. The person using the rock to bash somebody was evincing some quality of temperament. It might be "heroism," "wickedness," "insanity" or whatever, depending on circumstances and the bystanders' opinion, to say nothing of the victim's. Temperament is one of many, many things that cannot be measured, weighed or placed in evidence as Exhibit X. The definition of such a thing must necessarily be arbitrary, mutable by an infinity of factors and have a subtly or vastly different connotation to each individual.

Semantic confusion stems mainly from this: that any one word, instead of standing for one concrete thing, can evoke any number of images—and no number of words, however many, can evoke an accurate or universally consistent image of an abstract concept. For example, a man, asked by his little boy, "Dad, what is sex?" launched into a circumspect explanation, beginning with the flowers and bees. Twenty minutes later he had got to the "sanctity of the family unit" level, when the boy sighed, looking unhappily at the identification card in his new wallet and said, "I don't see how I can get all that in this little space under 'sex.' "

The innate imprecision of language would not be such a crippling handicap to communication if every man treated words with the respect, attention and sometimes caution they deserve. But the average person stands in awe or mistrust only of "big words," and uses everyday language with the carelessness of complacent familiarity. The demagogue and the propagandist—who almost never use "big words"— are well aware of the ambiguities inherent in "everyday language," and deliberately foster semantic confusion for their own ends. Language, originally created to express and transmit ideas, has increasingly become the means of muddling, distorting or smothering them altogether.

The seventeenth-century advocates of a "philosophical language" sought to end semantic confusion by adopting a whole new medium of communication. Modern-day semanticists maintain that the fault is not so much in the medium as in the users of it. Their line of attack on semantic confusion is to try to educate the average man to a new awareness of language and its effect on his life, both in his own use of it and others' use of it *on* him.

Technically, semantics is "the study of word meanings," as opposed to phonetics, the study of word sounds. For a long time, it was a rather dry and pedantic pursuit. But since the 1933 publication of Alfred Korzybski's *Science and Sanity*, semantics has broadened from a purely linguistic study into one (usually differentiated as "general" or "applied" semantics) that embraces both psychology and sociology. The difference between the older semantics and the new is like that between a coin-collector's concern with a silver dollar's mint mark and milling, and a realist's interest in what it will buy and how best it might be spent.

The basic tenet of general semantics is that "words are not things." At first glance this seems so self-evident as scarcely to need mentioning; it is patently impossible to use the word "spoon" to eat the word "soup." But it is in just this, the mistaking of words for things, that semantic confusion is most obvious in human behavior. We have already seen how many people will blush or bristle on encountering one of the taboo words for the sex act. These people identify the word so closely with the thing as to confuse the two, and they react on meeting the word as they would on opening the wrong bedroom door.

It has already been contended that the mistaking of words for things dates back to the primitive man's belief that the name of anything (himself and his deity included) had both the powers and the vulnerability of the thing itself. Five thousand years ago, the Israelites annually banished a scapegoat into the desert, bearing on its head all the sins of the tribe; that is, the goat was ritually cursed with the *words* for those sins. A thousand years ago, Teutonic witches "cast the runes," secreting in the thatch of an enemy's hut a scrap of paper inscribed with words warranted to inflict the curses they represented. Nowadays, to cite just one example of a similar belief in the essentiality of words, a Methodist church in Atlanta, Georgia, observes a certain ritual at every New Year's service. The members write down on bits of paper "the sins they would most like removed," and ceremoniously burn the papers in a pot at the altar.

Eskimos used to believe that, when they got old, if they changed their name it would give them a new lease on life. This we regard as quaint and childish nonsense, though there are among us several thousand descendants of immigrants who, on arriving in America, changed their name to Newman or Freeman for the very same reason. People collectively and individually have always given their enemies derogatory or derisive sobriquets, as a semantic device for "cutting them down to size." Americans have variously fought redskins, lobsterbacks, greasers, Rebs and Damyankees, heinies, Nips, gooks, and are currently embroiled with Commies. During

[238]

World War II quite a concerted propaganda campaign urged Americans always to refer to Hitler by his grandmother's surname. Who could fear a Schicklgruber? And the publisher of the *Philadelphia Daily News* decreed that the words "German" and "Jap" ("Japanese" was already unthinkable) would forever after be spelled in his newspaper with a demeaning lower-case initial.

To mistake a word for a thing, or deliberately to substitute it, is to operate at one remove from reality. But once that step is taken, others are possible and almost inevitable. When a word acquires whatever virtue rightfully belongs to its referent, this is fallacy enough (*vide* the various lists of the "most beautiful" words: "mother," "heaven," friendship," *et al.*). But when a word takes on whatever opprobrium is associated with its referent, the next step must be to invent an "innocent" euphemism. And, as has already been shown, one euphemism generally begets another and another, each a further remove from reality.

In World War I, one people (label: Americans) were fighting another (label: Germans). The enemy was real enough, the word was a convenient substitute for him. But everything else labeled "German," or even suggestive of "German," came to have for the Americans the same connotation of "enemy." Sauerkraut was renamed "liberty cabbage." Hamburger became "Salisbury steak." Dachshund owners gave up walking their dogs in public; grown men would kick them. A doctor even suggested renaming German measles "victory measles," but this was probably an ironical dig at the prevailing hysteria, as it actually went counter to the tradition of connecting the enemy with anything and everything baneful (e.g., "the French pox" for syphilis).

During World War II people in Washington, D.C., demonstrated their patriotism by taking hatchets to the famous Japanese cherry trees which decorate the Tidal Basin. The vandals were eventually pacified by a calculated semantic dodge when the fiction was put about that the trees had originally been stolen from Korea by the Japanese, and so were not really to be feared or hated after all. Around the same time, New York's Metropolitan Museum of Art had to remove a display of antique lacquered furniture from its galleries. Too many visitors would spit on the pieces because they bore the tag "japanned ware."

A recently published book on magic required the illustration of a swastika, a symbol of "good luck" used all over the world millenniums before Hitler made it infamous. But the book's author had to draw his own illustration with pen and ink; the printers confessed that they had melted down all the swastikas in their type fonts right after Pearl Harbor.

These are extreme examples of overwrought and unreasoning leaps from one level of abstraction to another. But we all make such jumps, all the time, in a less hysteric degree. If you utter such a simple remark as "It's a fine day," you are not stating a fact, but expressing an abstract opinion. The sun is shining, you feel good, and the combination spells "fine day" to you. But you may be addressing a farmer who is yearning for rain, who is worried sick about his crop, and who wishes he'd never got out of bed this morning. Even if you amend your statement to the apparently uncontroversial "The sun is shining," he may well reply, "Yes, damn it!" You have not communicated the cheery message you intended nor got the response you expected.

Every single word a man uses has a specific connotation— to the user and at the moment of use—compounded of its "meaning" as he first learned it, the personal emotions and recollections which it evokes in him, and the situation (as it seems to him) in which he now utters it. What it conveys to the hearer will depend on his own set of these references. When two men can contemplate the same seemingly concrete substantive—say, the word "dog"—and separately define it as "man's best friend" and "a nasty nuisance," it is hardly to be hoped that they will concur on the meaning of any more abstract word.

An added complication is the tendency of words to change even their "dictionary meanings" so rapidly and completely that people have a hard time adjusting. For one example, to speak of a man's "discrimination" only a few years ago was to compliment his good taste. Nowadays it oftener implies that he exercises some mean prejudice against some body of his fellow men. A person accustomed to using the word in its older sense runs the risk, now, of uttering it in some situation where it will be unappreciated and even actively resented.

We are prodigal with such words as "truth," "beauty," "good," "evil," but there are no such *things* that we can point to or draw pictures of, to show exactly what we mean. "Truth" no more exists in tangible actuality than "six o'clock" exists. Yet we not only give these words false corporeality, we too often employ them in an "either/or" capacity. The only alternative to "success" is "failure," the antithesis of "pretty" is "ugly." It is to be hoped that, when and if English does become an international tongue, it will by that time have de-

veloped a more flexible, multivalued structure like that of
the Chinese language, which avoids such rigid dichotomies
and tolerates a broader range of gradations between dead
right and dead wrong.

Meanwhile, we say one man is "good," another is "bad"—
without making plain in what respect he is, under what circumstances, in comparison to what other man or men, and
according to whose standard of goodness or badness. Good
King Wenceslaus had his evil moments, and Ivan the Terrible was loved by some of his subjects. The Aristotelian fallacy that everything must be either black or white, no shade
of gray, has had some notable partisans, including Jesus
Christ ("He that is not with me is against me . . ."). And
the Western languages, by providing a handy antonym to
every locution, have helped to perpetuate the either/or rigidity of evaluation.

Equally handy, and equally misused, are the innocent-
appearing words like "always," "never," "nobody," "everybody," etc. Semanticists generally shun them, pointing out
that any sweeping statement like "Everybody knows water is
wet" is vulnerable to disproof. Even if the only exception is
one single lunatic somewhere, he makes the statement a
false generalization and the speaker suspect. And a seemingly incontrovertible remark like "The sun always rises in
the east" is, when you think about it, merely a high-probability
extrapolation from past evidence. For that matter, who can
say for sure where "east" *is*? The world's first mapmakers,
the Arab seafarers, always put south at the top of their maps,
so east was on the left. It would again be there, if the Red
Guard zanies of China's 1965 Cultural Revolution had had
their way. They wanted all maps changed so that East always would be on "the Left." (They also wanted traffic rules
changed so that street stoplights' Red would signal "go
ahead!")

The lapses and loopholes prevalent in language are hardly
trivialities, even if semantic confusion seems to be most frequently evidenced in husband-wife squabbles of the "But you
said—!" "I never said any such thing!" variety. Language is
so vitally important to every one of us, at every level of communication from asking subway directions to holding summit conferences, that it behooves even the ordinary conversa-
tionalist and reader to take note of the weak spots in its
fabric.

All we ever really know about anything, beyond what we
can see and touch and smell, we get by means of question
and answer, remark and response. If we are unable to phrase

the query to ask exactly what we want to know, the answer we get is either misleading or meaningless. If we have a problem and can't put it into words, we can expect no practical solution. Wendell Johnson, in his *People in Quandaries,* quoted a psychiatrist as remarking that one symptom common to every one of his maladjusted patients was that "they were unable to tell him clearly what was the matter."

The little boy who asked, "What is sex?" phrased his question ambiguously, and so got a right response that was the wrong answer. Grownups do it, too. A friend of mine once applied for an insurance policy and submitted to an examination by the insurance company's doctor. The physician, filling out a medical-history blank, asked my friend's occupation. He replied, with some small vanity, "Advertising agency creative director and account executive." The doctor nodded and wrote down, "Occupation: sedentary."

In this case, at least, the questioner was able to translate the information he was given into the information he wanted and should have asked for in the first place. But too many times our questions are as skewed as the old childhood conundrum, "What's the difference between a duck?" and any answer* is bound to be jabberwocky.

When we ask a question, we deserve whatever kind of answer we get. But a lot of our information comes in the form of gratuitous answers to questions we haven't asked. Whenever we listen or read, we're opening our heads to somebody's attempt to get inside. Of course, much of the wordage uttered is the sheer noise of sociability. The words worth paying attention to are those aimed to produce an effect—to get a response, to evoke some emotion, to incite to some action, to persuade, teach, wheedle, threaten, demand, to make up our mind (or change it) regarding some issue major or minor. A semantic awareness can help us unscramble the real words from the background noise, and help us judge which of them we want to heed, respond to or act on.

To the Korzybskian semanticist, an abstract locution impossible of definition is a "blab." Thus a statement like "God is love," as it stands, devoid of qualification, must be translated, "Blab is blab." The word "god" here can refer to Jehovah, Allah, Baal, Manitou, Zeus, any one of a host of deities. Should the speaker explain, "Why, it means *our Lord,* of course!" it still can apply to the same one variously viewed. It can mean the august titan painted by Michelangelo, or the whimsy expressed in that story about an angel who was

* "Its right feet are both alike."

[242]

asked by a mortal for a description of God and began, "Well, She's black . . ." The word "love" can similarly refer to anything from divine grace to what goes on in the back seat of a parked car. The assertion "God is love" is meaningless because it has so *many* possible meanings.

But often the semantically oriented listener can find some content even in such a formless statement, by applying the question, "What do you mean?" (Faddists prefer the jargon: "Define your terms.") The question need not be voiced in so many words; thinking it to oneself will usually serve. But a conscious and conscientious iteration of "What do you mean?" and then the follow-up "How do you know?" can sometimes bring a semantic blab down the ladder of abstraction, rung by rung, to a level where it has some meaning. Socrates used this method; so do children, with their plaintively repeated, "Why?"

"Be good, or Santa won't bring you anything for Christmas."
"Why?"
"Because he doesn't bring presents to bad boys."
"Why?"
"Because he doesn't like little boys who are bad."
"Why?"
"Because! Now stop pestering me!"

Just so, repeating "What do you mean?" and "How do you know?" can make many a categorical assertion peter out into a feeble "because . . ." And even when the questions are unspoken, they can make many an asserter feel outrageously "pestered," as he watches a pet pronouncement get nibbled to death.

But the skillful and patient semanticist, assuming he doesn't get knocked unconscious during the inquisition, might persuade the man who asserts that "God is love" eventually to define his terms as something like: "The Two-Seed-in-the-Spirit Predestinarian Baptist concept of a Supreme Being, as Reverend Jones preached it last Sunday to our Maple Avenue congregation, and as I understand it in the light of my own knowledge and experience, can be defined as a personification of paternal benignity, tenderness, tolerance, etc., etc., etc. . . ." This is still full of static, but at least it says something more substantial than "Blab is blab."

The semanticist metaphorically feels beneath the shifty surface sands of language, both to find a solid walkway and to avoid the hidden snags and potholes. To do this, he uses a set of what Korzybski called "extensional devices," a number of which can be of service even to the nonprofessional. One device is quotation marks, used to bracket a multivalued word or phrase whenever it is used as a specific, or a locution that expresses the user's unverifiable opinion. For example, in the statement "My boss is a bastard," the semanticist would bracket "bastard." The boss may actually be one, but less forgivable factors than mere illegitimacy are implied: meanness, tyranny, Scroogism, Legreeism, etc.—and anyway the assertion is only the speaker's evaluation. The quotation marks around the word do not refute any of its implications, they merely serve to caution that it should not be taken too literally.

Another device is the *etc.*, meaning, as it does to everybody, "and so forth" or "and the like"—but the semanticist uses it oftener than others do. To him it is a reminder that no thing has a single and constant identity, and that no number of words can ever accurately and completely define another. ("Dog" means a mammal, a quadruped, a carnivore, a member of the genus *Canis*, a domestic pet, man's best friend, a nasty nuisance, etc.)

Probably the two most useful Korzybskian devices are the subscript index number and the superscript date. They serve, as well as any typographic tool can, to pin down abstractions. For example, there are 75 John Smiths listed in the Manhattan telephone directory. Chances are that John Smith$_1$ is not related to John Smith$_{75}$, has no connection with him, doesn't know him, and wishes the other Smith's friends would stop telephoning him by mistake. At any rate, the two John Smiths are not the same man, and if some philanthropist wants to bequeath money to a certain John Smith, or if the police want to issue a warrant for his arrest, they're going to have to add a string of qualifiers to the label "John Smith." The Korzybskian index number serves as a semantic code symbol for that string of qualifiers.

Say that John Smith$_1$ is fifty years old, a widower with two married children and three grandchildren. John Smith$_2$ or John Smith$_{66}$ may possibly duplicate him in those respects, but they can't be identical in everything: physique, temperament, fingerprints, etc. However, thirty years ago, John Smith$_1$ didn't have those grandchildren either. Hence the use of the superscript date mark, to distinguish grandfather John Smith^{1985} from bachelor John Smith^{1955} and even a putative great-grandfather John Smith^{2015}. A combination of the marks enables us to define John Smith in both space and time:

"In an Atlantic City hotel room, portly, bald, retiring conventioneer John Smith$_1$ $^{10:45 \text{ P.M., August 17, 1990}}$ put his teeth in a glass to soak."

The semanticist finds index and date marks handy for delimiting things even more abstract and amorphous than John Smith. Take "democracy" for instance—most writers on general semantics do, and it makes for a convenient example. While *democracy*$_1$ does not begin to define the concept, it can stand for "democracy" as the term is supposedly understood in the United States today, and can at least differentiate it from *democracy*$_2$, the version ostensibly practiced in the People's Democratic Republic of (North) Korea. Again, American *democracy*$^{\text{A.D. 1985}}$ can be distinguished from Athenian *democracy*$^{\text{430 B.C.}}$. And John Smith's personal definition of "democracy"—or a John Birchite's—can similarly be isolated for study.

Of course it's impractical to use all these devices in daily conversation, or to mutter them at political rallies, or even to scribble them on the pages we read. And if we interposed "What do you mean?" after every single word, nothing would ever get said, written, taught, learned or done. But general semantics is more a way of thinking than a system of rules, and its principles, consciously applied, can eventually come to be instinctive. By sharpening our eyes and ears, we sharpen our understanding, appreciation—and vigilance—of what we hear and read. That such a vigilance is much to be desired can be illustrated by numerous examples of both inadvertent and deliberate semantic confusion.

In his *Power of Words*, Stuart Chase averred that the Japanese might have stopped World War II short of the horrors of Hiroshima and Nagasaki, but for a high-level misuse of one ambiguous word. The word is *mokusatsu*, which has two meanings: "to ignore" and "to abstain from comment." According to Chase, when the Allies presented their demand for unconditional surrender in July, 1945, the Imperial Cabinet announced that it would follow a policy of *mokusatsu*. This was, in effect, a "no comment" which could conceivably have invited a popular mandate to surrender. However, the world's press carried the translation that "the Cabinet ignores the demand to surrender," and the Japanese could not issue a correction without losing face and forgoing any possibility of a negotiated surrender. So the war lasted another month, during which time two atomic bombs fell, and a new era in human history was irrevocably begun.

Another semantic misconnection, fortunately not such an epochal one, occurred in 1964, when Panamanian nationalists were rioting in the Canal Zone and demanding that the American military reservation there be ceded back to the country. American diplomats issued a placative communique using the Spanish word *negociar*, in the sense that they were willing "to discuss" the various points at issue. The Panamanians, however, chose to interpret *negociar* as a willingness "to bargain," presumably toward concessions. When the Americans insisted on a discussion only, Panama was able to clamor that the United States had gone back on its word.

Deliberately created semantic confusion is usually more corrosive than explosive. In the earlier chapter on euphemisms, we have seen some of the ways demagogues tailor language with tucks and padding to suit their purposes. It would seem that by now the techniques of propaganda should be so well known as to be useless as tools of persuasion. But the people most susceptible to demagoguery—which is most people—still have little semantic awareness, and can't be bothered to develop any. They are satisfied to judge headlines by their blackness and slogans by their sonority, without proper care for what they say, let alone what they mean.

"Propaganda" is another word which has undergone a change, the result of the general impression, during World War II, that it was the invention and personal property of the detested Dr. Goebbels. Since that time it has carried connotations of insidious deception and distortion. But originally "propaganda" simply meant the systematic propagation of any idea, doctrine or cause—making it close cousin to advertising and evangelism.

Wartime propaganda—and this includes Cold Wartime— seldom attempts distracting definitions of the principles and causes involved; explications are too hard to score for trumpet and drum. Instead, it wields glowing abstractions like The Flag, The Motherland, Our Way of Life, and Liberty (or *Svoboda, Freiheit, Libertad, Liberté*, etc.). The Communists have been propagandizing for their cause and against everybody else's for so long that even they must be tired of listening to it. But the "good guys" do it too.

The *New York Daily News* is read by more people than any other paper in America; it has achieved this circulation by brilliant editing to appeal to rather Neanderthal intellects. Unfortunately, at least from the standpoint of general semantics, it appeals to Neanderthal emotions as well. More than three million readers (Sunday circulation), or anyway as many of them as read the editorial page, have been told over and over again that "the only good Communist is a dead Communist."

A reader wrote to the paper some while back, not really hoping for any definition of "a Communist," but to ask whether the *News* advocated the extermination of *all* the approximately 1,004,000,000 people then inhabiting the Russias, mainland China and the satellite countries, or whether it favored annihilating just the provable Communist Party members, perhaps 5 percent of the total, a mere 50,200,000 people. An editorial writer replied, "The *News* does not go in for off-the-record arguments about or explanations of its editorials. It says what it thinks in the editorial column from day to day and lets it go at that." An admirably firm stand, but what *does* it "think," and what does it try to make its millions of readers think?

Advertising long ago outstripped all other forms of propaganda in its expert semantic manipulation, and it makes no apology for the fact. In 1964 an American advertising agency quite boldly, even arrogantly, took full pages in several newspapers to run a "house ad" congratulating itself on its talent at wielding "the tools that make advertising possible: language, and the readiness of people to believe what they read and hear."

Advertising can also profit from people's inclination to ignore things that they are, however subtly, discouraged from noticing. It is no secret to anybody that even the most prestigious companies have never been so lofty that they would hesitate to indulge in the measliest chicanery, wherever it might benefit them, and whenever they could get away with it. There is now extant one example of this, so often and everywhere displayed that I am amazed that no one has yet made public outcry against it.

For a couple of decades now, the U.S. government has enforced a regulation that every pack of cigarettes and every cigarette advertisement must display this printed caveat:

Warning: The Surgeon General Has Determined that
Cigarette Smoking Is Dangerous to Your Health.

Count the letters, punctuation marks and wordspaces in those two lines—48 in the first, 46 in the second. Any headline makeup man or composing room typographer (who doesn't just count characters, but also allows for the varying widths of them) would tell you that, in any type face, those two lines would "set" to an identical and balanced measure. However, the tobacco companies, and their advertising people, instantly perceived that to set the two lines thus might be dangerous to their sales and profits. It would leave the bald warning *Cigarette Smoking Is Dangerous to Your Health* as a line by itself, stark, declamatory, too readily readable and heedable.

So, with sly and callous ingenuity, the tobacco advertisers did some typographic toying with those two lines. They found that, by using an easily "squeezable" Alternate Gothic type face, they could get away with setting the mandated caveat differently—just 43 characters and spaces on the top line, 51 on the second—in such a manner that the imbalance didn't look too unwieldy and the ruse wasn't too obvious, thus:

> Warning: The Surgeon General Has Determined That Cigarette Smoking Is Dangerous to Your Health.

And so the intended message of that mandated label—the actual words of the warning—not only got mashed into lesser visibility, it also got sheltered behind the "That."

It might seem almost amusing: the vision of whole company offices and ad agencies full of grown men employing tweezers to tinker with tiny fragments of type proofs. But consider. You see those two lines, printed exactly as they are above, in every magazine and newspaper advertisement produced by *every* cigarette maker. The various companies have always competed viciously with each other, and still do, but in this case they made a concerted, industry-wide effort—however trivial the effort might appear—to gang up on the consumer of their goods and deliberately to obscure a message he was intended to see plainly and read easily.

Other examples of advertising's way with words and symbols have already been mentioned in earlier chapters; any reader can think of dozens more without straining; and still more hundreds are to be found in any periodical or at the twist of a television dial. The techniques range from brute repetition of a brand name, to innuendo ("Are You Satisfying Your Wife?") to scare tactics ("What About that Mortgage, When You're No Longer Here?") to virtue-by-association (having the product extolled, for a fee, by either an irresistible movie idol or a believable-looking Ordinary Joe) to deceptions like the open-end comparative (". . . gets clothes 30% whiter!") to sly insinuation ("Smirnoff Vodka leaves you breathless") to sheer static (that cigarette slogan, "You've come a long way, baby!" translates semantically as "You've blab a blab, blab!"). Advertising can even make semantic hay out of what it doesn't say or show, e.g., no chewing gum TV commercial ever shows anyone actually chomping gum; presumably that sight would revolt even the addicts.

Unlike advertising, which makes no bones about its manipulations, religion has the ticklish problem of dealing in semantic confusion without acknowledging that there is such a thing. Because, except on the pragmatic level of

Christmas-baskets-for-the-poor, religion treats of pure abstractions that have only an asseverated connection with reality. From its primordial beginnings in ritual magic and spirit worship, religion has been based on concepts with no discoverable existence outside men's heads.

These concepts, and the precepts preached from them, can be explained only in vague terms like "heaven," "hell," "sin," "redemption," etc.—and such terms, subjected to the semantic "What do you mean?" and "How do you know?" distill down at last to a "because . . ." that the devout defend as "faith." Theologians have given up trying to define the angel capacity of pinheads, but such modern innovations as the revivalist's call for "decisions for Christ" are just as defiant of definition. Depending on an observer's amount of indulgence, "decisions for Christ" either means nothing at all or has so many possible interpretations that it would require several reams of qualifiers to pin down one of them.

In the few instances where religion makes use of a fairly concrete concept, it can still exercise its prerogative of manipulating the references to suit circumstances. I recall that a Protestant chaplain, preaching to Korea-bound troops at Fort Dix in 1952, unostentatiously slipped into his sermon the Judaic version of the sixth commandment: "Thou shalt do no murder"—an expedient way to distinguish between patriotic killing and the sinful sort.

Early in 1965 the Vatican announced the formation of a new secretariat intended to establish contact with the world's atheists and, it was hoped, to convert them to Christianity. But the Church elders ran into a semantic problem when it came to naming this new department; "atheist" is a naughty word, even to atheists. "The Secretariat for Non-Believers" was suggested, but papal advisers feared this would repel those atheists who *do* profess an "idealistic belief in humanistic values." Last I heard, the new secretariat still had no official title, catchy or otherwise.

Lately some church bodies have been casting a similar realistic eye at the semantic weeds in their liturgical pastures. In 1964 the Roman Catholic Church finally gave individual bishops the discretion to decide whether the mass will continue to be said in Latin or will convert to the local vernacular. To the majority of today's Catholics, the spiritual content of the Latin service has resided mainly in its venerable familiarity, and the words might as well have been abracadabra. The use of the vernacular may not clarify the doctrinal abstractions, but at least the congregations will know what's being *said*.

The almost equally tradition-bound Church of England finally admitted that it had for too long been singing several fine old hymns simply because they were "fine old hymns." The Anglican hymnal is now minus such longtime sentimental standards as "Nearer, My God, to Thee" and "Lead, Kindly Light"—for the reason that their lyrics said little and meant less. In 1950 hymnologist Albert Edward Bailey had complained that "the frequent use of ['Lead, Kindly Light'] at funerals results from a total misapprehension of its meaning," but even he was at a loss to explain what it did mean.

It would be possible to fill several more books the size of this one with examples of semantic obscurity and obscurantism. All of human civilization was made possible by language, and still depends on language—and a good many of its shortcomings stem from disordered communications. Wars, depressions, pogroms, revolutions are more often caused by words than by actions, and are resolved the same way. Every society maintains its culture, customs and mores by means of language—and words uncaringly preserve both the traditions worth keeping and the ones that should long ago have been abolished. Practically all we can ever know of our world's history we must get by way of words; they long outlast artifacts and monuments. In an increasingly urban, industrialized and compartmented civilization, few of us get to see or experience more than a very little of our own present-day world. The rest—the far and foreign places—we often know only through others' reportage.

Barring blows or caresses, words are our only expression of aggression or affection. Words are often the first intimations of mental distress and derangement—and often, too, the primal cause. Potential suicides give notice of their intention in words (it is a myth that "suicides don't talk about doing it"; their hints may simply go unheeded). Our command and use of language do much to determine our individual place in the world—occupation, relations with others, social standing, achievements—and when we take our leave, quite often the words we've uttered or the words others have spoken about us are the only surviving trace that we ever passed this way.

It may seem that the general semanticists, and "realists" in general, are determined to trim all the fusty, lovely old gingerbread and filigree off our languages, and replace them with cold stainless steel. Not so. They merely hope that we will sometime learn to tell the difference between the ornamental and the functional, and use and appreciate them accordingly.

[250]

Common sense tells us that we should distinguish between a scat song and a stop sign, but heart sense tells us
that the silly ditty is no less necessary to our over-all well-
being. Even the semanticists would have small cause for
celebration if there were only one invariable meaning to be
discovered in a sonnet or a psalm, if a love letter did not
whisper a different endearment every time it was reread, if
jokes came tagged with ho-hum/funny/naughty/dirty ratings,
if every cuss-word exploded with a predictable bang, if the
map were all over Midvilles, and every man wore a name
like John Smith$_{928}$.

There are already too many words that tend to cue a consistent response in the ruck of people—the slogans, catch-
phrases, brand names, blurbs, war cries, mottoes, "humor"
backed by a laugh-track to cue its hearers that it's "hilari-
ous," words that will fit on a billboard or a campaign poster,
words that are easily bent into neon tubing, words that we
can recognize without having to take the trouble to understand. These are not language; they are symbols and prods
to actuate conditioned reflexes. Our obedience to them is like
that of the electronic computer, which reacts only to coded
impulses, not to any stimulus of intelligence.

The ambiguities and absurdities of any and every language are actually necessary to human functioning. The
slight mental gymnastics they require for comprehension
keep us awake, aware and alive. But even if we had no
practical need of them, the personality quirks and vagaries
of language would doubtless still be dear to us—like a hu-
manizing blemish in a great man: Lincoln's warts, not
Cromwell's.

The day may come when the computers and automata
reign supreme, when what is left of man lives by-the-numbers
and his language is as pale, precise and smooth as a pleat of
print-out. That may be a day devoid of misery and misunderstanding, but it will also be barren of all delight. And the de-
lights of language rank high among the indispensables. As
long as man is man and not a robot, it seems certain that
whatever language he employs will continue to reflect all his
happiest human foibles, follies, frailties and fancies, and enable him to rejoice in them, right to the end.

Bibliographical Notes

To cite every source that has contributed to this book, I would have to review practically every word I have ever heard, read, spoken or written. Instead, the bibliography lists only those works which were consulted during its preparation—and not all of those. Many of the contributory works simply would not interest the general reader, and even the literary detective checking up on my references would have a dreary time plowing through some of the source material. For example, the footnote item on page 25 came from an otherwise soporific history of bookkeeping. I have also omitted from the bibliography the innumerable published articles and periodicals of which I made use. These ranged from general-circulation magazines and daily newspapers to journals of various specialties. But comparatively few of them had anything to do with language per se, and anyway I feel that my listing them would not impel many readers to take the trouble of looking them up.

The best way of presenting a bibliography is to break it down according to which works contributed to which chapters. However, to do that here would require too many duplicate listings and complicated cross-references. Many of the works in the list supplied material for several different chapters, while others made no tangible contribution at all but did have an estimable influence on the book's treatment of various subjects. Since a categorized bibliography is impractical, let me just append these few notes on "further reading" for those interested in learning more about some favorite subject:

General Reading. Bloomfield's *Language* is recommended by many authorities, but the Bodmer-Hogben *Loom of Lan-*

guage is the best-selling introduction to the field. Mario Pei's numerous books (*The Story of Language, Language for Everybody,* etc.) range from the general to the particular, and are variously aimed at readers from grade school to postgrad; you can pick your starting level. Martinet's *Elements of General Linguistics* is an excellent guide to the technical study of language, but it will be best appreciated by those already well beyond the beginner stage.

Written Language. Gelb's *Study of Writing,* Moorhouse's *Triumph of the Alphabet* and Clodd's *Story of the Alphabet* are good and comprehensive studies for the layman. But Etiemble's *Orion Book of the Written Word,* though haphazard in its coverage, is a joy to read, both for its brightly erudite text and its stunning calligraphic illustrations. For the most readable story of the decipherment of unknown paleographies, I heartily recommend Doblhofer's *Voices in Stone.*

The English Language. On its history and evolution, there's an abundance; I'll mention just the Greenough-Kittredge *Words and Their Ways,* Pei's *Story of English* and again, Bodmer's *The Loom of Language.* On usage, there is of course Fowler's authoritarian and entertainingly acerb *Modern English Usage,* but equally wise and witty are S. Stephenson Smith's *Command of Words,* Bernstein's *Watch Your Language* and anything by Edwin Newman. It should be superfluous for me to recommend Mencken's *The American Language;* worth reading just for reading's sake, it could also be cited as an authority on the American aspects of almost every category listed here—etymology, semantics, slang, jargon, names, etc.

Etymology. Eric Partridge's *Origins* is the *sine qua non* of popular English etymology; I am not the only writer on language who is mightily beholden to it and to him. Since Engish is such an eclectic tongue, *Origins* serves also as an etymology of countless foreign words our language has borrowed. For the derivation of phrases, sayings and just plain odd words, I suggest Holt's *Phrase and Word Origins,* or any of the several works by Bergen Evans (*Comfortable Words,* etc.), Charles Funk (*Heavens to Betsy!,* etc.), Ivor Brown (*Words in Our Time,* etc.) and Willard Espy.

Jargon, Slang, Taboo Words. See Mencken, of course, but Partridge's *Slang Today and Yesterday* is probably the nearest thing to a definitive study of this field. The Berrey-Van den Bark *American Thesaurus of Slang* contains some 100,000 entries, admirably up to date, and the Wentworth-Flexner *Dictionary of American Slang* tells what they mean. Roback's *Dictionary of International Slurs*, if you can find it, is a grand guide to name-calling. The Wentworth-Flexner book is about the only decent compendium of "indecent" language. Other works have dealt less with taboo expressions than with their suppression; the Robert Downs compilation, *The First Freedom*, is an excellent study of censorship in this and other regards.

Onomatology. The study of names—of persons, places and things—has yet to see its Partridge (though Partridge himself has dabbled in it). Elsdon Smith's *Dictionary of American Family Names* is one of the more adequate items; expectably, it traces Old World names, too. I can't recommend anything dealing with given names; every such book simpers and coos like those what-to-call-baby pamphlets handed out by diaper laundries. Stewart's *Names on the Land* is the superlative study of American place-names. Other countries have similar works (e.g., Blackie's is one of the best for Britain), but none are so enjoyable as Stewart's. For thing-names, and a fantastic variety of other etymological lore and folklore, see Jacobs' diverting *Naming-Day in Eden.*

Pidgin and Play-Languages. Robert A. Hall, Jr., is the going authority on pidgin, but you may find his books (*Hands Off Pidgin English!*, etc.) hard to locate. See also Edgar Sayer's *Pidgin English* (Toronto, 1943). The play-languages are only occasionally mentioned in linguistic texts, and patronizingly; the sole work I could find devoted to the subject was *Playlanguages and Language Play* by "Artsid Otsikrev," whoever he or she is or was.

Code, Cipher, Computer Languages, etc. The Friedmans' *Shakespearean Ciphers Examined*, though focusing on a specialized aspect of the subject, is nevertheless one of the best introductions I've found to the whole field of code and cipher. Adler's *Thinking Machines* and Berkeley's *Symbolic Logic and Intelligent Machines* touch on informational computers, and my own *March of the Robots* (New York, 1962) gives a kindergarten course in the "binary language."

Universal Languages. Pei's *One Language for the World* is comprehensive and instructive, but the serious student may also want to see A. L. Guerard's *Short History of the Interna-*

tional Language Movement (New York, 1922). Bodmer gives a short but informative and interesting treatment of the subject in *The Loom of Language.* The only one of these artificial languages with an accessible literature of its own is Esperanto. Its grammar-*cum*-dictionary is called *Esperanto: The World Interlanguage.*

General Semantics. Korzybski's *Science and Sanity* is deservedly considered the Bible of this field, but it's more like the Dead Sea Scrolls for readability. I recommend any of Hayakawa's books (*Language in Thought and Action,* etc.), Stuart Chase's *Tyranny of Words* and Wendell Johnson's *People in Quandaries* as much more palatable and digestible for the newcomer.

Partial Bibliography

ADLER, IRVING. *Thinking Machines.* New York: John Day, 1961.

BALLARD, PHILIP B. *Thought and Language.* London: University of London, 1934.

BELL, RALCY H. *The Mystery of Words.* New York: Hinds, Hayden & Eldredge, 1924.

BERKELEY, EDMUND C. *Symbolic Logic and Intelligent Machines.* New York: Reinhold, 1959.

BERNSTEIN, THEODORE M. *More Language That Needs Watching.* Manhasset, N.Y.: Channel Press, 1962.

————. *Watch Your Language.* Great Neck, N.Y.: Channel Press, 1958.

BERREY, LESTER V. AND VAN DEN BARK, MELVIN. *The American Thesaurus of Slang,* 2nd ed. New York: Crowell, 1962.

BLACKIE, C. *A Dictionary of Place-Names, Giving Their Derivation.* London: Murray, 1887.

BLOOMFIELD, LEONARD. *Language.* New York: Holt, 1933.

BODMER, FREDERICK. *The Loom of Language,* ed. Lancelot Hogben. New York: Norton, 1944.

BOMBAUGH, C. C. *Oddities and Curiosities of Words and Literature* (*Gleanings for the Curious,* 3rd ed., 1890), ed. Martin Gardner. New York: Dover, 1961.

BRIGGS, HAROLD E., ed. *Language . . . Man . . . Society: Readings in Communication.* New York: Rinehart, 1949.

BROWN, IVOR. *Words in Our Time.* London: Jonathan Cape, 1958.

BROWN, ROGER. *Words and Things.* New York: Free Press of Glencoe, 1958.

CHARNOCK, R. S. *Local Etymology: A Derivative Dictionary of Geographical Names.* London: Houlston & Wright, 1859.

CHASE, STUART. *The Power of Words.* New York: Harcourt, Brace, 1953.

————. *The Tyranny of Words.* New York: Harcourt, Brace, 1938.

CLODD, EDWARD. *The Story of the Alphabet.* New York: Appleton-Century, 1938.

CONRAD, JACK. *The Many Worlds of Man.* New York: Crowell, 1964.

DEAK, ETIENNE AND SIMONE. *A Dictionary of Colorful French Slanguage and Colloquialisms.* Paris: Laffont, 1959.

DOBLHOFER, ERNST. *Voices in Stone: The Decipherment of Ancient Scripts and Writings,* trans. Mervyn Savill. New York: Viking, 1961.

DOWNS, ROBERT B. ed. *The First Freedom.* Chicago: American Library Assn., 1960.

DUNCAN, H. D. *Communication and Social Order.* New York: Bedminster, 1962.

ENTWISTLE, WILLIAM J. *Aspects of Language.* London: Faber & Faber, 1953.

ETIEMBLE. *The Orion Book of the Written Word.* New York: Orion, 1961.

EVANS, BERGEN. *Comfortable Words.* New York: Random House, 1962.

FINLAYSON, JAMES. *Surnames and Sirenames: The Origin and History of Certain Family & Historical Names; with Remarks on the Ancient Right of the Crown to Sanction and Veto the Assumption of Names, and an Historical Account of the Names Buggey and Bugg.* London: Simpkin, Marshall, 1863.

FINN, R. WELLDON. *An Introduction to Domesday Book.* New York: Barnes & Noble, 1963.

FIRTH, J. R. *The Tongues of Men.* London: Watts, 1937.

FRIEDMAN, WILLIAM F. AND ELIZEBETH S. *The Shakespearean Ciphers Examined.* London: Cambridge University Press, 1957.

FUNK, CHARLES EARLE. *Heavens to Betsy! and Other Curious Sayings.* New York: Harper, 1955.

GAINES, HELEN FOUCHÉ. *Cryptanalysis.* New York: Dover, 1956.

GELB, I. J. *A Study of Writing.* Chicago: University of Chicago Press, 1952.

GIBSON, H. N. *The Shakespeare Claimants*. New York: Barnes & Noble, 1962.

GOLDBERG, ISAAC. *The Wonder of Words*. New York: Ungar, 1957.

GRAVES, ROBERT. *The Future of Swearing and Improper Language*. London: Paul, French, Trubner, 1936.

————. *Mrs. Fisher; or, the Future of Humour*. London: Paul, French, Trubner, 1928.

GREENOUGH, J. B. AND KITTREDGE, G. L. *Words and Their Ways in English Speech*. New York: Macmillan, 1929.

HAYAKAWA, S. I. *Language in Thought and Action*. New York: Harcourt, Brace & World, 1949.

————, ed. *Language, Meaning and Maturity*. New York: Harper, 1954.

————. *Our Language and Our World*. New York: Harper, 1959.

HOLT, ALFRED H. *Phrase and Word Origins*. New York: Dover, 1961.

HUTCHINSON, ANN. *Labanotation*. New York: New Directions, 1954.

INGRAHAM, EDWARD D. *Singular Surnames*. Philadelphia: Campbell, 1873.

JACOBS, NOAH JONATHAN. *Naming-Day in Eden: The Creation and Recreation of Language*. New York: Macmillan, 1958.

JESPERSEN, OTTO. *Language: Its Nature, Development and Origin*. London: Allen & Unwin, 1922.

JOHNSON, BURGES. *The Lost Art of Profanity*. New York: Bobbs-Merrill, 1948.

JOHNSON, WENDELL. *People in Quandaries*. New York: Harper, 1946.

KORZYBSKI, ALFRED. *Science and Sanity: An Introduction to Non-Aristotelian Systems and General Semantics*. 4th ed.; Chicago: Institute of General Semantics, 1958.

KROEBER, A. K. *Anthropology*. New York: Harcourt, Brace & World, 1948.

KRUTCH, JOSEPH WOOD, compiler. *The World of Animals*. New York: Simon & Schuster, 1961.

LADO, ROBERT. *Language Teaching: A Scientific Approach*. New York: McGraw-Hill, 1964.

LAIRD, CHARLTON. *The Miracle of Language*. New York: World, 1953.

LARCHEY, L. *Dictionnaire de l'Argot Parisien: Eccentricities of the French Language, including All Recent Expressions whether of the Street, the Theatre, or the Prison, also those English Slang Words which have been adopted by the Parisians.* London: Hotten, *ca.* 1875.

LEVITT, JOHN AND JOAN. *The Spell of Words.* New York: Philosophical Library, 1963.

LEWIS, MORRIS M. *Language in Society.* New York: Social Sciences, 1948.

LOUGHEAD, FLORA HAINES. *Dictionary of Given Names.* Glendale, Calif.: Clark, 1958.

MARCKWARDT, ALBERT H. *American English.* New York: Oxford University Press, 1958.

MARTINET, ANDRÉ. *Elements of General Linguistics,* trans. Elizabeth Palmer. Chicago: University of Chicago, 1964.

MENCKEN, H. L. *The American Language.* 4th ed., 1936; Supplement I, 1945; Supplement II, 1948; New York: Knopf.

MILNE, LORUS AND MARGERY. *The Senses of Animals and Men.* New York: Atheneum, 1962.

MOORE, DAN T., AND WALLER, MARTHA. *Cloak and Cypher.* New York: Bobbs-Merrill, 1962.

MOORE, JOHN. *You English Words.* Philadelphia: Lippincott, 1962.

MOORHOUSE, A. C. *The Triumph of the Alphabet.* New York: Schuman, 1953.

MORRIS, CHARLES. *Signs, Language and Behavior.* New York: Braziller, 1955.

OGDEN, C. K., AND RICHARDS, I. A. *The Meaning of Meaning.* 8th ed.; New York: Harcourt, Brace, 1956.

OGG, OSCAR. *The 26 Letters.* New York: Crowell, 1948.

"OTSIKREV, ARTSID." *Playlanguages and Language Play.* Hillsboro, Oregon: Esperanto, 1963.

PAGET, RICHARD. *Babel; or, the Past, Present and Future of Human Speech.* London: Paul, French, Trubner, 1930.

PARTRIDGE, ERIC. *From Sanskrit to Brazil.* London: Hamish Hamilton, 1952.

———. *Origins: A Short Etymological Dictionary of Modern English.* New York: Macmillan, 1959.

———. *Slang Today and Yesterday.* 3rd ed.; New York: Macmillan, 1950.

PAUL, JAMES C. N., AND SCHWARTZ, MURRAY L. *Federal Censorship: Obscenity in the Mail.* New York: Free Press of Glencoe, 1961.

PEI, MARIO. *All About Language.* Philadelphia: Lippincott, 1954.

———. *Language for Everybody.* New York: Devin-Adair, 1957.

———. *One Language for the World.* New York: Devin-Adair, 1958.

————. *Talking Your Way Around the World*. New York: Harper, 1961.

————. *The World's Chief Languages*. New York: Vanni, 1960.

PHILLIMORE, W. P. W., AND FRY, E. A., compilers. *An Index to Changes of Name Under Authority of Act of Parliament or Royal License and including Irregular Changes from I George III to 64 Victoria, 1760 to 1901*. London: Phillimore, 1905.

RIEKEHOF. LOTTIE L. *The American Sign Language*. Springfield, Mo.: Central Bible Institute, 1961.

ROBACK, AARON A. *Dictionary of International Slurs*. Cambridge, Mass.: Sci-Art, 1944.

"SALVERTE, EUSEBIUS." *History of the Names of Men, Nations and Places, in Their Connection with the Progress of Civilization*, trans. L. H. Mordacque. London: Smith, 1862.

SCHLAUCH, MARGARET. *The Gift of Language*. New York: Dover, 1955.

SCHOTT, GEORGE F. *Strange Stories of Words*. New York: Vantage, 1954.

SHANKLE, GEORGE EARLIE. *American Nicknames: Their Origin and Significance*. New York: Wilson, 1955.

SHIPLEY, JOSEPH T. *Dictionary of Word Origins*. New York: Philosophical Library, 1945.

SLEDD, J. H., AND KOLB, G. J. *Dr. Johnson's Dictionary*. Chicago: University of Chicago Press, 1955.

SMITH, ELSDON C. *Dictionary of American Family Names*. New York: Harper, 1956.

SMITH, S. STEPHENSON. *The Command of Words*. 2nd ed.; New York: Crowell, 1949.

STEWART, GEORGE R. *Names on the Land*. Boston: Houghton, Mifflin, 1958.

SUMNER, WILLIAM G. *Folkways: A Study of the Sociological Importance of Usages, Manners, Customs, Mores, and Morals*. New York: Ginn, 1906.

TAYLOR, ISAAC. *Words and Places: Illustrations of History, Ethnology and Geography*. London: Dent, 1911.

ULLMAN, B. L. *Ancient Writing and Its Influence*. London: Harrap, 1932.

ULLMAN, STEPHEN. *The Principles of Semantics*. New York: Philosophical Library, 1957.

WALLIS, CHARLES L. *Stories on Stone: A Book of American Epitaphs*. New York: Oxford University Press, 1954.

WENTWORTH, HAROLD, AND FLEXNER, STUART BERG. *Dictionary of American Slang*. New York: Crowell, 1960.

WHITE, ALEX S. *Dictionary of German Slang.* Central Valley, N.Y.: Aurea, 1961.

———. *Dictionary of Hungarian Slang.* Central Valley, N.Y.: Aurea, 1960.

———. *Dictionary of Italian Slang.* Central Valley, N.Y.: Aurea, 1960.

WHITE, T. S. *The Book of Beasts: Being a Translation from a Latin Bestiary of the Twelfth Century.* New York: Putnam, 1954.

WHITNEY, WILLIAM D. *Life and Growth of Language.* New York: Appleton, 1901.